OPERA
& IDEAS

Also by the author

THE FREUDIAN LEFT

THE MODERNIZATION OF SEX

OPERA & IDEAS

From Mozart to Strauss

by Paul Robinson

CORNELL UNIVERSITY PRESS

ITHACA, NEW YORK

Copyright © 1985 by Paul. A. Robinson
Published by arrangement with Harper & Row, Publishers, Inc.

First published, Cornell Paperbacks, 1986.
Second printing, 1987.

International Standard Book Number 0-8014-9428-1
Library of Congress Catalog Card Number 86-47637
Printed in the United States of America

Grateful acknowledgment for permission to reprint excerpts from English language librettos is made to the following:

English translation of *The Marriage of Figaro* by Lionel Salter © Lionel Salter. Reprinted by permission from Phillips recording 6707 014.

English translation of *The Barber of Seville* by Peggie Cochrane © The Decca Record Company Limited. Reprinted by permission from London recording OSA 1381.

English translation of *Die schöne Müllerin* © 1962 Capital Records, Inc. Reprinted by permission from Seraphim recording 60140.

English translation of *The Trojans* by David Cairns © David Cairns. Reprinted by permission from Phillips recording 6709 002.

English translation of *Ernani* by William Weaver © William Weaver. Reprinted by permission from RCA recording LSC 6183.

English translation of *Don Carlo* by Gwyn Morris © Gwyn Morris. Reprinted by permission from Angel (EMI) recording SDL 3774.

English translation of *Die Meistersinger* by Peter Branscombe © Peter Branscombe. Reprinted by permission from Angel (EMI) recording SEL 3776.

English translation of *Der Rosenkavalier* by Walter Legge © Walter Legge. Reprinted by permission from Angel (EMI) recording 3563 O/L.

Designed by Ruth Bornschlegel

Librarians: Library of Congress cataloging information
appears on the last page of the book.

The paper in this book is acid-free and meets the guidelines
for permanence and durability of the Committee on Production
Guidelines for Book Longevity of the Council on Library Resources.

To the memory of
Amy Cook Robinson (1883–1963)
and
Mabel Cady Lippincott (1885–1961)

Contents

Introduction

Behind the chapters in this book lies the conviction that music is part of Western civilization, connected in numerous ways with the other intellectual and cultural artifacts that make up our history. Historians and musicologists would on the whole endorse this proposition, but they have not spoken with much precision about the nature of the connection. The grounds for their reticence are perfectly understandable: music is the least representational form of art, and we lack an accepted public vocabulary for articulating what it is about. We may *feel*, for example, that Beethoven's music is somehow of a piece with what the poets, painters, and philosophers of the early nineteenth century were doing in their respective realms. But we don't know how to specify that connection or to say how it works.

Opera offers an intriguing compromise—although a deceptive one as well. In opera, music is allied with language, and when we have language to guide us, the dimly sensed associations start to grow explicit. If—to stick with my example—we think about Beethoven's *Fidelio*, instead of his symphonies, piano sonatas, and string quartets, we begin to see the possibility of drawing lines of filiation between Beethoven and the larger cultural concerns of his day. *Fidelio* is manifestly an opera about oppression and liberation, about loyalty and treachery, about despair and ecstasy. It puts us in mind of the French Revolution and the tyranny of Napoleon, the philosophy of

Kant and the plays of Schiller, the poetry of Wordsworth and Byron and the paintings of David and Goya. Opera, it would seem, gives us a place to begin: it gives us words and stories, which we can then relate to other words and other stories, be they the explicit ones of playwrights and metaphysicians or the implicit ones of painters and sculptors.

Words and stories, however, are *only* the beginning, and if we confine ourselves to them, we may well draw many suggestive connections, but they will ultimately lack interpretive weight, because none of them will pertain to the principal thing that distinguishes opera from drama—namely, music. In the best operas, of course, music and language achieve a degree of unity that makes fatuous any mechanical separation of verbal and musical significances. Still, what we say about the intellectual content of opera will remain of only marginal interest unless we can show how it finds expression in a work's musical argument as well. Opera is first and foremost a musical phenomenon, and the operatic compromise won't get us off the musical hook.

The proposition, I confess, seems to me self-evident, and throughout the following chapters I have at all times forced myself to talk about music. The reader will perhaps find that I occasionally make the music say more than it really wants to, that I have extracted unearned intellectual capital from a phrase, a passage, or a modulation whose true significance remains ineffable—i.e., purely musical. I hope, however, that there will be many more times when my interpretations lend an extra resonance, a new layer of meaning, and, ideally, even increased pleasure.

I presume that I don't need to explain what I mean by "opera," but the other term in my title, "ideas," begs for specification. The ideas I have in mind are those with which intellectual historians concern themselves: the consciously articulated notions of professional thinkers, such as find expression in philosophical writings, political tracts, novels, plays, and poems. Naturally, such ideas take on greater significance when they escape the possession of an individual writer and become part of the shared intellectual resources of the age. In my first and last chapters, for example, I have sought to interpret two important operas in terms of intellectual constructs—those of the Enlightenment and of Modernism—whose currency became so widespread during their respective eras that one might more accurately speak of "assumptions" or "preconceptions." But even in the instances where an opera's intellectual pedigree strikes me as remarkably specific, I do not argue that the composer consciously tried to embody a set of propositions in his art. The process by which an idea moves from one medium to another is, I believe, virtually impossible to follow, since that movement is effected by means that are incremental, various, and, above all, invisible. Hence I have avoided the thankless task of trying to identify influences and chosen instead to speak of affinities. The measure of success in this sort of investigation is not whether a connection is demonstrable but whether it is illuminating.

In undertaking this study I have had several objectives in mind. The most important is to cast new light on the eight works to whose analysis the individual chapters are devoted. By showing how these works engage the intellectual concerns of their day, I hope to draw attention to a neglected conceptual dimension in their makeup and thereby to enrich our sense of their artistic logic. In "The Meaning of a Literary Idea," Lionel Trilling argues that the intellectual cogency of a work of literature is anything but irrelevant to its aesthetic effect. Much the same is true, I believe, of opera, and at its heart this book is an attempt to interpret several operatic masterpieces according to Trilling's dictum. The book is thus apt to be of greatest interest to persons who know and love opera and are eager to consider it from a novel perspective.

Although my principal aim has been to consider works of art from a particular interpretive standpoint, I believe that the book also has something of value to say about ideas. I have not sought to write intellectual history through an operatic prism—to reconstruct the story of Europe's spiritual evolution from the Enlightenment to Modernism by ransacking the operatic repertory for overlooked intellectual evidences. Rather, I hope these studies serve to broaden our sense of the scope of intellectual history by demonstrating its pertinence to an aspect of culture not generally considered intellectual. The life of the mind, I mean to suggest, enjoys a wider range of influence than we usually allow. At the same time, the studies also aim to breathe new life into the familiar ingredients of our intellectual heritage by showing how those ingredients become embodied in forms that are strikingly concrete and beautiful. Intellectual historians know how easily the subject matter of their discipline assumes an airy unreality; ideas that once engaged the passions of an age are forever threatening to degenerate into hollow clichés. But if we can experience those ideas as they give shape to great works of art, the desiccated abstractions come to life with the power and excitement they held for their original proponents. Just as operas assume an added richness, a new dimension, when their intellectual contents are identified, so, in turn, ideas shed their customary impersonality and achieve unexpected immediacy when they find expression in the sensuous realm of music. Such, at least, has been my own experience as both an operagoer and a teacher of intellectual history.

The chapters of this book are best thought of as discrete explorations of a common thesis about the relation between opera and ideas. To make my point I have found it convenient—indeed, unavoidable—to examine a limited number of operas in considerable detail. Needless to say, I have chosen examples that impressed me as especially rich in intellectual promise, although my assumption is that all operas could be profitably examined from the same point of view. In general, I have found the approach most revealing with operas that are not especially explicit in their intellectualizing. Mozart's *Magic Flute* and Wagner's *Ring,* for example, are rather too self-conscious in their devotion to "ideas"; an intellectual approach to them runs the risk of seeming both banal and superficial. Hence my choice of *The Marriage of Figaro* and *Die Meistersinger,* whose ideational content lies less close to the surface but is all the more rewarding to mine for being deeply buried.

Several other considerations have guided my choice of cases. Without exception, the works I examine are major artistic documents—indeed, masterpieces—and they are also works that I greatly admire. Perhaps my affection for Rossini's *Barber of Seville* and Strauss's *Rosenkavalier* is somewhat less than unqualified, but this book is nonetheless a labor of love. More important, I have picked works that span a fairly long stretch of cultural history—from the late eighteenth to the early twentieth century—which allows me to address a wide variety of ideas and intellectual concerns. Although I make no pretense to having exhausted the intellectual terrain from the Enlightenment to Modernism, the five chapters do aspire to sketch the important milestones in that progress. Of course, many important ideas never find operatic expression, and in my Postscript I offer some speculations about what might explain opera's affinity for certain ideas and its indifference to others.

It will perhaps be helpful to suggest, even at the risk of excessive schematization, the particular connections between opera and intellectual life examined in the book's individual chapters. In the first of them I compare Mozart's *Marriage of Figaro* (1786) with Rossini's *Barber of Seville* (1816), arguing that the former reflects the moral and social vision of the eighteenth-century Enlightenment while the latter gives musical voice to the early-nineteenth-century critique of the Enlightenment. Mozart, I suggest, was the operatic spokesman of the *philosophes,* Rossini the unwitting mouthpiece of their conservative opponents; where *The Marriage of Figaro* argues the operatic case for Reason and Humanity, *The Barber of Seville* mocks those very ideals.

The next chapter discusses Franz Schubert's two great song cycles, *Die schöne Müllerin* (1823) and *Winterreise* (1827), which I argue are devoted to a musical exploration of the Romantic subjectivity that Schubert shared with the famous lyric poets of his generation, above all Wordsworth and Keats. The Romantic self in its relation to nature provides the focus of this comparison. From a methodological viewpoint, the difference between an opera and a song cycle turns out to be less consequential than one might expect, since in the latter, too, music and ideas are united through the medium of language. I am not the first, moreover, to suggest that *Die schöne Müllerin* and *Winterreise* are distinctly operatic.

The third chapter makes perhaps the most explicit connection between an opera and an idea. In it, I examine Berlioz's undeservedly neglected Virgilian masterpiece, *The Trojans* (1858), with a view to showing how it embodies the distinctive historical consciousness of the nineteenth century. More particularly, I argue that Berlioz's great epic reflects the same conception of history that one finds in the philosophical writings of Hegel. The importance of this intellectual context for Berlioz's opera is suggested by a comparison with Henry Purcell's *Dido and Aeneas,* composed in the late seventeenth century.

Verdi is the central operatic composer of the nineteenth century, and for a while I contemplated devoting this study in its entirety to him. He is an especially inviting subject because, unlike Wagner's, his operas seem to be without intellectual pretensions. But in reality he was no less engaged with the intellectual life of his time than was his great German rival, and his operas were deeply influenced by nine-teenth-century ideas about romance, the family, and society. I have chosen to focus on a single preoccupation in his works: his long love affair with politics. Through an analysis of *Don Carlo* (1867), the greatest of his political operas, I seek to identify the affinities between his political ideals and the dominant realism, or *Realpolitik,* of the latter half of the century. In *Don Carlo,* I suggest, Verdi gives musical expression to a conception of politics strikingly similar to that found in such representative political thinkers of the age as Heinrich von Treitschke and Jacob Burckhardt.

In the last chapter I again turn to a comparison of two operas that span an important intellectual watershed. Just as the Mozart and Rossini operas are separated by the abyss of the French Revolution and the Napoleonic Imperium and, more important, by that great shift in sensibility that distinguishes the Enlightenment from its nineteenth-century critics, so Wagner's *Die Meistersinger* (1868) and Strauss's *Der Rosenkavalier* (1911) are separated by the no less traumatic break that marks the emergence of Modernism. Between Wagner and Strauss falls the ominous shadow of Sigmund Freud, and along with it the shadows of a host of lesser, but equally anxious, cultural prophets who usher in the age that we feel obliged to call our own. At the heart of *Die Meistersinger* and *Der Rosenkavalier* lies a remarkably similar story of romantic sacrifice. Yet the operatic results are extraordinarily different, and some significant part of that difference, I believe, reflects the changed intellectual climate that sets the twentieth century apart from the nineteenth. Where Wagner's opera is about art and society, mirroring ideas concerning their relation such as one finds in the writings of John Ruskin and his contemporaries, Strauss's opera is about the self and its struggle with the forces of time, mirroring, in turn, the obsession of modern artists and thinkers with the agonizing mystery of time's passing. It is the burden of my argument, here as throughout the book, that these intellectual differences find appropriate *musical* (not merely dramatic) expression in Wagner's and Strauss's operas. The focus of my attention, again, is on the score rather than the libretto.

There are many profitable ways in which to study operas. The most common approach—and for good reason—is to consider them in terms of the history of music: to compare an operatic composer with his forebears and successors, and to identify similarities and differences between opera and other musical genres. This is the way opera is discussed in the standard histories of music or in the specialized histories devoted to opera alone. Studies of individual operatic composers, such as the books of Edward Dent, Ernest Newman, Julian Budden, William Mann, and Spike Hughes, represent a yet further specialized variation on the same theme. I have no doubt that this musicological approach—which takes the boundaries of a particular artistic medium as its principle of unity—will remain the central one, as it ought to be. In the last analysis, we learn most about Beethoven when we set his achievement in historical relation to that of Mozart, Haydn, and his other great predecessors. Similarly, we learn most about Verdi's *Aida* when we follow its dramatic and musical evolution out of Verdi's earlier operatic projects.

But in addition to (and entirely compatible with) this dominant diachronic approach, there are a number of synchronic possibilities that promise to yield a certain amount of light. One of these, pursued intelligently by Gary Schmidgall in *Literature as Opera,* is to place operas against their literary sources and to explore the transformations that occur as an idea moves from the latter medium to the former. In some cases (for example, Donizetti's appropriation of Scott's *The Bride of Lammermoor*), the translation takes place more or less contemporaneously, but in others (such as Verdi's Shakespeare operas) the movement is not merely from one medium to another but from one age to another. In both cases, however, the analysis is apt to reveal things that don't become apparent when one sticks to the mainstream musicological tradition.

Another possibility is suggested by Joseph Kerman's *Opera as Drama,* which I still consider the most provocative book on opera I have read. Kerman, like Schmidgall, adopts an essentially extramusical starting point, but instead of examining operas from the perspective of their literary source, he measures them against the categorical requisites of drama. He asks, in effect, how dramatic values are transformed when a composer seeks to lend them musical expression, and he judges the success or (more often) failure of opera in terms of its ability to retain the essential logic and power of drama in its new medium.

I consider the approach taken in this book analogous to—though obviously distinct from—the approaches of Schmidgall and Kerman. Where the independent variable in their analyses is in the one instance literature and in the other drama, I have substituted the history of ideas. By examining operas in the light of more or less contemporary intellectual developments, I hope to achieve a comparable illumination of the artistic artifact. Operas will remain, I hardly need say, sources of musical and dramatic enjoyment whether or not one perceives them as intellectual events. But there is much satisfaction to be had when one recognizes that they are also—as I suggested at the beginning—part of Western civilization.

Enlightenment
and Reaction

Wolfgang Amadeus Mozart's
> *The Marriage of Figaro*
and Gioachino Rossini's
> *The Barber of Seville*

This book argues that operas reflect the intellectual climate of their age and that we experience them differently—indeed more interestingly—when this intellectual factor is taken into account. A comparison of Mozart's *The Marriage of Figaro* and Rossini's *The Barber of Seville* will serve to introduce my proposition. These are two of the most popular and admired operas in the repertory. *The Marriage of Figaro,* which had its premiere in 1786, is among the oldest operas regularly performed, and some consider it still the greatest. *The Barber of Seville* dates from 1816, making it among the earliest "bel canto" operas, a tradition whose chief adepts were Rossini, Bellini, and Donizetti.

The Marriage of Figaro and *The Barber of Seville* are particularly suited to comparison because they share so many things yet leave such remarkably different impressions. An important source of that difference, I'm persuaded, is intellectual in nature. But let me begin this comparison by considering their similarities.

First of all, one must note certain common dramatic and textual features of the operas. Both are social comedies, in which we laugh at absurd conventions about class, sex, power, and property. Both, moreover, are in Italian, lending them a shared vocabulary and an aura of linguistic continuity. More striking and unusual, both derive from plays by the same author, the French dramatist Beaumarchais (1732–1799). The plays are themselves intimately related to one another and even peopled by many of the same characters. This last fact has occasionally been a source of confusion, because Rossini, the younger of the two composers, set the first of the Beaumarchais plays, while Mozart, whose opera preceded Rossini's by exactly three decades, set the second—that is, the sequel. The explanation of this incongruity is quite simple: when Mozart came to write *The Marriage of Figaro*, the earlier play had already been made into an opera by the Italian composer Giovanni Paisiello (1740–1816), whose *Barber of Seville* (1782) was driven from the stage only by Rossini's incontestably superior version of 1816. Rossini's *Barber,* therefore, tells the chronologically prior story, namely of how a Spanish aristocrat, Count Almaviva, succeeds, with the help of the town barber, his former servant Figaro, in rescuing a young woman from her uxorious guardian. Mozart's opera picks up the story somewhat later, and, like the second Beaumarchais play, focuses on the marriage of the barber (once more a personal servant in the Almaviva household) and the philandering of the formerly romantic Count.

Besides their related librettos, *The Marriage of Figaro* and *The Barber of Seville* share a number of musical characteristics. The most general of these is their use of similar melodic and harmonic conventions: in both we hear the same fondness for regular, symmetrical, and clearly articulated phrases, the same steadiness of pulse, the same transparency and stability of harmonic organization. The operas, as noted, are separated by only three decades, and since Rossini was a relatively conservative composer, one could even argue that Mozart's opera seems the more advanced. The confluence of musical idiom between the two might be spelled out more precisely in terms of harmonic procedure, melodic construction, orchestration, and other matters as well. But for our purposes it is sufficient to say that to the average listener, moderately familiar with the operas that one is likely to hear in today's theaters, the works sound closely related.

A second musical similarity between the operas is that both are constructed of "numbers": arias, duets, trios, ensembles, and choruses. These numbers are separated by recitative, that is, by singing composed in a manner to approximate the rhythms and inflections of ordinary speech and accompanied only by the harpsichord. Thus the listener experiences both operas as a series of discrete musical events, each with its distinct beginning and ending—so distinct, in fact, that if well performed, the numbers are usually followed by applause. These fundamental musical units resemble one another in several ways. In both operas they normally last about four minutes. They are generally composed in a single key and to a fixed rhythm, tempo, and orchestral accompaniment—or, if not that, then in two clearly contrasted sections, one slow, the other fast. And they characteristically contain melodic material that is repeated several times over. Most of these numbers are sufficiently autonomous to be performed outside the opera as concert pieces, and many of them in *The Marriage of Figaro* and *The Barber of Seville* are so tuneful that they have become recital favorites: Mozart's "Dove sono" and "Voi che sapete," Rossini's "Largo al factotum" and "Una voce poco fa," to mention only the most famous.

Because of this method of construction (the common property of opera composers throughout the seventeenth and eighteenth centuries, but soon to give way to the "continuous" musical style of nineteenth-century opera), the audience's sense of theatrical time is the same in both operas: in both there are, so to speak, two clocks. When time is being kept by the first clock—that is, during the recitative—things move along more or less as they do in real life, and the actors on stage occupy the same temporal framework as does the audience in the theater. But during the numbers, as if by Einsteinian magic, a kind of "slow time" supplants quotidian time: people repeat themselves unconscionably, and, after having said what they have to say, go back, as if nothing had happened, and say it all over again— much to our delight, of course. There is a significant difference in Mozart's and Rossini's use of this convention: characteristically, Rossini is more self-conscious about it, and he draws on that self-consciousness for comic effect. No small part of the laughter in *The Barber of Seville* comes from Rossini's implicit suggestion that the conventions of his opera, with their two clocks, are absurd. His characters carry on in operatic time when the exigencies of the situation demand a prompt return to ordinary time. This bad faith (to put the matter in moralistic terms) is unfailingly funny, and it is entirely absent from Mozart's use of the same device. In effect, one sees in Rossini an operatic convention at the very end of its artistic life: he makes fun of it; the next generation simply abandons it. In the meantime, however, despite the satiric perspective unique to Rossini, the two operas are united in their general musical design.

This similarity extends to one further matter: the concerted finale. On two occasions in *The Marriage of Figaro* (the ends of Acts II and IV) and once in *The Barber of Seville* (the end of Act I), isolated numbers give way to long stretches of music uninterrupted by recitative. These finales remain segmental, and the listener has no trouble detecting when one segment ends and the next begins: usually the change is signaled by a new theme, rhythm, and tonality. The individual segments of the finale are about as long as a typical number, and the whole might contain ten or more such units. These finales lend concentrated musical expression to the dramatic climaxes of the operas. The finale to Act II of *The Marriage of Figaro* is among the most admired achievements in opera. But Rossini, in his more modest way, adopts the same ground plan, and the listener will come away from the two operas aware of having been treated to analogous musical experiences at their culminations.

In sum, *The Marriage of Figaro* and *The Barber of Seville* share a great many things in common, in both story and music. And yet they remain entirely individual. Their effect on us is altogether dissimilar, even antithetical. One leaves a performance of *The Barber of Seville* having laughed a great deal and delighted by its many musical felicities. But while the operagoer has also laughed—though probably not so uproariously—during *The Marriage of Figaro,* and while its tunes also return to haunt him, it is not uncommon to leave Mozart's opera profoundly moved, and this Rossini's can never achieve.

Let me now consider the possible sources of this striking emotional difference. I am of course most interested in the ways it reflects a difference of worldview, and above all the changes in the European climate of opinion over the thirty-year span separating the two works. I think those changes crucial, but it would be foolish to overlook some fairly obvious musical and dramatic reasons for our dissimilar reactions to the two works.

At the risk of banality, one must begin by noting that the operas do, after all, tell different stories, with different themes, even though the choice of story and theme already reveals something of the composer's preoccupations. Speaking broadly, *The Marriage of Figaro* is about infidelity, while *The Barber of Seville* is about courtship. By their very nature, these two subjects necessarily elicit different responses from their composers.

One must note further that although many of the same characters appear in both operas, they appear at different stages in their lives, entertain different concerns, and exhibit different qualities of heart and mind. All these differences, as one would expect, result in rather drastic musical transformations. To give but one example, the music teacher, Don Basilio, appears in both works, but he is a basso profondo in the Rossini opera, while an effete, oleaginous tenor in the Mozart. Certain important characters in Mozart's opera do not yet exist in Rossini's, notably the page Cherubino, Figaro's fiancée, Susanna, and his mother, Marcellina. Most important of all, virtually every character assumes a different dramatic stature in the two operas: Rossini's Dr. Bartolo is a major figure—the guardian of the opera's prima donna—but is relegated to a secondary role by Mozart; the Count in *The Barber of Seville* is the romantic lead (and a tenor), but the heavy (and a baritone) in Mozart. These differences—and others like them—mean that, while the names remain the same, we don't think of these characters as identical, or even as earlier and later versions of the same persons. It is inconceivable—to give a final example—that Rossini's unflappable heroine Rosina (a coloratura mezzo) could have matured into Mozart's melancholy Countess (a spinto soprano). Everything we know about the continuity of character, not to speak of the limits of vocal evolution, simply prohibits the thought.

To these textual or dramatic differences one must add certain striking musical differences. Doubtless the most important musical consideration to be borne in mind is the simple but awesome fact that Mozart was a greater composer than Rossini. However much we might admire Rossini, there remains a quantum leap in sheer compositional skill, never mind emotional depth, that must always separate these two composers, and hence part of the "difference" one senses when attending *The Marriage of Figaro* and *The Barber of Seville* reflects the brute fact of the earlier composer's musical superiority. Mozart's greater skill shows up most clearly in those moments that require the greatest technical control. It is thus above all in the finales that one becomes fully conscious of his advantage.

Considerations of sheer talent aside, Mozart and Rossini display significant musical idiosyncrasies that probably reflect nothing further than the mystery of artistic inspiration. I don't intend to catalogue those differences, but they might be subsumed under the general (and frankly impressionistic) proposition that Mozart's music is more rounded, complex, and inward, whereas Rossini's shows a predilection for mechanical-sounding and angular effects, as well as a brilliant compositional surface. Another way of saying the same thing is that Mozart draws one's attention to the core of the musical process—to matters of rhythm, harmony, and melody—whereas in Rossini one attends to detail—to ornament, dynamic changes, and the exquisite and humorous particulars of his orchestration.

I can perhaps convey the difference by way of an example—namely, the opening scenes of the two operas. In the first few moments of *The Barber of Seville* the listener is apt to be transfixed by Rossini's wonderful orchestral articulations and mechanical rhythms—the inevitable tread of bassoon and pizzicato strings, clarinets chirping their sixteenth-note harmonies, rapid triplet figures highlighted by the flute. All these make the passage sound as if it were emanating from some huge music box. The effect is delicious, and one can never hear it often enough. At the corresponding moment in Mozart's opera one hears something altogether different: though the rhythm is no less steady, the instruments don't call attention to themselves, and their agitated rustlings quickly dissolve into a composite sonic picture at the back of our minds. The whole is more of a piece, and one thinks not of a huge music box but of a real world of space and time in which two people speak to one another (or, as it turns out, past one another) with great excitement. The difference is not without its intellectual implications, as I will argue in a moment. But it is also a purely musical difference: Rossini milks his embellishments for every last drop of aural pleasure, while Mozart strives for a more organic effect.

Needless to say, I have merely hinted here at the musical differences that determine our varying responses to these composers. But even when all such matters are taken into account, neither they nor the textual differences alluded to earlier entirely explain the dissimilar effect of the two operas. There remains an element of intellectual disparity that also must be acknowledged. Some significant portion of the difference between *The Marriage of Figaro* and *The Barber of Seville* mirrors the fact that the first was written in the eighteenth century and embodies the characteristic intellectual concerns of its time, while the second was written in the early nineteenth century and embodies ideas and attitudes that achieved ascendancy only in the wake of the French Revolution.

That Mozart's music and his operas in particular are products of the European Enlightenment is a commonplace of cultural history. And like all good commonplaces, it is also true. The connection is most transparent in *The Magic Flute,* which is fully explicit in its Enlightenment values, even down to the particulars of Freemasonry. If I have something to add to the commonplace, it will be that the Enlightenment is to be found not merely in Mozart's texts—whether penned by Lorenzo Da Ponte or by Emanuel Schikaneder—but in his music as well. Indeed, it is only because he succeeds in realizing its values musically that the question is of enduring interest.

The Enlightenment was a complex intellectual movement about

whose essential nature scholars are by no means agreed. Furthermore, the thinkers of the Enlightenment, like thinkers of any generation, concerned themselves with many issues that do not allow of musical— or even theatrical—realization. Empiricism, deism, and anticlericalism are hardly the stuff of great tunes, although Musorgsky, a century later, did rather handsomely by the last of these with his drunken monk Varlaam and evil Jesuit Rangoni in *Boris Godunov*. Nonetheless, certain of the Enlightenment's fundamental intellectual and moral beliefs lend themselves quite readily to musical embodiment, at least in the hands of a great composer who himself shared those beliefs. Mozart manifestly was such a composer, and his commitment to the values of the Enlightenment was as complete as Voltaire's or Rousseau's or Kant's.

The most important of those values is the conviction that human beings can overcome the antagonisms that separate them from one another. Like the *philosophes*, Mozart believes that we have within us the intellectual and emotional resources to transcend our hostilities. To put the matter in a word, he believes in the possibility of reconciliation. Reconciliation—or what Herbert Marcuse called "the pacification of existence"—is, in my view, the fundamental theme of *The Marriage of Figaro*, of both its story and its music. As Freudians or post-Freudians, we can perhaps no longer fully accept the proposition, for we've come to think of egoism and aggression as intractable elements of our psychic makeup—a point of view shared, significantly, by the composer of *The Barber of Seville*. But to feel the completeness with which Mozart believed in reconciliation is an exhilarating experience. That, above all else, is why we leave the theater so profoundly moved.

One might be inclined to object that reconciliation is the theme of almost all music, and of much literature as well. Does not the typical work of music or literature begin by establishing tensions and end by resolving them? Is not reconciliation, after all, the very essence of "plot" (to view the matter in literary terms) or of harmonic and melodic resolution (to view it musically)? In other words, is there any reason to consider this theme unique to *The Marriage of Figaro* or to tie it to the worldview of a particular period, such as the Enlightenment?

To these questions the answer must be: "It's all a matter of degree." Reconciliation is indeed a perennial theme of art and thought. But in *The Marriage of Figaro* the theme is accorded such prominence, explored in such detail, exhibited in so many guises, and allowed to permeate the musical and dramatic action so thoroughly that whereas in other works of art we experience particular *instances* of reconciliation (the reunion of separated lovers, let us say, as in *Fidelio,* or of separated parent and child, as in *King Lear*), in *The Marriage of Figaro* reconciliation itself, almost as if it were an abstraction, lodges itself in the memory as the essence of what we have seen. It is, so to speak, the argument of the opera, both at the episodic level of the work's many incidents in which reunion is the underlying issue, and in the overarching structure that builds toward the Countess's epiphanic act of forgiveness at the opera's close.

If reconciliation is the argument of the opera, one might say that Reason is its means. And Reason, of course, is also among the great battle cries of the Enlightenment. What the thinkers of the eighteenth century meant by Reason is not always easy to say, for they were not necessarily consistent in their use of the word. But Ernst Cassirer and Peter Gay have shown us that their conception of Reason was above all critical: Reason for them was the faculty of mind that disputed the unargued claims of tradition, revelation, and authority. As has often been noted, this conception of Reason is in many ways quite modest, at least when compared with the intellectual presumptions of the Continental metaphysicians of the seventeenth and the nineteenth centuries—thinkers who aspired to construct an adequate view of reality largely by deductive means. Thus the Enlightenment at once celebrates Reason—as man's last best hope in an unfriendly world—and cautions about its limitations: if not checked by the more humble powers of observation and common sense, pure rationality eventuates in fiction. Just such untethered rationalism was the source of Voltaire's famous critique of Leibniz.

The Marriage of Figaro is the musical embodiment of this eighteenth-century conception of mind. The opera celebrates intelligence, dramatically in the machinations of its protagonist, and musically in the cleverness of its composer. In the finale to the second act, these two elements are brought together in a moment of supreme intellectual and musical exhibitionism, a veritable tribute to the powers of intellect. And yet at the same time, indeed at that very moment, intelligence is also mocked and its pretensions deflated, in the best Enlightenment tradition. Viewed psychologically or ethically, then, the opera is an eighteenth-century essay on conflict and reconciliation. Viewed intellectually, it is an Enlightenment tract on Reason.

In linking *The Marriage of Figaro* to the Enlightenment I have merely followed common practice. But in arguing, as I wish to now, that Rossini's *Barber of Seville* reflects European intellectual life in the early nineteenth century I am treading on virgin territory. My contention, as will be seen, must be carefully qualified.

The early nineteenth century can be justly described as a period of reaction against the Enlightenment. That reaction, however, was extremely complex, resulting in a cultural and intellectual era of great richness. We are perhaps most familiar with the aspect of the reaction that goes by the name of Romanticism, which, among other things, involved an intensified subjectivity. In music it is best represented by Franz Schubert, who will be examined in my next chapter. But there was another aspect of the reaction, which gave rise to an intellectual perspective in many ways just the opposite of Romanticism. I have in mind the aversion to intellect and to political enthusiasm that one finds in the great conservative thinkers of the age: Thomas Malthus, Joseph de Maistre, Friedrich von Gentz, and above all Edmund Burke, who, though dead in 1797, cast a long shadow over the European political imagination of the early nineteenth century. At the heart of this tradition was a critique of the intellectual ambitions of the Enlightenment, especially as they related to politics. The Enlightenment came to be considered an act of intellectual hubris: men had overreached themselves in believing that injustice could be eliminated by a simple effort of mind and goodwill. In reality, conservatives argued, the insufficiencies of our existence were firmly rooted in human nature and the precariousness of communal survival. To ignore these unpleasant facts was to invite disaster—such as the French Revolution. Wisdom, therefore, called for a withdrawal of intellect and passion from the overextended positions they had staked out in the eighteenth century. A modulated cynicism, in other words, was the only sensible attitude.

The Barber of Seville is the perfect operatic realization of this mood of intellectual and emotional retreat. It is relentlessly unserious, displays human viciousness in all conceivable guises, and refuses any kind of psychological or moral investment. The argument of both libretto and music is that life can be managed only by laughing at it. For the rounded characters and human conflicts of *The Marriage of Figaro* Rossini substitutes superbly exaggerated caricatures and incidents of the utmost archness. *The Barber of Seville,* in effect, is a musical joke, perhaps the greatest piece of musical slapstick ever written. It stands in relation to *The Marriage of Figaro* much as *The Comedy of Errors* stands in relation to *Twelfth Night.* And while this difference can be attributed in part to the peculiarities of Rossini's character and to his distinctive musical gifts, his opera is nonetheless inconceivable outside the intellectual atmosphere of post-Napoleonic Europe. How little the difference is to be explained in terms of Rossini's literary source can be established by comparing not merely Beaumarchais's two plays, which are remarkably similar, but also Rossini's own opera with what Giovanni Paisiello made of the same material in 1782. The qualities of exaggeration, self-assertion, and outrageousness that make Rossini's opera unforgettable are quite absent in Paisiello's agreeably tuneful and almost gentle rendering of the story. Only by locating *The Barber of Seville* against the background of European conservatism, I believe, can one understand why this work of 1816 is, paradoxically, the least Romantic of all important operas. Its horror of affect makes it almost the perfect inversion of the great song cycles that Franz Schubert was composing in the same period several hundred miles to the north.

I am particularly eager to show that the contrast I have drawn between Mozart and Rossini is a musical contrast, though, obviously, it cannot be entirely separated from text and story. In the remainder of this chapter I wish to examine four aspects of the operas that will serve, I hope, to make my point.

THE FIRST SCENE

Many of the essential differences between *The Marriage of Figaro* and *The Barber of Seville* are already on display in their opening scenes, and those differences reflect opposite conceptions of art and human nature—in short, two different worldviews. The Enlightenment and the reaction against it are neatly adumbrated.

The Marriage of Figaro begins with two duets and a brief recitative for the protagonist, Figaro, and his fiancée, Susanna. The action takes place in a room intended by Count Almaviva to be the newlyweds' bedroom, though Susanna is still unaware of this. In the first duet (or "duettino," as Mozart calls it), Figaro is observed measuring to see whether the bed will fit in a particular part of the room, while Susanna admires a hat, which, she says, looks as if it had been made just for her (she has in fact made it herself). She urges Figaro to take note of it as well; eventually she captures his attention, and they sing together in praise of the hat.

The Marriage of Figaro is a long opera, and if the music to this duet were not so delightful, an impatient listener might wonder why Mozart has wasted the opening minutes of his show on a vignette that makes no contribution to the action. But precisely its uselessness invites inspection. It is, I believe, an inspired cameo of the opera as a whole. *The Marriage of Figaro* opens with two individuals in a state of mild alienation, the sort of alienation that comes from a simple failure to pay attention. Figaro is doing one thing, Susanna another, and the latter is eager to draw the former into her "mental sphere." That this element of alienation is intentional is disclosed by the music: Figaro sings one melodic line (a sequence of downward intervals that move stepwise up the scale as the measurements increase: "Five . . . ten . . . twenty . . . thirty . . . thirty-six . . . forty-three . . ."), and while he repeats his words, Susanna imposes a countermelody on top of them. The melodies, needless to say, are compatible, but they move in ignorance of one another, mirroring the mutual insouciance of the characters. We are shown a world in which people don't listen to one another.

But of course they do: Figaro comes to attention, seizes Susanna's melody, admires her hat, and the duet ends with them singing in harmony of its beauty and appropriateness. The independent—even antithetical—movement of voices gives way to parallel thirds and sixths. A tiny reconciliation has been effected, prefiguring the great moment of reconciliation at the opera's end. I cannot stress too emphatically that this little melodrama is embodied not merely in the text, but in the music as well: Mozart has devised musical means for expressing an idea about human relations.

In his discussion of *The Marriage of Figaro* in *Opera as Drama*, Joseph Kerman comments on our awareness, at the conclusion of the opera, that "the Count will soon be philandering again," thus necessitating further acts of forgiveness and further reconciliations. We may absolve—and be absolved—but there will be yet other alienations. Mozart, in short, is a psychological realist, though a hopeful one. It is thus altogether appropriate, indeed symbolic, that the tiny reconciliation brought about in the opening duettino should be followed immediately by a new antagonism, which is the subject of the second duet and the intervening recitative.

Unlike the matter of the hat, the new source of friction *is* germane to the plot, and it won't allow of resolution until the final act. Accordingly, it is given more substantial musical representation. The specific matter is Susanna's discovery that the room in which the two are speaking has been reserved as their bedroom. In a passage of amusing banter, she reveals to Figaro that its location (right between the rooms of the Count and the Countess) is not so advantageous as he had imagined. Mozart keeps his protagonists at musical odds in this recitative and in the duet that follows: if Figaro sings in the major, Susanna sings in the minor; if Susanna sings high, Figaro sings low. At the same time he introduces, in characteristically ambiguous fashion, the second eighteenth-century theme that I have associated with the opera: Reason. The ambiguity might be formulated as follows: although Figaro is the self-appointed wit of the opera—a claim he will set forth in his first aria, "Se vuol ballare"—it is Susanna who here pretends, and rightfully, to superior intelligence, a pretension that she validates musically by her ingenious manipulation of the duet's melody. The piece focuses on the matter of bells: Figaro explains the room's virtue in terms of Susanna's being able to respond quickly to a ring from the Countess ("din din" on the F above middle C) and he to one from the Count ("don don" on F an octave below). The "din din" is delicate and feminine, the "don don" pompous and masculine, a musical representation of the tension between the sexes that pervades the opera. But in controverting him, Susanna wittily sounds the "don don" for herself—just as the Count may be expected to do if the couple in fact take up housekeeping in the room—and she does so at a moment in the score when both Figaro and the audience have been set up musically for a repetition of her innocent "din din." The effect is deliciously jarring, as the awful truth of the situation suddenly dawns on Figaro. (A close musical parallel occurs in Act II of Verdi's *Otello,* where a solo E sharp for the cellos unmistakably marks the first instant of Otello's jealousy.) Much of the moment's pleasure, I'm convinced, resides in the coincidence of Susanna's insight and the composer's cleverness: she surprises Figaro with a piece of unpleasant intelligence just as Mozart surprises us with a brilliant frustration of our musical expectations. Moreover, Susanna's wit and Mozart's compositional skill effect a musical critique of received opinion about sexual roles: they conspire to deflate Figaro's pomposity and, by implication, the pomposity of all men. The moment is at once funny, incisive, and beautiful—a musical demonstration of intelligence. We can almost sense a mind at work—two minds, for that matter.

At the risk of dwelling excessively on what might appear to be insignificant details, I would also like to call attention to the role of objects and their musical representation in this opening scene. The opera discloses a world of things—a bed, a hat, a room, a bell—and these things immediately identify the drama as one of social relationships. This sociable world—the world in which the tensions of sex, class, and temperament are played out—is precisely the world of the eighteenth-century *philosophes*. It can be contrasted with the ideological world of Beethoven's *Fidelio*, the mythical world of Wagner's *Ring*, the heroic world of Berlioz's *The Trojans*, the transcendental world of Gounod's *Faust* and Boito's *Mefistofele*, or the intrapsychic world of Debussy's *Pelléas* and Berg's *Wozzeck*. It is also a contemporary world: Europe at the end of the eighteenth century. Almost as the curtain goes up, we know that the opera will treat of people and things, and of nothing else—neither religion, nor politics, nor the unconscious. All of this seems so obvious that we hardly stop to recognize that the opera has in fact bracketed off a particular realm for examination and implied thereby that that realm is the most worthy of our attention. The presupposition of the opera, as of eighteenth-century thought in general, is secular humanism.

One might characterize the universe of the opera as a kind of middle-level reality: above nature and below God. And to depict it, Mozart composes music that, as many critics have remarked, is distinguished above all by its equipoise: it balances male and female, fast and slow, major and minor, loud and soft, high and low (but, be it noted, never very high or very low: voice fetishists can never quite forgive Mozart for having written a masterpiece without a single part that, from a purely vocal point of view, is truly difficult). Perhaps one can best appreciate the extraordinarily measured character of the opera's music if one makes mental comparisons with the extremes to which other composers are inclined: the apoplectic frenzy of Beethoven, the exhausting length of Wagner, the sheer loudness of Verdi, the female bias of Strauss and Puccini, the male bias of Britten. Mozart is, above all, a centrist composer.

Thus in two short duets and a snatch of recitative Mozart has introduced us to the essential theme of his opera and located it in the real world as it was conceived of by the eighteenth-century Enlightenment, a balanced world of physical objects and personal relationships. Moreover, the burden of his introduction has been carried as much by the music as by the text or the action on stage.

Let us turn now to the opening scene of Rossini's *Barber of Seville*. No less emphatically than that of *The Marriage of Figaro*, it announces the theme and manner of the entire opera and exhibits most of the musical means that Rossini will use to entertain his audience. The action consists of the early-morning appearance, outside of the house of Dr. Bartolo, of a band of musicians, who accompany Count Almaviva in serenading his future bride. Reduced to its essentials, it is a series of verbal and musical gags, whose subjects are rapaciousness, self-indulgence, and stupidity—in short, a demonstration of mindless egoism. It initiates an evening's entertainment of psychological and musical preening.

The orchestra begins its droll commentary, establishing itself, unlike Mozart's orchestra, as an independent voice, which seems to stand at an ironic distance from the characters whose musical lines it is meant to support. This drollery is conveyed, first of all, by a tempo that sounds unnaturally deliberate, as if the orchestra were listening to itself, and then by the manner in which the smooth upward contour of the opening phrases gives way to an unexpected rush of descending triplets as the melody reaches its climax: like so many tunes in this opera, it dissolves into a decorative figure of wondrous triviality. Even before a word has been sung, the listener knows that he has entered the universe of the mock-heroic.

As the melody repeats itself, the Count's servant Fiorello enters, followed by the band (and the Count himself), and he begins immediately to discuss the most important theme of the opera: dynamics. His first words come right out of the score: "Piano, pianissimo." The theme is never far from anyone's lips: "Senza parlar" ("Without a word"), "Fate silenzio" ("Be quiet"). The gag bears full comic fruit in the chorus after the Count's serenade, when, having been paid off, the musicians express their thanks ever more vehemently, while the Count and Fiorello, making the greatest racket of all, enjoin them to shut up:

> *Basta, basta! Non parlate,*
> *Ma non serve, non gridate. . . .*
> *Zitti, zitti! Che rumore!*
> *Maledetti, via di qua!*
>
> Enough, enough! Don't talk,
> It's quite unnecessary, don't shout. . . .
> Silence, silence! What an uproar!
> Cursed fools, get out of here!

The comic possibilities of noise crop up throughout the opera, most spectacularly in Don Basilio's famous calumny aria, with its litany of dynamic terminology ("piano piano, ... sottovoce ...") and its musical evocation of calumny as a murmur that grows slowly but inevitably into a thunder of cannon fire. Indeed, the subject's only rival in the composer's affections is the gag about taking a long time to hurry up. The joke finds ideal musical articulation in the most famous of all Rossinian devices: the crescendo. Thus the unwanted chorus of gratitude after the Count's serenade is constructed, essentially, out of a single (repeated) crescendo. Its melodic and harmonic content couldn't be less interesting: except for a brief passage in the remote key of E flat, it consists of little more than rocking back and forth between tonic and dominant. What musical interest the passage boasts—outside, that is, of the magnificent crescendo itself—resides, characteristically, in the decorative obbligato for Fiorello and the Count. Musically, in other words, the piece is as arch and frivolous as are the emotions of the singers.

Thus if the opening duets of *The Marriage of Figaro* introduce a world of things and relationships—a world of alienation and reconciliation—the beginning of *The Barber of Seville* introduces a world of gestures, from which thought and feeling have been banished, a world where issues such as alienation and reconciliation can't even emerge. It is, I would contend, the safe, cynical intellectual landscape of European conservatism, into which many thinkers and artists of the early nineteenth century had been frightened by the excesses of the French Revolution. The single most powerful effect of Rossini's opening pages (as of his entire opera) is a sense of withdrawal, of pulling in one's intellectual and emotional horns, of depositing one's entire affect at the service of laughter.

Between the entrance music and the chorus of thanksgiving comes, as noted, the Count's serenade, "Ecco ridente." It is cast in a similar mold, except now the gag is not noise but exaggerated yearning (in the largo) followed by exaggerated ecstasy (in the allegro). It is, in a word, a *mock* serenade, and we never for a minute take the Count's assertions at face value. "Ecco ridente" is a splendid piece and a great challenge for the coloratura tenor. But it is also no more than that: a piece and a challenge, and it can be ripped from the fabric of the opera to be sung on the concert platform without its suffering even the slightest damage. In the largo, phrases of improbable grandiosity (leaps of a sixth and a seventh) give way to sudden coloratura bagatelles, ridiculing the text's pomposities. The succeeding allegro is ludicrously difficult, and the listener's attention is riveted on the tenor's effort to negotiate its treacherous runs. (In the "music lesson" scene of Act II, Rosina's aria "Contro un cor che accende amore" gives us the female counterpart of "Ecco ridente." It, too, represents itself explicitly as a "song"—thus allowing the prima donna to substitute an aria from another opera, if she so chooses—and it consists of mock-romantic utterances in which the audience listens primarily to the singer's technical accomplishments.) Rossini thus uses all his skill as a composer to eliminate even the possibility of our taking a genuine interest in the Count's predicament. Music, one might say, conspires to deny the reality of human emotion.

In sum, Mozart begins his opera by establishing real characters drawn from the imagination of the Enlightenment. Rossini begins his with a sequence of jokes, which serve as a defense mechanism against the Enlightenment's dangerous humanism.

THE REPRESENTATION OF FIGARO AND ROSINA (THE COUNTESS)

Figaro and Rosina (the Countess in *The Marriage of Figaro*) are central characters in both operas, but Mozart and Rossini represent them in strikingly different ways. Part of this difference, as noted, stems from their dissimilar functions in the two operas. In *The Barber of Seville* Figaro is the Count's factotum: he aids and advises the Count in procuring the latter's bride. In *The Marriage of Figaro* he is more integrally involved in the drama: the opera's subject is his own marriage and the threat posed to it by his libertine master. Rosina, on the other hand, has a more consistent relation to the action in both operas: in the first she is wooed, in the second neglected. These changes in dramatic function, of course, call for different musical handling, as would be the case even if the operas had been the work of the same composer. But Mozart's and Rossini's musical representations of both Figaro and Rosina diverge more radically than anything required by the stories. They reflect, once again, differences of worldview.

I will confine my observations here to the way Figaro and Rosina are presented in their arias. The portraits in both cases, and especially in *The Marriage of Figaro,* are modified by their appearances in recitative, duets, trios, and ensembles.

Figaro

Mozart writes three arias for his protagonist. The first two, "Se vuol ballare" and "Non più andrai," occur in Act I, the third, "Aprite un po' quegli occhi," in Act IV. The common theme of the arias is aggression. In them Mozart reveals various aspects of his character's hostility: the first aria, directed at Figaro's master, the Count, is menacing; the second, directed at his potential rival, the page Cherubino, is gently sadistic; and the third, directed against his fiancée,

Susanna, is hysterically vengeful. To put the matter schematically: the first is about class hatred, the second about erotic rivalry, the third about romantic betrayal.

"Se vuol ballare" is preceded by a recitative in which Figaro bitterly rehearses the Count's plan to seduce his bride. Mozart achieves the proper tone of menace (with a hint of anxiety) by setting the recitative to a unison accompaniment of cellos and basses, which comment angrily on each of Figaro's reflections:

> *Bravo, signor padrone! Ora incomincio*
> *A capir il mistero . . . e a veder schietto*
> *Tutto il vostro progetto: a Londra, è vero?*
> *Voi ministro, io corriero, e la Susanna . . .*
> *Segreta ambasciatrice . . .*

> Well done, my noble master! Now I begin
> To understand the secret . . . and to see
> Your whole scheme clearly: to London, isn't it?
> You as minister, I as courier, and Susanna . . .
> Confidential attachée . . .

The aria itself begins and ends with a superbly deliberate and threatening melody, to which Figaro sings:

> *Se vuol ballare,*
> *Signor Contino,*
> *Il chitarrino*
> *Le suonerò.*

> If you want to dance,
> My dear Count,
> It is I
> Who will play the guitar.

The disingenuously simple F major tune suggests an anger so disciplined, so just, and so sublime that it has no need for recourse to the hectoring gestures of, say, Don Pizarro in Beethoven's *Fidelio,* or Alberich in Wagner's *Das Rheingold.* In particular, the untranslatable and contemptuous diminutive "Signor Contino"—sung with almost sweet nonchalance—has the effect of turning established class relations on their head, putting the servant in psychological control of his master. Before the melody repeats itself there intervenes a vicious presto, in which Figaro announces that his chief weapon in this warfare will be nothing other than his wits, against which the Count, he assures us, will be defenseless. Here he is not so persuasive (nor is the music on the same level of inspiration), and he is decidedly more impressive when he returns to the *faux-naïf* simplicity of the aria's opening melody. Mozart's Figaro, we see, is a man of strong emotions and unusual self-confidence.

"Non più andrai," the bravura aria that closes the first act of the opera, is the most famous of Figaro's monologues. It is the tune quoted by Mozart's stage band in the last act of *Don Giovanni*. On first hearing, it seems rather a jolly affair, but it, too, is nasty enough in its own way. The aria, as mentioned, is addressed to the hapless page Cherubino, who has been banished to the Count's regiment for his amorous indiscretions, and Figaro takes obvious satisfaction in reminding him of the courtly pleasures that he must now forgo and the military agonies that await him. The "gloria militar" that Figaro commends to the page, and that Mozart evokes so wonderfully in the fanfares at the aria's conclusion, could easily spell the end of the page, whom Figaro has reason to dislike as a younger member of the leisure class who aspires to the same sexual intimacies with Figaro's fiancée as does the Count. (Several commentators have noted that Cherubino is simply the Count as a teenager.) Properly rendered, the bouncy C major melody of "Non più andrai" assumes unexpected bite, as when Figaro tells the page to anticipate

> *Molto onor, poco contante,*
> *Ed invece del fandango,*
> *Una marcia per il fango.*

> Lots of honor, little money,
> And instead of the fandango,
> A march through the mud.

Musically, it is made of the same deceptively harmonious stuff as "Se vuol ballare": it is somewhat foursquare and relies heavily on the least ambiguous harmonic progressions from tonic to dominant and back again. However, the absence of musical ambiguity suggests not dimwittedness but mastery. It is the confident tune of a man in charge. The aria is in fact the high water mark of Figaro's control in the opera, and the next three acts find him slipping badly. In it he is once again revealed as a fellow of strong views and equally strong, and not always altruistic, emotions. The man of reason, we learn, is also a man of passion, and Figaro's ironic discourse would not sound at all out of place on the lips of Voltaire.

The last of the three arias, "Aprite un po' quegli occhi," is probably the least well known, but it is also the most powerful.

Moreover, it dramatically enlarges our sense of Figaro's emotional life. Whereas in the first two arias his hostility is strictly controlled—a control suggested by the measured pace of the first and the equally steady, though more relaxed, jauntiness of the second—here he is quite beside himself. Figaro is not, we discover, merely a man of intelligence and reasonable anger (that is, anger based on the reality of his exploited situation), but one open to the full range of irrationality. Under other circumstances, we sense, the Figaro of "Aprite un po' quegli occhi" could well become an Otello: he is abjectly in love, he has (he thinks) been betrayed by his bride, and, in effect, he loses control. The threatening manner of "Se vuol ballare" and the easy sarcasm of "Non più andrai" give way to a pitiful, babbling calumniation of women. Like "Se vuol ballare," the aria is introduced by an accompanied recitative. But where the prevailing mood in the earlier recitative was disgust, here all is despair:

> *O Susanna, Susanna,*
> *Quanta pena mi costi!*

> O Susanna, Susanna,
> What anguish you cost me!

The aria itself is forced and breathless, with Figaro repeating over and over the deadly allusion to sexual infidelity, "Il resto nol dico" ("I need say no more"), which he sings on a desperate low B flat—desperate in the purely vocal sense that it seems to draw the singer down below his comfortable range, suggesting thereby a painful aside. The aria culminates in a hectic scramble of triplets up to repeated high E flats, which again find the singer straining at the borders of his comfortable range:

> *Colombe maligne,*
> *Maestre d'inganni,*
> *Amiche d'affanni*
> *Che fingono, mentono,*
> *Amore non sentono,*
> *Non senton pietà.*

> Malign doves,
> Mistresses of deceit,
> Friends of distress
> Who cheat and lie,
> Who feel no love
> And have no pity.

Largely through his music, Mozart lends this denunciation of women just the right aura of bogus cynicism—the sort of misogynistic outburst that betrays only too clearly the bad faith of its author. The aria has an exact counterpart in Ford's great monologue on jealousy in Act II of *Falstaff,* where Verdi also uses musical means to call the singer's bluff.

Of course, there is more to Mozart's Figaro than anger and hostility. If I were to conduct a similar examination of his function at other points in the opera, we would find him displaying nearly the full repertory of human attitudes: love, good humor, inventiveness, stupidity, gratitude, and more. But even within the single theme to which his arias are primarily devoted, he shows himself to be a figure of considerable depth and complexity.

Rossini's Figaro in *The Barber of Seville* is given only a single aria. One might be inclined to argue that if he had been granted more time at the microphone he would have revealed as many facets of his personality at does Mozart's Figaro. But it is no accident, I believe, that he holds forth only once, because he really has only one thing to say. He says it brilliantly, of course, and his aria, "Largo al factotum," is among the most famous in all opera.

"Largo al factotum" tells us everything there is to know about Rossini's barber. And what there is to know is that he thinks a great deal of himself. He is pure ego. To be sure, he also complains of being put upon, but that's only because everybody wants to avail him- or herself of Figaro's extraordinary talents. In his aria he catalogues those talents, names his clients, and generally celebrates himself.

If one thinks too much about *The Barber of Seville* (as I will doubtless be accused of doing), and especially about the barber himself, the opera begins to take on qualities of the theater of the absurd. Who is this barber after all? And what is he up to? In most ordinary respects, he is entirely without an emotional life. For instance, he has neither sexual nor romantic interests—at least none that we learn about. There's a suggestion at the beginning that he feels oppressed by the Count (a hint of the resentment felt by Mozart's Figaro), but that soon passes, and he enters into the Count's enterprise with as much relish as the Count himself. No one has been silly enough to propose that Figaro is motivated by the injustice of the situation: Rossini's Figaro would be the last candidate in the world for the role of operatic social critic. One might think he is driven by greed, for when the Count promises to reward him financially, he expresses delight at the golden prospect:

All'idea di quel metallo
portentoso, onnipossente,
un vulcano la mia mente
già comincia a diventar.

At the mere idea of that
portentous all-powerful metal
my mind becomes
a spouting volcano.

This is of course funny, but it's hard to believe that Figaro means it seriously, for not only does he express himself here with characteristic musical exaggeration (wide mock-heroic leaps followed, as in the Count's serenade, by coloratura high jinks), but the idea passes rather quickly from mind. Greed in the opera is represented by the music teacher Don Basilio, who must be repeatedly plied with money. Nor do we have any sense of what Figaro would do with the money. Would he buy new clothes? A house? Would he retire from his onerous job? His economic life, in other words, is as implausible as his romantic and sexual life. The more one examines him, the more he reduces to a single emotion: self-glorification. That emotion is realized through a single capacity: his superb intelligence. Here—and only here—he comes close to his Mozartean counterpart. He is an idea man. "Un'altra idea!" ("Another idea!") he exclaims to the Count in their duet. One might even say that he is pure mind, an abstraction. Small wonder that many commentators, mystified by his disembodied nature, have proposed that he is Gioacchino Rossini himself.

"Largo al factotum" is admirably designed to represent this "character." We experience the aria not as a revelation of this or that emotion, but as a masterpiece of vocal display. That is, we hear not a character emoting, but a baritone singing. It is the sort of aria—unlike any of those sung by Mozart's Figaro—that one collects recordings of, in order to hear how each of the great baritones of the century has met its challenges. First of all, we want to hear how he copes with its several high G's, a note that, if freely produced and sustained with tonal integrity by a true baritone voice, is among the most glorious sounds emitted by the human throat. (Mozart's Figaro sings nothing above F, and never sustains a note above E.) We also want to hear whether the singer attempts a high A—a note of tenorial altitude—on the word "Bravo," or settles for the lower option. When he comes to the line "Colla donnetta ... col cavaliere" ("With the young ladies ... with the young gentlemen"), does he fatten his voice for the men while slimming it to a near falsetto for the women? And, finally, we want to hear how he negotiates the treacherous patter and the difficult triplets near the aria's end. We listen for other things as well, but all are of the same sort: all pertain to the demonstration of vocal technique, not the revelation of character. Moreover, our attention to such matters reflects no fundamental unseriousness on our part. Rather, they are forced on us by the composer himself, who seeks in the aria, as he did in the opening scene, to create not a figure who might experience tensions and reconciliations (or any other human emotions), but a caricature, exaggerated almost into abstraction. Rossini's Figaro virtually prohibits our entertaining serious thoughts about him, and that prohibition is effected as much by the music of his aria as by anything he says or does. In sum, the representation of this character shows the same emotional withdrawal that I have detected in the opera's opening scene, and I would again suggest that the transformation Figaro has undergone between 1786 and 1816 is emblematic of a larger shift in European intellectual life over the same period.

Rosina (the Countess)

The two Rosinas offer a similar contrast. No commentator on Mozart's opera has failed to note that the Countess is a serious figure, despite the fact that in much of the opera she adopts the same comic tone as the other characters. Less nicely observed is the way Mozart elaborates her seriousness, allowing her to become more complex and admirable as the opera progresses. As with Figaro, this revelation comes primarily through her solo utterances—her two arias and her act of absolution at the end.

Though we don't see the Countess in the first act of *The Marriage of Figaro,* we hear a great deal about her, and we know from the Count's shenanigans—in the scene where Cherubino is discovered hiding in a chair while the Count presses his suit with Susanna—that she has excellent grounds for complaint. Appropriately, the second act opens with an aria, "Porgi, amor," devoted entirely to that complaint.

Here we might pause for a moment to imagine what kind of figure Mozart and Da Ponte could have set before us. It would not have been inconceivable, for instance, for the curtain to go up on a woman in a state of high dudgeon, barnstorming in the manner of, let us say, Norma when she discovers Pollione's infidelity, or Brünn-hilde when she discovers Siegfried's. But what we see, of course, is a melancholy creature who thinks not of revenge but of death:

> *Porgi, amor, qualche ristoro*
> *Al mio duolo, a'miei sospiri;*
> *O mi rendi il mio tesoro,*
> *O mi lascia almen morir.*

> O love, bring some relief
> To my sorrow, to my sighs;
> Either give me back my loved one,
> Or at least let me die.

These unremarkable words are set to a melody whose hushed arcs, when sung by the proper kind of voice—substantial, steady, pure, and with unflawed legato—suggest a magical stillness, a sense of repose and resignation such as one finds in certain of the poems of John Keats. The phrases, hovering in the upper-middle part of the voice and infinitely drawn out, rest on a woodwind-dominated orchestral base of superb languor. Though short, the aria nonetheless creates a vivid picture of the Countess's personality.

So the Countess is sorrowful. But she also emerges from this lovely aria as ever so slightly self-indulgent. The phrases seem to caress her sorrow—in contrast, for example, to the sorrow of Orfeo in the opening pages of Gluck's opera, which is abject and unqualified. The Countess, we remember, is the prototype for Richard Strauss's Marschallin, a figure whose long-suffering is checked only by her heroic stoicism.

But the Countess is also a richer figure than the Marschallin, just as Mozart's conception of human nature is richer than Strauss's. In her second aria, "Dove sono," the melancholy of "Porgi, amor" is supplemented by a new emotion, one as characteristic of the eighteenth century as it is uncharacteristic of our own—namely, hope. The andante of the aria ("Where are those happy moments of sweetness and pleasure?") covers much the same emotional ground as "Porgi, amor." Moreover, in harmony, pace, and general atmosphere, its music is remarkably like that of the earlier aria. Once again we hear the magical stillness and the sustained melodic arcs that, with a voice of the right weight and purity, can be breathtaking. But unlike "Porgi, amor," "Dove sono" transcends its melancholy beginnings in a concluding allegro of bracing hopefulness. The text is ambiguous:

Ah! se almen la mia costanza
Nel languire amando ognor
Mi portasse una speranza
Di cangiar l'ingrato cor.

Ah! if only my constancy
In yearning lovingly for him always
Could bring the hope
Of changing his ungrateful heart!

But Mozart's music, with its confident passagework, its unexpected and exhilarating rise through a C major arpeggio to a high A, and its grand concluding trill, banishes all ambiguity. The aria is one of the vocal and emotional high points of the opera, dramatically enlarging our sense of the Countess's psychology and admitting us into the inner sanctum of the eighteenth-century mind. Though no Pollyanna (this we know from the first half of her aria), she will not be defeated by her circumstances.

To the seriousness and hopefulness revealed in her two arias, the Countess's last solo appearance adds yet another dimension of character, and it, too, reflects an ideal of the Enlightenment, though the thinkers of the eighteenth century did not always succeed in living up to it. It might be called, simply, humanity: a generous response to one's fellowmen, a tolerance of their shortcomings, a readiness to forgive. It is the virtue celebrated in Sarastro's great aria "In diesen heil'gen Hallen" from *The Magic Flute:*

In diesen heil'gen Hallen
Kennt man die Rache nicht,
Und ist ein Mensch gefallen,
Führt Liebe ihn zur Pflicht.

Within these holy walls
Revenge is unknown,
And should someone fall,
Love leads him back to duty.

One's first intimation of this quality in the Countess comes in her beautiful "letter duet" with Susanna: a woman of the aristocracy and her chambermaid sing together as absolute equals, their thirds and sixths and their gently interwoven phrases suggesting two human beings in complete union. Music strips away all social distinctions and reveals them in their pure humanity.*

The Countess's final display of magnanimity is even more powerful, because it is extended to a person from whom she is separated not by the abstract distinctions of class but by personal neglect and offense. Over the course of the opera we have observed the Count's repeated betrayals, all of them deeply wounding to her. In the last act, disguised as Susanna, she suffers the ultimate indignity of her husband's making love to her under the misapprehension that she is another woman. When, therefore, at the opera's close the Countess steps out of the garden shadows to forgive her wayward spouse, we are overwhelmed by her act of unimaginable grace. There is, we discover, no pettiness in her, no poisonous resentment, only an exemplary tolerance and love. Her gesture bespeaks resources of human feeling that belong to a forgotten moral dispensation.

The Countess's generosity of spirit at this epiphanal moment, be it noted, is conveyed not by Da Ponte's text but again by Mozart's music. Her words in response to her husband's plea for forgiveness are somewhat less than memorable:

> *Più docile io sono*
> *E dico di sì.*

> I am kinder:
> I will say yes.

But Mozart composes these lines in a manner altogether consistent with the musical portrait he has created for the Countess in her two arias. In particular it has clear melodic and harmonic ties to the concluding phrases of "Dove sono": a twice-repeated upward leap of a fifth, followed by a suspension on the sixth above it, and then resolution by way of passagework along the classic and inevitable harmonic route through subdominant and dominant. This description makes it seem fairly complicated, but the effect couldn't be more elemental. There is the same slow pace, the same elongated melodic

---

* In the recitative preceding "Dove sono" the Countess seems to regret the social familiarity forced on her by the Count's infidelity:

> *Prima amata, indi offesa, e alfin tradita,*
> *Fammi or cercar da una mia serva aita!*

> Once loved, then insulted, and finally betrayed,
> I am obliged to seek help from one of my maids!

But the musical egalitarianism of the "letter duet" leaves a far more lasting impression than the aristocratic sentiments expressed here.

arc through the upper-middle portion of the soprano range, the same sense of stillness that one hears in "Porgi, amor" and the first part of "Dove sono," documenting, one might say, the Countess's musical integrity. Finally, and unforgettably, the entire ensemble takes up the Countess's phrase to the words "Then let us all be happy," suggesting that her goodness has touched everyone present. I am probably not the only person who cherishes this moment above any other in opera. But I may be unique in experiencing it as the perfect symbol of an age—an age that believed, with alarming lack of ambiguity, in the possibility of human virtue.

The Rosina of *The Barber of Seville* is an altogether different affair. Rossini treats her in much the same way he treats his Figaro. She, too, gets only one proper aria (the aria in the "music lesson" scene already referred to is a put-on), and it reveals a character that for all intents and purposes is indistinguishable from Figaro. That is, she, also, has but a single emotion, and it is the same emotion that exhausts Figaro's inner life: egoism. And to display it Rossini settles on the same musical device: a bravura aria in which we listen above all else to the singer. "Una voce poco fa," like "Largo al factotum," is one of those magnificent creations for the human voice that we want to hear essayed by all the great coloratura sopranos and mezzo-sopranos on record. If there is a distinction between the egoism of Figaro and that of Rosina, it is that the former resorts primarily to bluster, the latter to guile. But the characters remain strikingly similar, and just as it would be difficult to confuse the psychic lives of Mozart's Figaro and his Countess, it is no less difficult to distinguish, in terms of fundamental qualities of mind and personality, the corresponding figures in Rossini's opera.

Save for a brief appearance on her balcony, Rosina, like the Countess, doesn't enter the action until the opera is about a quarter over. Also like the Countess, she has good reason for complaint: she is being kept hostage by her doddering guardian, who hopes to marry her. Once again it is useful to imagine the range of possibilities available to the composer in introducing his aggrieved heroine. The person actually set before us could hardly be more different, both characterologically and musically, from the melancholy author of "Porgi, amor."

The scene is Rosina's room in Dr. Bartolo's house. There is a grandiloquent orchestral prelude, which, were it not for the gently mocking woodwind commentary, could serve to introduce any mythological figure from the world of *opera seria:* a stately tempo, rich sonorities, dotted rhythms, and trills. The aria itself has slow and fast portions. In the former, Rosina declares that she will not be frustrated in her romantic objectives: the line "Lindoro [the Count's pseudonym] shall be mine; I swear it, I shall win" is repeated four times. Rossini conveys her sense of resolve and sassiness with a heroic upward leap (first of a fourth, then of a sixth), followed by a descending volley of coloratura scalework. In performance, every Rosina takes the opportunity to elaborate the already highly decorated vocal line, until the final repetition culminates in a cadenza of preposterous length, complexity, and vocal extension, usually rising to a sustained high B natural. None of this is in the score, of course, but it is probably what Rossini would have expected. The joke is the familiar one of extravagant musical material squandered on egoistic trivialities.

In the allegro (actually marked "moderato," in contrast to the opening "andante"), Rosina abandons her immediate concerns— Lindoro and her tyrannical guardian—and offers us a general self-portrait, which is as gratuitous as the self-portrait Figaro offers in "Largo al factotum." Listening to an aria of this sort, one is apt to think, "Well, who asked you, anyway?" In other words, one is apt to wonder whom the character is singing to. In this respect there is a striking difference between Rosina and the Countess. The Countess, in her two arias, is obviously speaking to herself: she is musing, and we overhear her. Rosina, on the other hand, speaks directly to the audience. She ticks off her virtues as if she were being interviewed for a job: "I'm docile, I'm respectful, I'm obedient, gentle, loving; I let myself be ruled and guided." This is composed in an appropriately genial fashion, the tempo moderate, the coloratura relatively restrained. We are being set up, both musically and textually, for the inevitable qualification, "the ominous *but*." That "but" ("ma" in Italian) is in a way the high point of the aria: the action is brought to a halt, the orchestra is silenced, and the word is allowed to float freely out into the theater. It becomes an autonomous musical entity, summing up with unrivaled conciseness the essence of Rosina's contrariness. A good singer can do wonders with this seemingly innocuous B natural in the middle of the scale (the very fact that it is a B natural—the fifth or dominant of the key in which the aria is set—announces musically that an important qualification is about to follow). The score reveals that Rossini has left the matter largely in the performer's hands: the orchestral pause is indicated, but nothing differentiates the

B natural eighth note to which "ma" is set from the B natural eighth notes for the next two words ("se mi"). As often happens in the casual world of bel canto opera, some of the most striking musical effects result from performance practice. The score to the "mad scene" from *Lucia di Lammermoor*, for example, reveals only a rough outline of what one actually hears in the theater or on record. Thus in the present instance it would perhaps be most accurate to say that Rossini creates an opportunity, which no Rosina in my listening has failed to exploit.

The qualification, of course, is that if someone crosses her on matters of romance, Rosina will become a viper:

> *Ma se mi toccano dov'è il mio debole,*
> *sarò una vipera, sarò.*

> But if you hit me in a weak spot,
> I'll be a viper.

The coloratura turns aggressive, plunging down beneath the staff to a low G sharp, and after the whole has been repeated (and, according to convention, elaborately decorated by the singer), the final phrase carries the voice up over a thrillingly sustained high B. Rosina has "displayed" herself for our benefit, and when she is finished we are entirely convinced of one thing: she is incontrovertibly an opera singer.

It might appear from the text that "Una voce poco fa" is an aria about love, and that Rosina's celebration of self is thus distinguished from the barber's in having a higher purpose—i.e., romance. But if not the text, then the music tells us quite otherwise: love is not the subject, merely the occasion. It would make no difference—indeed, it would make a good deal more sense—if Rosina were singing about her resolve to become a coloratura soprano. Again, as in the case of Figaro, we are given a figure that for all practical purposes is affectless. She can engage in the action only in terms of an abstracted egoism. The closest Mozart came to creating such a character is Fiordiligi in *Così fan tutte* who sings "Come scoglio," an aria also cast in the mock-heroic vein. But Fiordiligi goes on to sing "Per pietà"—to become, in effect, a fully real creation with a complex inner life that one would never dream of attributing to Rosina. Like Figaro, then, Rosina exhibits that emotional withdrawal that seems a typical defense mechanism of European culture in the early nineteenth century.

THE CENTRAL ENSEMBLES

Although *The Marriage of Figaro* is in four acts and *The Barber of Seville* in two, from a structural standpoint both operas are divided into halves. Neither the first nor the third act of Mozart's opera ends in the sort of concentrated musical event that seems to demand an intermission, whereas the second act most assuredly does. True, the third act does technically conclude with a finale, but it is a modest affair—about a quarter as long as those of the second and fourth acts—and lacking in the cumulative effect of the great Mozart finales. Indeed, it is among the least satisfying parts of the opera.

Thus one experiences *The Marriage of Figaro*, just as one does *The Barber of Seville*, as essentially a two-part music drama. Within these extended stretches of musical and dramatic activity—lasting up to two hours—one musical number often functions as a kind of centerpiece. I don't mean this in any precise or technical sense, but audiences rarely fail to feel the weight of these central ensembles. They achieve their peculiar status by virtue of their strategic location, their size and complexity, and the compositional energy that has been lavished on them. Mozart and Rossini handle these ensembles in characteristically different fashion.

In the first half (i.e., the first two acts) of *The Marriage of Figaro*, the musical and dramatic centerpiece, it seems to me, is the "giudizio" trio for the Count, the Countess, and Susanna. Its rough counterpart in the first half of *The Barber of Seville* is the so-called letter duet between Figaro and Rosina (which is not to be confused with the letter duet—"Sull'aria"—between the Countess and Susanna in *The Marriage of Figaro*). In the latter halves of the two operas, the function of "central ensemble" devolves on the "sua madre" sextet in *The Marriage of Figaro* and on the "buona sera" quintet in *The Barber of Seville*. These four ensembles will be the objects of my discussion in the following pages.

The "Giudizio" Trio and the Letter Duet

The "giudizio" trio (the label is my own, based on the prominence of the word in the trio's text) occurs in Act II of *The Marriage of Figaro*. It establishes in our minds the depth of antagonism between the Count and the Countess.

We find the Countess in her room with Cherubino. She has just sent Susanna on an errand. Because of her nervousness about dressing the page as a girl, she has had the doors to the room locked. The stage is thus set for the confrontation with her husband.

The Count arrives outside, tries the door, and, finding it locked, demands to be admitted. The Countess stalls him while frantically depositing Cherubino in a closet. When finally allowed into the room, the Count is immediately suspicious and starts berating his wife, and does so all the more vehemently after he hears some furniture knocked over in the closet. Susanna returns unnoticed, and the trio (Count, Countess, and Susanna—the last audible, in theory, only to the audience) begins. The Count demands that the closet be opened; the Countess refuses indignantly; and Susanna marvels at the conflict to which she is witness and, with characteristic brightness, deduces its cause. We are at the emotional center of Mozart's opera.

From a distance of nearly two hundred years it is difficult to appreciate the sheer musical violence of this number. The dynamic range of Mozart's music seems narrow when heard alongside Berlioz, Verdi, or Wagner. But within that range this trio must have sounded tremendous to eighteenth-century audiences. The orchestration doesn't include heavy brass or percussion, but it is nevertheless extremely full and sonorous, with especially vigorous writing for the strings. The three-four "allegro spiritoso" moves at an almost brutal pace, and the music passes through distant harmonies, creating an atmosphere of anxiety and disorder.

First there is an alternation of shouted commands, contradictory imperatives from the two antagonists:

> COUNT: *Sortite!*
> COUNTESS: *Fermatevi!*
> COUNT: *Parlate!*
> COUNTESS: *Tacete!*
>
> COUNT: Come out!
> COUNTESS: Stop!
> COUNT: Speak!
> COUNTESS: Be silent!

There follow allusions to "disaster," "scandal," and "catastrophe." The atmosphere is further intensified by an upward modulation of a fourth as the main melody of the trio is repeated. The Countess's terrified and angry cries of "No, no, no" ("Nemmen, nemmen, nemmeno") ride fiercely up the scale to high A. Each party then concludes by commending prudence to the other: "Consorte mio (mia), giudizio!" The word "giudizio" is repeated more than a dozen times. Just before the end, the rush of the music is halted as first the Count and then the Countess hisses a final "Giudizio!" unaccompanied and to a menacing upward interval. Properly rendered, it is a chilling moment.

"Giudizio" long remains in the mind because of the musical prominence Mozart has assigned it. The word, as noted, means "prudence," and hence the mutual admonitions of the Count and Countess would seem to imply a concern for appearances: if tempers are not controlled there will be talk around the castle. But the music tells us that something more than reputation is at stake. Mere decorum could not have elicited music of such intensity. We have no trouble discerning the deeper issue so far as the Count is concerned: he is violently jealous. Moreover, he is not a prudent man and would hardly shy away from making a scene; indeed, he makes one in the last act when he publicly accuses his wife (in reality Susanna in disguise) of infidelity. But the Countess, who is essentially a sanguine and forgiving creature, is no less vehement in her reiteration of "Consorte mio, giudizio!" What is the source of her anger, which inspires Mozart to such assertive musical gestures?

Most everyone who has seen or listened to the opera knows the answer to this question. Admittedly, part of the Countess's indignation is feigned, as she is trying to bluff her way out of an embarrassing situation. But at a deeper level she is angry because she has been wrongly accused; she protests the injustice of her situation. When she sings "Giudizio!" we are inevitably in mind of its cognate "giustizia," that is to say, "justice." The trio carries a subliminal political text, which, I believe, is the source of its great energy. Mozart has gone to the violent heart of the situation.

Few are likely to disagree with this general construction of the trio's effect: we all feel the anger of the parties, we detect the Count's barely concealed jealousy, and we also have no doubt about the Countess's outrage. There will be more resistance, however, to the proposition that this trio documents Mozart's emotional identification with the political radicalism of the eighteenth century—that it captures in musical and dramatic form something of the spirit of the French Revolution. Notice, I say "emotional identification": as Georg Lukács has shown, one does not take an artist's political temperature by attending to his explicit political pronouncements. Rather, an artist's politics become interesting only when they achieve artistic expression. In Mozart's case, the consensus has been that he watered down the political criticism of Beaumarchais's play, especially the class conflict between the Count and his valet. This is all very true. But the "giudizio" trio, I would maintain, provides *musical* evidence that Mozart shared the Enlightenment's political vision. That vision is here filtered through a domestic prism and is in no sense ideologically correct, as the Count and Countess are of course both members of the ruling class. But in the Count's unfair treatment of his wife, Mozart sensed an instance of the general phenomenon of injustice, and he reacted to it, musically, with the warm indignation typical of the thinkers of his time. This affinity with the political imagination of the Enlightenment is, I believe, the deeper source of the number's powerful effect.

Until now I have spoken of this number as if it were a duet. But of course it is in fact a trio, for Susanna participates in it from the start. One might well ask why it is such. Why not simply a duet? To this there are a number of possible answers. The least interesting is that Susanna's presence furthers the plot: in the course of the scene she deduces that Cherubino is in the closet, which allows her, after the Count and Countess have left the room, to spring him, substitute herself in his place, and thereby set up the superb moment (in the finale) when she emerges demurely from the closet, to the astonishment of Count and Countess alike. But had Mozart been concerned only with the plot, he could easily have brought Susanna in to overhear just the end of the argument. Or he could have had her present throughout, but as a silent observer. There is, in other words, no compelling dramatic reason why the piece should be a trio.

There are better musical reasons. Susanna's participation lends the music a denser texture—the vocal weight and complexity, one might say, necessary to create an appropriately violent atmosphere. Indeed, I suspect that purely musical considerations weighed most heavily in Mozart's thinking. But there is a psychological element as well: Susanna is shown as witness to (and musical participant in) a scene that, to a person in her position, must have been at once terrifying and revelatory. She observes two members of the nobility, husband and wife, stripped of their dignity and accosting each other like savages. Musically speaking, she shares the horror of the moment by echoing the Countess's phrases at the trio's outset. But as the piece progresses, she achieves a kind of psychological distance, and her musical line grows more independent and decorative (factors emphasized by the performance practice of assigning to her the two difficult runs up to high C that Mozart had originally intended for the Countess). The effect is to suggest, musically, a kind of political education: the higher orders, she discovers, are, underneath their fine clothing, subject to the same violent emotions as the rest of humanity. Although she, too, continues to fret about "a scandal, a catastrophe," her increasing musical autonomy betrays a distinct irony. "Capisco," she sings, meaning of course that she has figured out the situation with respect to the page in the closet. But she has also figured out something more profound. In the course of the trio the myth of class has been exploded. I won't insist too strenuously on this interpretation, as its effect is largely subliminal, and undoubtedly most listeners experience the trio first and foremost as a musical event. But the theme is nonetheless there, and it recurs throughout the opera, starting with Figaro's rude awakening, in the first act, as to the Count's designs on Susanna. It is, moreover, one of the great themes of Enlightenment social thought, which might fairly be described as a protracted assault on the idea of aristocracy, the notion that humanity is naturally divided into distinct social orders, each with its peculiar rights, manners, and even qualities of character. When, as in the "giudizio" trio, the lower classes find out the truth about their betters, the whole notion of a society of orders is drawn into question. Again one sees that Mozart's opera is deeply imbued with the ideas of its age, and it expresses those ideas with an emotional precision known only to music.

The musical centerpiece of Act I of *The Barber of Seville* is the letter duet, "Dunque io son," between Figaro and Rosina. It occupies that place by virtue of its compositional brilliance and the dramatic excitement created by its being the first meeting in the opera between these characters of unmistakable force. Considering what an elaborate musical event it is (with its introductory recitative it lasts between seven and eight minutes), we might be struck at first by certain oddities.

For one thing, these two characters, who sing at such length, have no emotional interest in each other whatsoever. As opposed to the Count and Countess, neither love, nor hate, nor anything else binds them together. They can't even be called friends. At best one might say that Rosina has reason to be grateful to Figaro for his efforts on behalf of her romance, even if those efforts are unrelated to any feelings he might have for her. The essential neutrality of their relationship can be appreciated if one considers, for a moment, another operatic encounter between heroine and romantic intermediary: Cio-Cio-San and Consul Sharpless in the second act of *Madame Butterfly*.

Sharpless and Butterfly are even less well acquainted than Figaro and Rosina. So far as we know, they have met only once—at Butterfly's wedding—and the encounter was brief. Yet their interview in Act II proves the most wrenching moment in an opera not short on such events: the Consul's affection and stifled pity, Butterfly's elation and exquisite hospitality, the excruciating reading of Pinkerton's letter, the muffled curse, and finally Butterfly's uncompromising dismissal of the Consul when he suggests that she marry her wealthy Japanese suitor, Yamadori. Even listeners not especially sympathetic to Puccini are unlikely to make it through these passages unaffected. Butterfly's situation, of course, is tragic, while Rosina's is promising: Figaro has come to tell her that Lindoro loves her. But in the duet she exhibits none of the delight one might expect her to feel, or even the gratitude she ought properly to show this man who has brought her such good (albeit fully anticipated) tidings.

There is an excellent reason for her relative indifference, and this is the second odd thing about the duet: for all its considerable length, virtually nothing happens. Or, to speak more precisely, its seeming events cancel one another out—which explains why the typical operagoer, even one who knows the text, can with difficulty remember what supposedly occurs in the course of this number. By way of contrast, not even the most inattentive listener will forget what happens between Butterfly and Sharpless.

On first inspection, two things might appear to take place: in the recitative Figaro reveals to Rosina that Lindoro (the Count) loves her, and in the duet proper he urges her to write the young man a note arranging an assignation (hence the name "letter duet"). But we sense from the start that the "revelation" is no revelation at all. Indeed, the funniness of the moment stems largely from the fact that both parties to the discussion are merely pretending to ignorance. And if anyone is still in doubt, Rosina announces explicitly, in the duet, that she already knew what Figaro came to tell her. In the duet we also learn that the proposed letter is just as bogus as the supposed intelligence delivered in the recitative, for (and this is the point of the joke) Rosina has already written the letter and in fact produces it for Figaro on the spot.

So we have seven or eight minutes of music devoted to two characters who have no particular feelings for one another and in which nothing happens. How does it work?

Not surprisingly, by a ruthless exploitation of the very emotional and dramatic vacuum I have just described. Essentially the scene presents a spectacular confrontation of egos, a kind of coloratura warfare.

The introductory recitative, which never fails to amuse, consists of Rosina's asking a series of questions to which she already knows the answers, while Figaro either pretends to have forgotten or gives intentionally misleading replies. The subject of the interview, naturally, is Rosina herself and her various merits. It culminates in the unforgettable moment when the barber spells out, then sounds out by syllable, and finally sings out—usually at the top of his lungs—the heroine's name: *ROSINA*. The moment invites every sort of hamming, and in most performances Rosina herself joins in the spelling bee.

The duet, "Dunque io son," registers in the mind primarily as a piece of fiendishly difficult coloratura, especially for the baritone, who must imitate many of the rapid figures executed by his naturally more flexible soprano or mezzo-soprano partner. Only one baritone in a hundred can manage it with dignity. Characteristically, the most elaborate vocal displays are reserved for each singer's self-congratulatory asides:

> ROSINA: (Già me l'ero immaginata: lo sapevo pria di te.)
> FIGARO: (Oh, che volpe sopraffina, ma l'avrà da far con me,
>   sì, ma l'avrà da far con me.)

> ROSINA: (I'd already guessed it: I knew it before you did.)
> FIGARO: (Oh, what a sly minx, but she'll have to deal with
>   me, yes, she'll have to deal with me.)

There follows Figaro's urging that Rosina write a note—"just two lines"—which in turn elicits, first, a show of mock modesty and, then, the already completed missive. This little *coup de théâtre* marks a decisive turning point in the war. Indeed, it would not be inaccurate to call it an unqualified victory for Rosina, and in the second half of the duet Figaro sings as if he had suffered a musical defeat. Gone is the effort to keep up with Rosina's vocal antics—the "Anything you can do I can do better" routine. Instead he retreats to the role of accompanist, singing a delightful countermelody (which, however, poses no technical challenges) to the words "Women, women . . . ye eternal gods," while the triumphant Rosina undertakes coloratura acrobatics of ever more spectacular difficulty.

In other words, Rossini has written a duet entirely suited to a confrontation between the singer of "Largo al factotum" and the singer of "Una voce poco fa": a singers' duet, whose only real subject is the self. We are still in the affectless world of abstracted egos, colliding like electronic particles to create a magnificent display of vocal fireworks, and we are, needless to say, light-years removed from the angry, mortifying engagement of Mozart's "giudizio" trio. The injustice of Rosina's situation never crosses our mind. Even though, objectively speaking, she is no less abused than the Countess, the thought we are least likely to entertain on leaving the theater is "Something ought to be done about things!" On the contrary, such thoughts have been positively discouraged. The duet is the perfect symbol of an age that has decided to take nothing other than the self too seriously.

The "Sua Madre" Sextet and the "Buona Sera" Quintet

The central ensembles in the second halves of the operas—the "sua madre" sextet from *The Marriage of Figaro* and the "buona sera" quintet from *The Barber of Seville*—have at least two important things in common: except for the finales, each is the most complex musical number in its respective opera; and each is based essentially on a gag. But again the differences turn out to be far more important than the similarities.

The sextet in Act III of *The Marriage of Figaro* is occasioned by the discovery that Figaro is the long-lost son of Marcellina and Bartolo. Up to this point in the opera, the latter have figured as villains: Marcellina as the vitriolic "other woman" whom Figaro has passed over for Susanna, Dr. Bartolo as the vengeful former guardian of the Countess. But when they discover that Figaro has a birthmark on his right arm, Marcellina embraces him as her bastard son "Raffaello" and introduces Bartolo as his father. The Count and his "judge," Don Curzio, until now allies of Marcellina and Dr. Bartolo in their campaign against Figaro, greet the news balefully: "Sua madre!" and while they continue to grumble, the members of the reunited family—father, mother, and son—express their genuine delight.

The slapstick, both physical and musical, is provided by Susanna's entrance just at the moment when Figaro and his mother are embracing. Naturally, Susanna misinterprets the situation and boxes him on the ears. But Marcellina explains, and Susanna, in a kind of rhetorical daze, can utter only "Sua madre?" To which everyone responds, first sequentially (to a rising harmonic progression) and then in unison, "Sua madre!" At the end of the progression, where we are prepared for a pause, Figaro jumps in with "And this is my father," thus allowing the entire musical sequence to be repeated. The ejaculations of "sua madre" and "suo padre" (each is repeated eleven times) create an appropriately broad and surefire comic effect.

But, as Joseph Kerman has noted, although the sextet is a joke, it is also a moment of reconciliation: a son has been reunited with his parents, a once-scorned future daughter-in-law is accepted with affection by her fiancé's mother and father. This is reflected in both text and music: the Count and Don Curzio grouse in the musical background, but Figaro, Susanna, Marcellina, and Bartolo unite to sing of their "sweet contentment" in warm and ingratiating harmonies that seem to float freely above the sextet's steady pulse, deaf to the mean thoughts of the Count and his legal henchman. Their tune suggests a realm of well-being in the midst of squalid intrigue. As so often happens with Mozart, the joke turns serious: we witness a display of authentic emotion. One is back in the world of the Enlightenment, where human relations—in this instance, the relations between parent and child—are taken seriously and where antagonisms allow of resolution.

The reconciliation effected in the sextet is set up in part by an earlier number in the opera, the Act I duet between Susanna and Marcellina. The duet's main dramatic function was to establish the antagonism between these two characters and thus to heighten both the humor and the pathos of their union in Act III. (In the final act there comes an even more touching moment between them, when Marcellina sides with Susanna against her own son; it marks a 180-degree shift in their relationship.) Taken by itself, however, the duet in the first act has always seemed to me a failure, though a revealing one. It fails, I believe, because, unlike the sextet just discussed, it consists of nothing more than a gag. To be specific, the duet is a contest of insults—disguised as courtesies—arising out of the question of which of the two women should leave the room first. Marcellina says that precedence should go to Susanna, because she's "the Count's favorite." No, says Susanna, Marcellina should lead the way, because she's "the love of all Spain." The supposed *coup de grâce* is delivered by Susanna when she suggests that Marcellina be given precedence because of her "age."

On paper, I suppose, this is amusing enough. But as set to music by Mozart, the two women sing along in attractive harmony, and one would never guess that they were quarreling. The piece is charming, but it's not funny. Mozart can't seem to muster the brutal musical caricature necessary to bring off a joke of this sort. The supple contours of his music evoke characters too full-bodied to behave in so stylized a fashion.

In such matters, Rossini is altogether his superior. One need think only of the duet between Count Almaviva and Dr. Bartolo that launches the second act of *The Barber of Seville*. Like that between Susanna and Marcellina in *The Marriage of Figaro,* it turns on an exchange of civilities that are in reality insults. Over and over, the Count, dressed as a music teacher, whines his hypocritical greeting of "Peace and Joy! Joy and Peace!" until his host becomes so infuriated that he starts parodying him. The situation is hilariously captured in the oily plangency and mincing gait of Rossini's tune. It usually makes us laugh out loud, whereas the duet between Susanna and Marcellina elicits only forced smiles.

The central ensemble in Act II of *The Barber of Seville*, like the duet I have just mentioned, is again a superb piece of musical slapstick. As with Mozart's sextet, it is built around a comic arrival: in this case the unexpected (and undesired) entrance of the music teacher Don Basilio. Ernest Newman calls it "one of the most effective entrances in all opera." The source of its effectiveness could hardly be more rudimentary: the interloper threatens to explode a ruse whose first prerequisite is his absence. Count Almaviva has made a second penetration of the Bartolo household, disguised as an apprentice music teacher sent to substitute for the supposedly ailing Don Basilio. The object of this quintet, therefore, is to prevent Basilio from blowing the Count's cover.

The number is in three parts. In the first Rossini milks everybody's astonishment at Basilio's arrival. In the second the Count and Figaro mount a campaign to convince Basilio that he is indeed ill: text and music are devoted to diagnosis and prescription. In the third all present join in a concerted "Good night" ("buona sera") to Don Basilio, who, properly bribed, takes his leave. Even in the most routine performance the scene can't fail to entertain. Well done, it elicits belly laughs.

The three parts of the quintet rely on a single comic device: in all of them, Rossini achieves his desired effect by means of ironic imitation and repetition. One character's statement is transformed into another's question, and vice versa. This to-ing and fro-ing is nicely reflected in the music, which shifts back and forth from tonic to dominant with remarkably little fuss. Thus, for example, the opening part of the quintet is set to an unctuous tune (ultimately repeated four times), whose first phrase is a descending sequence from the tonic chord (violins), followed by an upward scale (clarinets in thirds) to the dominant, where the descending sequence is repeated to the notes of a dominant seventh chord (violins), followed by a downward scale (clarinets in thirds again) back to the tonic. The harmonic simplicity and perfect thematic symmetry of the tune—and the symmetry of the orchestration as well—seem an exact musical translation of the neat, mechanical repetitions of the text:

> BARTOLO: *Don Basilio, come state?*
> BASILIO: *Come sto?*
> BARTOLO: *E . . . il curiale?*
> BASILIO: *Il curiale?*

> BARTOLO: How do you feel, Don Basilio?
> BASILIO: How do I feel?
> BARTOLO: What about the lawyer?
> BASILIO: The lawyer?

It is a world of automatic binary polarities where both words and music sound as if they came from a computer.

In the second part of the quintet—that devoted to diagnosis and prescription—the pattern continues, but now the music abandons its prefabricated antitheses in favor of repetitions that might be called onomatopoeic: wherever possible Rossini gives musical representation to the various physical disorders attributed to Don Basilio. Thus:

> ALMAVIVA: *Siete giallo come un morto.*
> BASILIO: *Sono giallo come un morto?*

> ALMAVIVA: You're as yellow as a corpse.
> BASILIO: I'm as yellow as a corpse?

This is set to a sinister phrase in F minor, rising only half a tone and repeated by Basilio, suggesting both the final agony and rigor mortis. Then:

> FIGARO: *Che tremarella!*
> *Questra è febbre scarlattina!*
> BASILIO: *Scarlattina!*

> FIGARO: What shivers!
> It's a case of scarlet fever!
> BASILIO: Scarlet fever!

This diagnosis finds Figaro singing with tremulous agitation and scrambling feverishly to a high E flat. The contrasting musical representations nicely suit the pigmentary incompatibility of Almaviva's and Figaro's diagnoses.

There follows the prescription: "Quick to bed," urged by all and acquiesced in by Don Basilio (who, however, isn't totally decrepit: "I'm not deaf," he protests). And finally we reach the third section of the quintet: the prolonged farewells—"Good night, my good sir," sung by each of the principals in turn. Like the opening melody of the quintet, it is based on a simple alternation of tonic and dominant arpeggios, but with an important difference: in this instance the tune is launched on a sustained note lying outside the major chord—namely, the sixth. By thus leaning on what is in effect a foreign tone, Rossini breaks up the harmonic and rhythmic regularity and lends the ensemble a comic asymmetry. One might say that this note insults the musical fabric in the same way that the words of the text—the farewells—insult Don Basilio: Rossini achieves what could be called musical rudeness. The ultimate gag comes when Don Basilio himself latches onto both tune and phrase, reciprocating the farewells, so to speak—first on a stupendous high E natural (which, delivered by a basso profondo, sounds like a blast from the trombone), and then at the opposite end of the singer's range, on two arpeggios rising, respectively, from low B and low A, cavernous tones that play off once again the fundamental alternation of tonic (G) and dominant (D). The funniness of the scene is not unrelated to the extraordinary economy of Rossini's musical means. Almost the whole of this sustained musical joke has been constructed out of repetition and the simplest form of harmonic antithesis.

The quintet serves up a typical Rossinian confection of stupidity, greed, and mendacity—and the greatest of these is mendacity. From start to finish the characters lie to one another with abandon. Admittedly, when Don Basilio first arrives, the Count is mainly discomfited and Dr. Bartolo confused, but the former soon recovers himself and the latter is persuaded that his interests, also, rest in Basilio's swift departure. Thenceforth follow a string of outrageous deceptions: everyone misrepresents Don Basilio's condition to him, all prescribe unnecessary and probably not very efficacious therapies (assuming he were sick), and all conclude with unctuous farewells, which, save in the case of Dr. Bartolo, express feelings that couldn't be more foreign to the characters' true sentiments. A comparison with Mozart's sextet is instructive. Mean-spiritedness is represented there too, in the complaints of the Count and Don Curzio. But Mozart's

emotional spectrum is dramatically broader, as it includes also sentiments of gratification, relief, and love. Characteristically, moreover,
the sextet turns not on a lie but on the revelation of a truth: the
discovery of Figaro's parentage.

One might be inclined to protest that this comparison is all very
interesting but rather pointless: Rossini's quintet, after all, deals with
one situation, Mozart's sextet with another, and thus it is not a bit
surprising that the first is about lying and aggression, while the second
is about truth and love. Or, to put the objection in more general
terms, the comparison is not especially revelatory since the common
denominator necessary to any meaningful analogy hasn't been established.

I would suggest, however, that it has. My contention is that
these two ensembles occupy comparable structural positions in operas
that are representative works of their composers and that, for reasons
identified in the first section of this chapter, might well be expected
to show marked similarities. When Mozart comes to the center of his
Beaumarchais opera, he composes a little musical essay on truth and
love. For exactly the same place in *his* Beaumarchais opera, Rossini
composes a musical essay on lying and hostility. The earlier composer
states the case for humanism, whereas the later composer expounds
his misanthropy. The respective librettos of the two operas, of course,
provide the occasions for these contrasting utterances, but their
argument is at bottom musical. Needless to say, the comparison I
have mounted here doesn't constitute definitive proof—whatever that
might mean—that Mozart is the composer of the Enlightenment while
Rossini is the composer of the Reaction. To me, however, it is a
matter of some significance that at just about the same moment in
the evening's entertainment, each artist pulls out all the compositional
stops to such radically different ends.

The contrast touched on here also helps explain a curious
discrepancy in our response to Mozart and Rossini. I don't believe
I've ever heard the beginning of a Rossini opera without thinking
something along the lines of: "This is too good to be true. Why don't
I listen to this splendid music more often? And why aren't these
wonderful operas staged more regularly?" By comparison, a Mozart
opera can seem just slightly lacking in bite; one occasionally wishes
for more of Rossini's snappiness. But in the long run Mozart proves
more satisfying: he tolerates repeated exposure in a way that Rossini
doesn't. The main reason for this, doubtless, is Mozart's larger musical
vocabulary: Rossini's range is limited, and charming though his music

is, we eventually tire of it. But the discrepancy in sheer skill also reflects a discrepancy of spirit: Mozart gives us more of life, a wider canvas, the virtues as well as the vices. He is the more capacious artist. We can listen to him more often because his comedies (Rossini's serious operas are another matter; their deficiencies are of a graver sort) don't insist so relentlessly on a single psychological perspective, which, no matter how much truth it might contain, ultimately grows wearisome.

Both because of its different dramatic purpose and because of Rossini's unambiguously farcical intent, the quintet in *The Barber of Seville* assumes a shape quite different from Mozart's sextet in *The Marriage of Figaro*. Where the latter ends in a moment of reconciliation and musical integration—Figaro's reunion with his family—the outcome of the quintet is just the opposite: it terminates not in union but in separation. The offending party—Don Basilio—is ushered out of the house. To be sure, a problem has been solved, a danger passed, and everyone can catch his or her breath. But after Don Basilio has left, the remaining characters stand in exactly the same relation to one another as before his arrival, and the intrigue picks up where it left off. There has been no transformation, no reordering of fundamental relationships. Viewed musically, the whole scene is composed in a style analogous to that Mozart adopts for his sequence of comic "sua madres" and "suo padres," a style that he of course abandons as the issue of his sextet turns earnest. In Rossini, on the other hand, the musical unseriousness is brilliantly sustained. Indeed, the quintet is among the most striking musical evidences of the postrevolutionary generation's emotional retreat. How else is one to account for the enormous compositional energy lavished on an event of such human inconsequence?

THE FINALES

The Marriage of Figaro has three finales, *The Barber of Seville* two. As noted, however, the Act III finale of *Figaro* is a modest creation. Similarly, the second finale to *The Barber of Seville* exists largely on paper: it consists of a sextet with chorus and is even briefer than the third-act finale of *Figaro*. In the theater, however, what one hears at the end of *The Barber of Seville* usually sounds like a finale: that is, one hears a longish stretch of "composed" music, uninterrupted by recitative. The effect might be described as an aural illusion. The penultimate number of the opera, an elaborate aria for the Count, is virtually never performed, being far too difficult for contemporary tenors to negotiate without vocal embarrassment. Thus the concluding sextet is juxtaposed—save for a passage of recitative that lasts little more than a minute—to a long, two-part trio for Figaro, the Count, and Rosina. And since these three characters are also the only ones to hold forth individually in the final sextet (the others simply sing along with the chorus), the opera leaves the impression of ending with three consecutive trios for its principal tenor, baritone, and mezzo-soprano (or, as often happens, soprano). The middle of these, "Zitti, zitti," is the most famous and also the most representative: while making their escape by ladder from Dr. Bartolo's house, the three pause to caution one another—at considerable length and volume—to keep quiet and hurry up. It is the quintessential Rossinian gag, the last and funniest version of the routine that makes its debut with the noisy musicians in the opera's first scene. That *The Barber of Seville* should open and close on the same joke says a good deal about its psychological range. Stripped of the Count's preposterous coloratura aria, the act does, however, achieve a sense of musical concentration toward the end, if not on the scale of a full-fledged finale.

By way of contrast, the finale to Act IV of *The Marriage of Figaro* is the genuine item: long, complex, and terminating in the Countess's rending apotheosis. Both finales take place at night, but only Mozart draws on the psychological resonance of night, as would later composers (notably Berlioz, Verdi, and Wagner), to conjure up his own distinct blend of balminess and anxiety. With Rossini, there is merely "the cover of darkness."

The first finales to *The Marriage of Figaro* and *The Barber of Seville* are more strictly comparable. In this instance Rossini attempts a musical construction on roughly the same scale as Mozart's. His finale is nearly as long as Mozart's, and, also like the latter's, it incorporates a wide range of events: arrivals, departures, discoveries, confrontations, and (as with Mozart) ultimate confusion. These finales mark the beginnings of the "continuous" style of nineteenth-century opera: discrete numbers give way to uninterrupted (if still segmental) music, which encompasses under one compositional roof the separate tasks previously assigned to recitative and numbers—i.e., action and reflection. Since these are ambitious musical structures, comparable in length and complexity to a symphony or a concerto, a full analysis of each would require more space than I'm prepared to allot them. The finale to Act II of *The Marriage of Figaro*, for example, contains no fewer than ten distinct sections, each with its own musical profile, and each embracing a stretch of plot that would take several paragraphs just to summarize. Here I wish to consider only one segment from each finale, a segment that I find particularly revealing of its composer's worldview.

Figaro's Cross-Examination

About midway through Mozart's finale comes a musical sequence that might be called "Figaro's cross-examination." To appreciate its significance one needs some knowledge of the dramatic circumstances. Following the "giudizio" trio, and while the Count and Countess were out of the room, Cherubino had managed to escape from the closet by jumping out the window into the garden. In the course of the finale, we learn that he was observed in that emergency exit by the Count's gardener. Figaro, the *soi-disant* wit, now proposes to save the day by insisting that the person who jumped from the window was in fact himself, not the page. The music of his "cross-examination" begins as he lays down this claim, for he is quickly confronted with the embarrassing task of explaining a piece of paper that had fallen from the jumping man's pocket. The next few minutes of the finale are devoted to his effort to extricate himself from this situation by identifying the document. The wit, in short, is put on trial.

Mozart organizes the cross-examination around an orchestral theme of remarkable simplicity: a four-bar phrase distinguished by hypnotizing repeated triplets in the second and fourth measures. From its first sounding, the theme suggests the process of deliberation: its self-consciously measured pace (reminiscent of the droll orchestral figure that accompanied Susanna's unexpected emergence from the closet earlier on), its steady pulse, and its harmonic wanderings as the cross-examination proceeds convey the impression of a mind at work, a brain ticking away as it wrestles with the intractable material. And of course that is precisely the subject of Mozart's drama here: the feverish workings of Figaro's mind as it brings all its resources to bear on fielding the Count's questions. When the gardener suggests that the paper is most likely a list of Figaro's debts, Mozart interrupts the cross-examination—while continuing to exploit the same musical material—to drive the gardener from the stage. It has always seemed to me a slight flaw in the structure of the finale to have given such prominent musical articulation to his exit.

The distraction of the gardener eliminated, Figaro's situation becomes truly desperate. He has, of course, no idea what the paper might be. At this point, however, the women come to his rescue—providing, incidentally, yet further evidence of the feminist ethos of the opera, a fact that should be borne in mind when contemplating the misogynistic elements in *Così fan tutte* and *The Magic Flute*. The Countess manages to observe that the document in question is Cherubino's military commission. She passes this information on to Susanna, who in turn whispers it to Figaro. The last-named then responds proudly:

> *Uh che testa! quest'è la patente,*
> *Che poc'anzi il fanciullo mi diè.*

> Oh, what a head! It's the commission
> The boy gave me a while ago.

He is far from being out of the woods, however. The cross-examination continues: why, asks the Count, had the boy given the commission to Figaro? Again Figaro is saved by the women: in a magnificent passage, in which the little orchestral figure makes its way through a series of resounding resolutions at ever greater volume, he stumbles triumphantly into the right answer, much to the Count's dismay.

> FIGARO: *Vi manca . . .*
> COUNT: *Vi manca?*
> COUNTESS (aside to Susanna): *Il suggello!*
> SUSANNA (aside to Figaro): *Il suggello!*
> COUNT (to Figaro, who pretends to be thinking): *Rispondi!*
> FIGARO: *È l'usanza . . .*
> COUNT: *Su via, ti confondi?*
> FIGARO: *È l'usanza di porvi il suggello.*

> FIGARO: It lacks . . .
> COUNT: It lacks?
> COUNTESS *(aside to Susanna):* The seal!
> SUSANNA *(aside to Figaro):* The seal!
> COUNT *(to Figaro, who pretends to be thinking):* Answer!
> FIGARO: It's usual . . .
> COUNT: Come, you're confused?
> FIGARO: It's usual to seal it.

The moment plays off the joke of the witless wit, as first suggested in the opening duets between Figaro and Susanna, when the latter bested the former on his own ground. We have been treated to a little triumph of intelligence. Figaro may not be as smart as he seems to the Count, but he does, after all, show good sense when he "pretends to be thinking," for had he failed to do so the Count would have figured out that his answers were being prompted. The situation inspires Mozart to an awesome musical display, as he works his modest little phrase—the primitive unit of cerebration, one might say—into a thrilling climax, suggesting a series of mental processes brought to a fully satisfying conclusion. Whether consciously or not, he seems to be presenting us here with a demonstration of his own intelligence, an exhibition in music of the sort of mental prowess that Figaro only aspires to as he wrestles with the Count's challenge. It is the sort of passage that makes one exclaim, "What a genius Mozart was!" Moreover, I half suspect that Mozart himself may have entertained the same thought as he composed it.

But of course Figaro's intellectual achievement is of questionable authenticity. His triumph has been as much a matter of luck as wit, and he would have been lost without the goodwill and resourcefulness of the women. Appropriately, therefore, no sooner has Figaro "solved" the riddle than Mozart reverts, as if nothing had happened, to the little theme in the same apprehensive and indecisive form in which we first heard it. The music has moved forward boldly to suggest a mind on the march, but the pretension to intelligence dissolves almost before it has made its claims. Mozart's sudden musical reversal perfectly captures this sense of intellectual deflation, as it does the Count's embarrassment. Indeed, from the perspective of the revived little theme, we are likely to look back on the harmonic resolutions and the orchestral crescendo of the climactic moment—so satisfying when they occur—as just a bit pompous. In other words, we are given a heavy dose of musical irony, which makes us conscious of how ridiculously people can behave. Thus the powers and pretensions of mind have been displayed and criticized in the best Enlightenment fashion. The effect is similar to that of Voltaire's *Candide,* where ingenuity and mental paralysis, speculative indulgence and cynicism, appear as opposite sides of the same coin. Moreover, as usual, Mozart's display and critique have been realized largely by musical means.

The "Picture of Stupefaction" in The Barber of Seville

The most striking moment in the finale to Act I of *The Barber of Seville* is what Rossini labels the "quadro di stupore" or "picture of stupefaction." It is a device to which he was especially partial. An even more splendid example is provided by the sextet "Questo è un nodo" ("What a snarled knot") from *La Cenerentola* (1817). The idea is as follows: when developments grow impossibly confused toward the end of the act—with more entrances, revelations, accusations, and raised tempers—the composer calls a kind of musical time-out. There is a sudden caesura, everything grows unexpectedly hushed, and all the characters turn to the audience, in a collective soliloquy, to express their stupefaction at the course of events. The whole thing has the effect of a grand musical parenthesis.

In *The Barber of Seville* this moment comes when the troops stationed in Dr. Bartolo's house refuse to arrest the troublemaking "Lindoro," because he has surreptitiously shown them documents identifying himself as Count Almaviva. Rosina, Bartolo, Basilio, and the maid Berta unite to sing, one after another:

> *Freddo(a) ed immobile*
> *come una statua,*
> *fiato non restami*
> *da respirar.*

> Frozen and motionless
> as a statue,
> I hardly have
> breath to breathe.

The Count and Figaro know what's going on. Therefore they remain outside this mesmerizing stupefaction and observe it, the Count simply repeating the above words but changing "I" to "he," while Figaro offers the following commentary to a countermelody:

> *Guarda Don Bartolo,*
> *sembra una statua!*
> *Ah, ah, dal ridere*
> *sto per crepar!*

> Look at Don Bartolo,
> still as a statue!
> Ha, ha, I'm ready
> to burst laughing!

The musical construction of this ensemble is extremely complex. It is the sort of vocal writing sometimes called instrumental: the voices are treated very much as if they were individual instruments in a woodwind or string sextet. The lines are highly mechanical (though Figaro's, appropriately, is slightly less so: he, after all, is conscious of what's happening), giving way to elaborate but strictly rhythmical coloratura. The result is to make the singers sound like puppets, as if their mental processes had been reduced to the subsistence level.

Both in its argument—if it can be called such—and in its musical impact, the "quadro di stupore" is the exact opposite of Figaro's cross-examination in *The Marriage of Figaro*. Where Mozart's subject was intelligence, and his music tailored to convey an ongoing mental process—namely, the evolution of the cross-examination—Rossini's subject is precisely the failure of intelligence, and his music charts not a process but a state of mind: the incomprehension in which the characters are frozen. I think it no exaggeration to say that the "quadro" is a musical celebration of stupidity. Indeed, the wit of the ensemble derives from the incongruity between the characters' professed incomprehension and the manifest genius of the music to which their professions are set. Strictly as a piece of music the "quadro" bears comparison to a Bach fugue. And yet its agents sound as if they couldn't compose a C major scale. The composer has monopolized all intelligence for himself, and he employs it to abuse his characters. By way of contrast, the wit of Figaro's cross-examination in *The Marriage of Figaro* comes not from a discrepancy but from a correspondence between the mental endeavors of the characters and those of their creator.

CONCLUSION

It will perhaps have occurred to some readers that I have neglected an important critical undercurrent in *The Barber of Seville*, which contradicts my thesis that it is the opera of the Reaction. That is, one could well argue that the work's unrelenting cynicism represents a more radical and pointed critique of the values of Western civilization than does the rationalist humanism of *The Marriage of Figaro*. *The Barber of Seville* is a deeply irreverent opera. It takes nothing seriously, not God, not society, not love, not loyalty, not enmity—and in certain important respects not even music. It exhibits something of the nihilism one associates with thinkers like the Marquis de Sade or Friedrich Nietzsche. No true conservative, committed to the values of religion and tradition, would be likely to take much solace in it. Moreover, this irreverence is not simply a matter of its story. One feels it also in the characters, the music, and the structure of the opera. The piece, one senses, could easily have been written by an atheist or a traitor, if he had sufficient talent. It sticks out its tongue at the endeavors of Rossini's musical contemporaries, such as Beethoven and Schubert. Only in chronological terms does it stand midway between Mozart's piano concertos and Beethoven's late quartets. Musically it ridicules the formal complexity and ponderous introspection of the entire Viennese classical school.

Admittedly, all comedy depends on a degree of irreverence. But in works such as *The Marriage of Figaro, Die Meistersinger,* Shakespeare's romances, and Jane Austen's novels, irreverence is modulated by strong positive convictions. The irreverence of *The Barber of Seville* is unremitting. It does not serve as a vehicle for expounding deeply held constructive values. Instead it virtually exhausts the opera's intellectual energy.

This unrelenting cynicism gives the opera a curiously modern flavor. I have already noted that reflecting on Figaro's entrance aria, "Largo al factotum," can lead one to thoughts about the theater of the absurd. There is indeed something quite mad about *The Barber of Seville,* just as there is about Rossini's career as an operatic composer, which he terminated voluntarily thirty-nine years before his death. Furthermore, I think it fair to say that although one experiences this madness, this nihilism, when one listens to his operas, one experiences it only at a semiconscious level. It remains semiconscious, or subliminal, precisely because it is so radical, so sweeping. By way of contrast, the nicely delimited injustices of *The Marriage of Figaro* are easily absorbed. Without too much trouble one might draw up a platform to correct the abuses on display in Mozart's operatic world: it would be, approximately, the platform of the French Revolution. But what is one to do about the abuses on display in *The Barber of Seville?* They are inoperable. And besides, as everybody knows, it is only a farce. It doesn't aspire to represent the real world, merely to amuse, and we are not supposed to react to it politically.

If the irreverence and cynicism of *The Barber of Seville* are too extreme to have any practical effect, they do reveal an important truth about the conservative reaction of the early nineteenth century, one usually hidden by the pious exterior of conservative ideology. Beneath all the talk about God, tradition, and authority—whether in Burke, or Maistre, or Metternich—one senses an imperfectly repressed awareness that the intellectual machinery of conservatism stands in the service of privilege and self-interest. Rossini's opera has the virtue of making that moral bankruptcy explicit. It does not try to disguise its amorality or its aesthetic disrespect. Rather, it tells the truth about Europe's moral estate in the early years of the nineteenth century, and perhaps nowhere more incisively than in its untempered egoism. Here, I think, we have the deeper meaning of the memorable (if hyperbolic) sentence with which Stendhal began his biography of Rossini, first published in 1824:

Napoleon is dead; but a new conqueror has already shown himself to the world; and from Moscow to Naples, from London to Vienna, from Paris to Calcutta, his name is constantly on every tongue.

If I were to sum up the difference between *The Marriage of Figaro* and *The Barber of Seville*, I would say that Mozart's opera is intellectually richer—just as it is also compositionally richer—than Rossini's. The mind that inspired it impresses me as more encompassing and supple. Rossini is rather like Daumier: brilliant but limited, whereas (to take an example from a different field) Mozart's art resembles Dickens's in its range of sympathy and understanding. I don't wish to imply that this discrepancy mirrors the relative intellectual richness of the eighteenth and early nineteenth centuries as a whole. If anything, I think rather the opposite. Rossini's narrowness stems from the fact that he represents only one strand in the larger cultural fabric of his time, whereas Mozart comes as close as any single figure to representing the full spectrum of eighteenth-century sensibilities. In the chapters that follow, I will examine two composers who reflected elements of Europe's nineteenth-century cultural heritage ignored by Rossini. Only when one takes the accomplishments of Rossini, Schubert, and Berlioz together does one obtain a portrait of their age comparable in its breadth to that which Mozart gives of the Enlightenment.

The Self and Nature

Franz Schubert's
Die schöne Müllerin
and Winterreise

In his book *Natural Supernaturalism*, M. H. Abrams draws attention to striking parallels between the lyric poetry of the early nineteenth century and the often obscure philosophical speculation of German Idealism. He shows, in effect, that Romanticism, properly understood, encompasses both the poetic work of Wordsworth and the conceptual work of Hegel. Common qualities of heart and mind—a common sensibility—inspired these seemingly dissimilar, though contemporaneous, cultural enterprises. Both, he insists, reflect the spirit of the age.

My argument in this and the next chapter might be considered a musical variation on Abrams's theme. As in the world of letters, musical Romanticism expresses itself in both lyric and heroic forms. Or, if you prefer, it has both subjective and objective manifestations. In the first instance, human psychology is the focus of attention, and real events serve primarily as the occasion for its representation. In the second, the matter set before us is historical reality, and psychology is explored as it reflects that reality.

Two of the finest musical examples of the former—of Romantic subjectivity—are Schubert's song cycles *Die schöne Müllerin* (1823) and *Winterreise* (1827). These works are not, of course, operas, but, as I will argue in a moment, they have legitimate claims to be considered operatic. For the sake of consistency I might have chosen to examine a work like Carl Maria von Weber's *Der Freischütz* (1820), which shares many of the qualities of Schubert's song cycles. But I have settled on Schubert, both because his subjectivity impresses me as more radical than that of any of the other great Romantic composers, and because his song cycles are among the supreme achievements of European culture and—so it seems to me—insufficiently appreciated.

My reasons for devoting the next chapter to Berlioz's opera *The Trojans* (1858) are analogous. Any number of operas from the nineteenth century reflect the epic vision that Berlioz shares with German Idealism. But no other opera realizes that vision so powerfully, and none approaches its artistic heights. *The Trojans* is a masterpiece whose neglect has mystified other listeners besides myself. Donald Jay Grout, the author of the most satisfactory general history of opera and normally an even-tempered judge, grows impassioned on the subject:

Les Troyens is incomparably the most important French opera of the nineteenth century, the Latin counterpart of Wagner's Teutonic Ring; its strange fate is paralleled by nothing in the history of music unless it be the century-long neglect of Bach's *Passion According to St. Matthew*. One can account for this in the case of Berlioz's work: it is long, it is extremely expensive to stage, and its musical idiom is so original, so different from the conventional operatic style, that managers (no doubt with reason) have felt unable to take the redoubtable financial risks involved in mounting it. There is no overwhelming public in any country for Berlioz as there is for Wagner, Verdi, or Puccini; and not even all connoisseurs are agreed about Les Troyens. But, public or no public, the work ought to be produced regularly at state expense until conductors, singers, and audiences are brought to realize its greatness.

Grout's charmingly utopian proposal well captures the sense of frustration felt by anyone who has taken this opera to heart. That we almost never see it, while we have apparently unlimited time and money for the workmanlike stuff of Berlioz's fellow countryman Massenet, is one of the more incomprehensible anomalies of contemporary operatic life.

Unlike Mozart's *Marriage of Figaro* and Rossini's *Barber of Seville*, Schubert's song cycles and Berlioz's opera don't invite direct comparison. But I introduce them here together in order to underline my conviction that Romanticism involves both a distinctive conception of the self and a distinctive conception of history. It operates, one might say, at microscopic and telescopic levels, in the first instance examining the nuances of individual emotion with loving exactitude, in the second limning the historical panorama in the boldest possible strokes. Perhaps not surprisingly, Romanticism is somewhat undernourished at the middle level of domestic and social analysis—the level of reality, in other words, that was the primary subject of European art and thought in the eighteenth century and that Mozart explored so trenchantly in *The Marriage of Figaro*. Among the accomplishments of European Realism in the latter half of the century was the restoration of domestic and social concerns to the heart of the creative imagination. In the Romantic Age the study of society atrophied; it assumed the stylized and exaggerated form one hears in Rossini's *Barber of Seville*. Instead the Romantics attended to the extremes: to the self and to universal history, the smallest and largest units of humanistic study. Mozart's famous equipoise gave way to the antithesis of the lied and grand opera, the one almost excruciatingly private, the other shamelessly public. Such extremism—a kind of schizophrenia of scale—is itself of the very essence of Romanticism, which inclines simultaneously to the minute and the monumental, whether in painting, in literature, or, as we shall see, in music.

Die schöne Müllerin and *Winterreise*, as noted, are song cycles. Simply put, a song cycle is a group of related songs that, taken together, tell a story. Normally such a cycle is sung by one person, accompanied on the piano.

Having offered this definition, I must immediately qualify it, since many song cycles violate it in one way or another. To begin with, in some cycles the individual songs aren't clearly separated—as they are in Schubert—and musical material from one part of the cycle may show up elsewhere. Thus, for example, in Beethoven's cycle *An die ferne Geliebte* (1816), the six individual songs are united by a continuous piano accompaniment (and by formal key relationships as well), and the last song reverts at its close to the melody with which the cycle began. Similar reversions or recapitulations (though only in the accompaniment) occur in Robert Schumann's two most famous song cycles, *Frauenliebe und Leben* and *Dichterliebe* (both from 1840). In all these cases, as one might expect, the return of earlier material serves a narrative function. In the Beethoven cycle, for instance, the reversion occurs when the narrator imagines his mistress receiving and singing the songs that her absence has inspired him to compose. But *Die schöne Müllerin* and *Winterreise* contain no such reversions. None of the songs borrows musical material from another, with the exception of two brief melodic and textual echoes in the earlier cycle.

In contrast to the Schubert cycles, some cycles are composed to orchestral rather than piano accompaniment. Among such are Berlioz's *Nuits d'été* (1856, though written originally—two decades earlier—for piano), Mahler's *Kindertotenlieder* (1902), and Britten's *Serenade for Tenor, Horn and Strings* (1943). A further variation finds the individual songs assigned to more than one performer, as in Mahler's *Lied von der Erde* (1908). There is, moreover, great leeway in performance practice: cycles written for a single voice are sometimes divided between two singers; songs written for a man are sometimes undertaken by a woman (though I've never heard the inverse); and cycles are transposed up and down the scale to suit the range of particular voices.

The narrative density of a song cycle also varies greatly from case to case, so that even my stipulation "tells a story" mustn't be insisted on punctiliously. The stories of *Die schöne Müllerin* and *Winterreise* are themselves more sketched than told, more indicated than articulated. In other cycles the narrative is so elusive as to be little more than a vague psychological progression, sometimes only a mood. Such, for example, is the case in Schumann's *Dichterliebe* (based on poems by Heinrich Heine), a wonderful mixture of passion, irony, and bitterness, but hardly a story. Likewise with the last Schubert cycle, *Schwanengesang* (1828), also based partly on Heine poems, and also unified by atmosphere rather than story. It thus makes no great difference in what order the songs in *Schwanengesang* are performed, whereas a reordering of those in *Die schöne Müllerin* or *Winterreise* would be aesthetically catastrophic.

By now it might seem that my definition is honored mostly in the breach. That may be the case. But the preeminence of Schubert's two great cycles is such that they remain the standard against which all deviations are measured.

The ways in which a song cycle differs from an opera are, I trust, fairly obvious: no scenery, no costumes, no orchestra, and only one singer (although, as Schoenberg's *Erwartung* and Poulenc's *La voix humaine* have shown, it is also possible to write an opera for a single voice). Moreover, the songs in a cycle—while roughly comparable in length to the basic musical units of an opera—are bound together neither by recitative, as in the works of Mozart, Rossini, and their predecessors, nor by the "continuous" musical language of nineteenth-century opera. Inevitably, therefore, the narrative line is less sequential than in opera. A song cycle might be said to resemble an opera stripped of its connective tissue: the singer indulges in isolated moments of reflection, and the listener must reconstruct a course of events that in an opera would be spelled out explicitly. Indeed, this increased demand on the participation of the listener is itself a distinctive feature of the cycles.

On the other hand, the similarities between opera and song cycle, though perhaps less obvious, are still remarkable. The most important of these has already been touched on: the telling of a story. Among other musical forms, only the oratorio approaches opera in its narrative aspirations, and an oratorio differs from an opera in much the same way as does a song cycle. Oratorio, however, was a moribund form in the nineteenth century; Mendelssohn's *Elijah* and Elgar's *Dream of Gerontius* are pale replicas of their Handelian forebears. By way of contrast, the nineteenth century was the great age of the song cycle, just as it was the great age of opera. Program music might be considered a significant rival, but its narrative powers are extremely generalized and depend often on an extramusical gloss. The "story" of Berlioz's *Symphonie fantastique* is barely adumbrated in the music, and the same holds for the tone poems of Richard Strauss. Without the composer's explanation, Berlioz's score would invite a wide variety of interpretations. I doubt that even the much more rudimentary story of Beethoven's *Pastoral* Symphony could be divined without the labels the composer has given its movements.

Schubert's song cycles, however, share the literary and dramatic qualities that distinguish opera as a musical form. They create, often with operatic precision, a sequence of events and human responses. They also share something of opera's visual quality, although in an entirely vicarious form. In the cycles, the piano carries the burden of the stage scenery in opera. No small part of the effectiveness of these works lies in the pictorial ingeniousness of their accompaniment. Listening to them, we enter a drama of human emotions, and at the same time a vivid panorama rises before our inner eye. We can even imagine how they might be staged, and we understand, retrospectively, how opera as a genre came into existence when narrative songs, such as Monteverdi's madrigals, were acted out with ever greater explicitness.

I have called *Die schöne Müllerin* and *Winterreise* supremely great works, and some justification for that claim is in order. The principal source of their greatness is unanalyzable, yet far from mysterious.

Time after time the poems in these cycles (written by Schubert's contemporary Wilhelm Müller) inspire melodies of extraordinary beauty. Schubert is one of the great melodists in the history of music, and these cycles find him at the height of his powers. Virtually nothing can be said about this achievement other than that it is there. I have listened to the cycles hundreds of times, and repeatedly I come back to the same basic truth: the songs are beautiful. About the only way in which that unhelpful judgment might be specified is to say that their beauty is of a simple and seemingly effortless variety, particularly in the earlier cycle. They are artless—or so they sound. In this respect they are at polar opposites from a work like Beethoven's Quartet Opus 132, whose beauty is extremely complex, almost intellectual.

With respect to this fundamental attribute one can only point to examples. A passage that sticks in mind is the phrase to which Schubert sets the words "O Bächlein meiner Liebe" ("O brook of my love") in the sixth song of *Die schöne Müllerin:* it consists of a mere eight notes—only four of them on different pitches—its rhythm is regular and unremarkable, its harmonies are conventional (only two chords: tonic and dominant), and the piano accompaniment is unpretentious. Yet once heard, the phrase is unlikely to be forgotten. All by itself, one feels, it would earn Schubert a secure place in the history of music. Moreover, phrases of such distinction occur over and over in the cycles, to the point that one almost becomes sated with them, as with an outrageously rich dessert.

Schubert's two cycles have other virtues beyond sheer melodic fecundity. A good part of their effectiveness comes from their cumulative emotional power. They are not just a random sequence of exquisite moments, but organic wholes that invite the listener into a distinctive sonic and psychological universe for the full length of their duration—about an hour in the case of *Die schöne Müllerin,* an hour and a quarter in the case of *Winterreise.* This structural effect is managed very much as it is in opera: by creating characters who set out on an adventure, and by establishing an identifiable and consistent musical vocabulary—the single voice, the piano, and a delimited range of melodic, harmonic, and decorative procedures. Because of Schubert's unqualified belief in his lyricist and because of the purity of his artistic impulse, the cycles seduce us into a complex emotional process, even when the particular difficulties faced by his protagonists are quite unlike our own. Their experiences and feelings engage us in much the same way as those of a Hamlet, a Macbeth, an Othello, or a Lear—also creations whose predicaments are unlike those that we ourselves confront.

There is, however, an important difference in the manner of our engagement, which distinguishes Schubert from most of his predecessors. It is a difference he shares with the great Romantic poets of his generation: we experience the drama entirely from inside the protagonist's head. The song cycles reflect the unprecedented subjectivity of the Romantic movement. This is not simply a question of more emotion, more introspection, or more agonizing. Rather, the transformation is structural: the actual location of the drama has been moved from the external world of objects and relationships to the internal one of consciousness. A passage from one of John Keats's letters nicely sums up this great revolution in the order of things: "My own being," Keats writes, "becomes of more consequence to me than the crowds of Shadows in the shape of men and women that inhabit a Kingdom. The soul is a world of itself, and has enough to do in its own home."

The song cycle is particularly well suited to effect this process of internalization. Its sheer physical austerity eases the movement from the realm of things to the realm of thoughts. We hear nothing except a single voice and a piano. At a live recital (as opposed to a record) there are also the singer's physical self, the pianist (and his instrument), and the always slightly comic page-turner. But all of this is as nothing compared with the visual distractions provided by an opera or even by a symphony concert. Thus we enter the protagonist's imagination with surprisingly little fuss. Indeed, it all happens so naturally that we are apt to forget what a watershed these cycles mark in our cultural history. But in fact *Die schöne Müllerin* and *Winterreise* are representative documents in the emergence of a radically new sensibility, in which consciousness has displaced both God and society as the principal object of artistic and intellectual contemplation.

DIE SCHÖNE MÜLLERIN

The first of Schubert's two great cycles is generally considered the lesser. Musically it lacks the complexity of *Winterreise,* and its text recounts a plain and sentimental story with none of the later cycle's self-conscious irony. But the poems of this cycle speak directly to Schubert's strongest suit, his unexcelled lyricism. Thus while I appreciate the compositional and literary grounds on which *Winterreise* has been pronounced the superior work, I find the earlier cycle more affecting, and I think the public has judged rightly in taking it more readily to heart. Indeed, I suspect that critics have been afraid to like *Die schöne Müllerin* too much, or afraid to admit liking it as much as they do. It has the disarming effect of making sophisticated people experience the most unsophisticated emotions, of moving us with a hopelessly obvious tale set to uninspired and often trite verses. In the face of this sustained Romantic outcry, no amount of urbanity or cynicism is adequate defense. Schubert's music is so heartfelt that one has little choice but to go along.

The twenty songs of *Die schöne Müllerin* tell a story of adventure, love, betrayal, and death. A young miller leaves home to make his fortune in the world. ("Make his fortune" must be understood in strictly psychological, not economic, terms, for the young man is untouched by greed.) He follows a brook, because he knows that brooks eventually lead to mills. And indeed he soon happens upon a mill, where he is taken on as a worker. He then falls in love with the miller's beautiful daughter, courts her, and eventually wins her. But his bliss is relatively short-lived, for her affections are alienated by a young hunter, who is recommended to her, we are made to feel, less by qualities of character than by his superior social position. The sociology of the cycle, however, remains in a typical Romantic haze, and the hunter may simply be more dashing. The only certainty is that the young miller's love is deep and true while the hunter's is shallow. In his bitterness and despair the miller ultimately drowns himself in the brook that has served as his guide. In the final song the brook welcomes him to his true home, where he will find release from the aggravations of his short and unhappy life.

This account of the story will already leave the modern reader ill at ease. Even a soap opera is apt to sound more nuanced. That such a narrative inspired Schubert to some of his best melodies should remind us of how radical the Romantics were—psychologically radical, that is. They had access to more primitive emotions than we do—indeed, more primitive also than those accessible to their immediate predecessors in the eighteenth century. A comparison with Mozart is instructive in this regard. *The Magic Flute* is, I believe, the most direct and earnest of Mozart's great operas; its subjects are truth, goodness, brotherhood, and all those other admirable things that make us moderns nervous. They don't make Mozart nervous, of course, and his opera is one of the high points of Western culture. But if one compares the musical and mental universe of *The Magic Flute* with that of *Die schöne Müllerin*, it is to recognize what a sophisticate

Mozart was, even at his most ardent. Schubert's miller could no more fill Tamino's shoes than he could Hoffmann's or Faust's. Even the relatively uninflected moral scheme of Mozart's Enlightenment is beyond the ken of this profoundly simple man. Schubert gets beneath civilization, as it were, in a way that Mozart never tried to. His effort is of a piece with those of Rousseau and Wordsworth.

The songs of the cycle divide naturally into groups. The first three songs portray the miller's wandering and discovery. They convey hope, movement, and a hint of anxiety, and they grow increasingly animated as the miller approaches his new home. The next seven songs describe the stages of his courtship. As one would expect, they are predominantly slow and their mood is reflective. The eleventh song stands by itself: it marks the young man's success, and it is fittingly jubilant. It is followed by two extraordinarily peaceful songs that signal his newfound happiness (although even here there are hints of the tragedy to come). The hunter enters in the fourteenth song and the dream is shattered. The next three songs (mostly fast and in minor keys) are distinguished not only by their bitterness but also by the single manifestation of irony in the cycle (in *Winterreise,* by way of contrast, irony is the dominant mode). In the last three songs bitterness gives way to despair (some might say self-pity) and finally to the consolation of death. Their enervated escapism brings to mind the closing couplet of Keats's "Sonnet to Sleep":

> Turn the key deftly in the oiled wards,
> And seal the hushed casket of my soul.

Die schöne Müllerin has no formal design in the sense of a symphonic movement or an operatic finale. One can compile numerous tabulations of its elements, but they don't add up to the sort of structural whole that invites musicological analysis. The cycle provides little occasion for a discussion of key relationships, thematic development, or architectural effects. Thus, for example, when one learns that thirteen of the songs are in the major and four in the minor, while the remaining three modulate from minor to major, one has done little more than specify the general tonality of the cycle (i.e., major). If there is a structural significance in the progression of keys, it is lost on the listener—as is not the case, for instance, in the sonata movement of a classical symphony, where the harmonic tension between the first theme in the tonic and the second theme in the dominant is very much a part of our aural experience. Most of the early songs in the cycle are composed in 3/4 and 6/8, while those in the latter half, with two exceptions, are in 4/4 and 2/4. Nine of the songs are strophic (numbers 1, 7, 8, 9, 10, 13, 14, 16, and 20), but in only one instance does there seem to be any particular logic to their placement in the cycle. Similarly, knowing that eleven of the songs are slow and nine fast tells us very little about the work's artistic logic. As one would expect, the fast songs come at moments of exuberance or anger, the slow ones at moments of thoughtfulness, bliss, or despondency.

In broad musical terms, then, the cycle consists of twenty seemingly random components, each as autonomous as a traditional operatic aria. Nonetheless, the work exerts unmistakable structural pressures. One of these is a feeling of circularity. The miller doesn't return to his point of departure in the literal sense of the prodigal son—a metaphor of considerable importance to the Romantics. But he does move from the security of home to the security of death: his life is portrayed as a "circuitous journey" (to borrow M. H. Abrams's phrase)—a bold move out into the world followed by a retreat when the world's burdens prove too great. This sense of going out and coming back is central to the cycle's emotional effect, and it makes an interesting contrast with the geographical and psychological trajectory of *Winterreise*. The latter also, as its title indicates, is a journey. But it is not a circular journey. Rather, it is a journey without end.

Musically, the sense of circularity is conveyed by means of a rough symmetry. Perhaps most important in this respect is the decidedly strophic character of both the first and the last songs. The listener is conscious of hearing the same *kind* of song at the end of the cycle that he had heard at the beginning. In both, a single melody is repeated five times, always to different words, and in both we are aware of an insistent rhythmic pulse—assertive in the first song, elegiac in the last. None of the other strophic songs—which are concentrated toward the middle of the cycle—is so transparently repetitious, and none contains more than four verses. The crucial placement, then, of two extended strophic songs—one at the beginning, the other at the end—establishes a musical framing of the story.

If I am not mistaken, the image of the mill, around which the drama unfolds, also exerts a subliminal circular pressure: a mill, after all, is a set of wheels, and in his opening song the young miller explicitly identifies their turnings with his own wanderings:

> *Das sehn wir auch den Rädern ab,*
> *den Rädern!*
> *Die gar nicht gerne stille stehn,*
> *die sich mein Tag nicht müde drehn,*
> *die Räder.*

> We see it in the mill wheels too—
> the mill wheels!
> That never like to stand still,
> but turn all day and never tire—
> the mill wheels.

This theme finds musical support in the arpeggios of the piano. The arpeggio, as we shall observe, has another meaning as well, but little imagination is needed to see that an arpeggiated chord is the perfect musical representation of a circle: in its simplest form it moves up through a specific set of notes and then back down through the same notes, only to begin the cycle again. As song after song is accompanied by these broken chords, we are reminded of the never-stopping wheels of the mill, as well as the larger circle—the circuitous journey—of the miller's life.

There is also a felt symmetry in the division of the cycle into emotional halves, the turning point marked by the eleventh song, "Mein." This pivotal song—the young man's ecstatic shout of success—is beautifully set off by the slow tempos of the three songs that precede it. The listener thus has no doubt of its centrality, and he knows, on the basis of musical evidence alone, that he has come to a point where the story of romantic adventure must shift directions. Moreover, just enough hints have been dropped in the previous songs to make him anxious about the future course of events.

The cycle contains further internal demarcations, which lend the whole its shapeliness. But they must not be insisted on with analytic ferocity, because if pressed too hard *Die schöne Müllerin*, like its modest heroine, will demur and become, once again, just a series of beautiful tunes. The cycle has the kind of casual unity that one finds in the narrative poetry of Wordsworth: by classical standards neither will pass muster, but one feels their wholeness every bit as much as one does the more explicitly articulated unities of a Pope or a Haydn. Romanticism effected a revolution in our notions of form, discovering new ways of organizing experience so as to allow for more intimate and discursive expression. But the aesthetic announced in the Preface to *Lyrical Ballads* is hardly anarchic, and Schubert's song cycle might be considered the musical reflection of the more latitudinarian, but nonetheless orderly, conception of form propounded in that epoch-making document. "No work of true genius," Coleridge remarked, "dares want its appropriate form."

I propose here to examine four themes in *Die schöne Müllerin*, each of which, I feel, reflects an important and characteristic aspect of Romantic subjectivity; each, in other words, pertains to the way Schubert represents the self. I am especially eager to show that Schubert's distinctively Romantic characterization of the self—as well as his characterization of nature in its relation to the self—is achieved largely through his music. The text of *Die schöne Müllerin*, though of course essential, ultimately tells us no more about the work's artistic meaning than does the libretto of an opera.

The Innocent Self

Schubert's miller is an innocent. One hesitates to call him good because goodness implies more awareness than he possesses. He is, I suspect, precisely the sort of creature Jean-Jacques Rousseau has in mind, in his *Discourse on the Origin of Inequality*, when he talks about man in a state of nature. There is indeed an almost animal insouciance about him: he is the very embodiment of unselfconsciousness.

Schubert, however, is not the least embarrassed by this rude creation. His capacity to believe in the most unqualified emotions reflects an aspect of Romanticism from which we have become entirely estranged. We are comfortable with the Romantics' irony, but not with their sentimentality. Characters like Esther Summerson in *Bleak House* are "problematic," and we are ill at ease when a great poet like Wordsworth writes about dancing daffodils, as he does in "I Wandered Lonely as a Cloud." This extraordinary emotional directness is the single most striking feature of *Die schöne Müllerin*, whose protagonist is denied all traces of worldly wisdom.

Schubert creates this impression, I believe, largely by his reliance on the simplest musical procedures. The music of the cycle constantly draws our attention to elemental processes; ambiguity is held to a minimum; there is a kind of musical reduction appropriate to the psychological reduction of the character. Musical innocence is thus made to reflect characterological innocence. Schubert's gifts as a melodist are ideally suited to this procedure. Unlike Brahms, or Mahler, or even Schumann, he needs very little compositional space to work his effects.

One way to suggest innocence and unselfconsciousness is through repetition: children and fools repeat themselves, adults (if they care about the impression they make) try to say things only once. Music is full of repetitions, but surely one of the most blatant examples of musical repetition is the strophic song—that is, the song whose music is reduplicated in its entirety for each verse of the text. Thus the strophic form of nearly half the songs in *Die schöne Müllerin* plays an important role in creating our sense of the miller's psychology. Schubert and his miller aren't ashamed to sing the same tune over and over. Furthermore, there are repetitions within repetitions. Consider, for example, the opening song, "Das Wandern." A moment ago I noted that the miller sings this tune five times in a row. I can now add that each of the song's three phrases is subjected to an immediate restatement (or, in the case of the second phrase, an echo that amounts virtually to a restatement), so that before the song has run its brief course we have heard each of its phrases ten times. We know, without any doubt, that we are in the company of a very simple fellow.

Nor should one assume that repetition of this sort was a musical fixture of the age. In reality the strophic song was nearing the end of its career: the great lieder composers after Schubert will occasionally revert to it, but for Schumann, Brahms, Wolf, Mahler, and Strauss, the standard form of the song will be through-composed. Moreover, the instances of strophic composition are much rarer even in Schubert's own *Winterreise* (written only four years after *Die schöne Müllerin*), and accordingly the protagonist of the later cycle impresses us as a much more self-conscious man than the young miller. It seems fair to conclude, then, that Schubert intentionally used repetition in *Die schöne Müllerin* to create a musical portrait of artlessness. Indeed, if he were a less skillful composer the repetitions of a song like "Das Wandern" might easily sound satirical. But of satire or authorial distancing there is not a trace. The composer of Heine's "Doppelgänger"—one of Schubert's masterpieces of tragic irony—is nowhere in earshot.

Another musical device used to suggest his hero's innocence is rhythmic and melodic regularity: the establishment of a steady pulse and the construction of phrases that are even in length and that fall predictably on the ear. In almost all the songs, a fixed tempo and accompaniment are set at the start, and the melodies, which are usually short, divide audibly into symmetrical parts, with easily recognizable echoes, inversions, and imitations. The miller is not allowed the emotional complexities implied by the free compositional style of a Hugo Wolf, in whose songs rhythm and melody (as well as accompaniment) are adjusted to every shade of feeling. The miller's emotions are direct, uncomplicated, and stable throughout the course of each song.

Naturally, some of the most wonderful moments in the cycle come when Schubert violates this prevailing conceit. Because it is such a firmly established expectation, the cycle's occasional irregularities are all the more affecting. The first of these occurs in the fifth song, "Am Feierabend" ("On a Holiday Evening"). At its beginning the young man indulges in a slightly desperate fantasy about how he might bring his feelings to his beloved's attention. Here Schubert establishes the sort of unambiguous rhythmic and melodic pattern that we have come to associate with his simple-minded hero: up to this point in the cycle not a beat has been dropped, and the melodic material of each song—usually announced in the first few moments—has been held to with remarkable fidelity from start to finish. But in the middle of the fifth song the tempo relaxes and new phrases are introduced as the young man recalls a summer evening spent with his fellow apprentices in the company of the master and his daughter:

> *Und da sitz' ich in der grossen Runde,*
> *in der stillen, kühlen Feierstunde,*
> *und der Meister spricht zu allen:*
> *Euer Werk hat mir gefallen;*
> *und das liebe Mädchen sagt*
> *allen eine gute Nacht!*

> And there I sit in the large circle,
> In the quiet, cool evening,
> and my master says to all:
> Your work has pleased me;
> and the dear maiden
> bids all a good night!

The music dips down to catch the deep tones of the father, then rises poignantly to suggest the voice of the daughter; it lingers on the word "allen," thus conveying unmistakably the young man's frustration at being treated to so democratic a farewell. Thereafter the song reverts to the more vigorous and regular material with which it began, enclosing the episode, as it were, in musical parentheses. The effect of this interruption is to make us feel the bewildering power of romantic love. Passion breaks in on the miller's unselfconscious existence, diverting him from his simple and regular ways.

Again, one should not make the mistake of thinking that the rhythmic and melodic regularity of these songs, like their repetitiousness, is merely standard operating procedure for Schubert. That he could write complex and irregular songs when he wished is amply demonstrated by the corpus of his lieder (which number over six hundred) and above all by those in *Winterreise,* where the pulse often varies dramatically and the melodies seldom "breathe" in the predictable four-bar units of *Die schöne Müllerin.* Schubert, in other words, must not be thought a musical innocent merely because he wrote music that portrays innocence. Rather, he believed in the psychological legitimacy, even desirability, of innocence—so much so that he repressed the inclination to write music that by its sophistication might compromise the integrity of his creation. This capacity to believe in innocence is among the great common themes of Romanticism—one thinks almost instinctively of the celebration of childhood in the poetry of the age—and Schubert's cycle ranks with Blake's *Songs of Innocence* as perhaps the most sustained realization of that belief.

The Anxious Self

The above might imply that Schubert's miller is one of those people who sail through life with an open heart, a generous mind, and very little to worry about. Yet from his ultimate fate we know that can't be the case, since openhearted, resilient people, while they may fall in love, don't throw themselves into brooks when their romantic ambitions come to grief. And of course the miller is not just another stout fellow with a genial disposition. Rather, he exhibits a characteristic Romantic fragility, a delicacy of spirit such as one associates with Keats or Shelley. He is an anxious man, with a soft, epicene vulnerability. One can easily see how he might be broken on the rack of life.

In one respect, this proposition will seem implausible. After all, our hero is a common laborer, and millwork, which is strenuous and repetitive, hardly encourages a refined sensibility. In his opening song the miller draws our attention to the humble objects that are the elements of his livelihood: water, stones, and wheels. Elsewhere we get glimpses of his rough daily routine. The fifth song, which I have just discussed, begins with a rugged workingman's fantasy that Schubert sets to an appropriately energetic tune:

> *Hätt' ich tausend Arme zu rühren!*
> *Könnt' ich brausend die Räder führen!*

Könnt' ich wehen durch alle Haine!
Könnt' ich drehen alle Steine!
Dass die schöne Müllerin
merkte meinen treuen Sinn!

Had I a thousand arms to work with!
Could I guide the roaring wheels!
Had I breath to blow through every grove!
Could I turn every millstone!
That the beautiful miller's daughter
might perceive my true intent!

Only the subjective construction takes something of the braggadocio off these lines; set in the indicative they would be intolerably muscular.

Still, both text and music insist that this seemingly bold young man is nonetheless fragile. Literary Romantics typically convey such delicacy by showing a character's sensitivity to nature, and Schubert's poet has provided ample evidence of such sensitivity. Not only does the miller appreciate nature, he even talks to it; he speaks to flowers, to stars, and above all to the brook. These disquisitions occur in no fewer than thirteen of the songs, and in the final two the brook actually speaks back. Again, there is no hint of incredulity in Schubert's setting of these conversations. The music is entirely straightforward. The eighteenth song, entitled "Trockne Blumen" ("Withered Flowers"), is especially noteworthy in this regard:

Ihr Blümlein alle, die sie mir gab,
euch soll man legen mit mir ins Grab.
Wie seht ihr alle mich an so weh,
als ob ihr wüsstet, wie mir gescheh?
Ihr Blümlein alle, wie welk, wie blass,
ihr Blümlein alle, wovon so nass?

All you flowers that she gave to me,
you shall be laid with me in the grave.
Why do you look at me so sadly,
as if you knew my fate?
All you flowers, so withered and pale,
all you flowers, why so moist?

The young man who intones these artless lines—in a plaintive G minor—simply lacks the defenses necessary to survive in the world of human relations. The vulnerable Romantic is at ease only among the guileless forms of nature.

Schubert also uses a strictly musical device to render the miller's anxiety. I have in mind his distinctive treatment of the harmonic antithesis between major and minor. Save for his brilliant lyricism, it is perhaps the single most remarkable feature of his music. The device is so pervasive that one is apt to overlook it. Yet it is responsible for some of Schubert's most haunting effects, and in particular his musical representation of the miller's doubt.

Major and minor serve all tonal composers as basic elements of musical language. They are harmonic conventions whose general emotional significance is transparent to every listener, just as is the antithesis between fast and slow or loud and soft. Major suggests happiness, minor sadness; or major suggests benevolence, minor evil. Of course, there are many shadings and exceptions: Gluck's Orfeo, for instance, laments his Euridice in the major, and does so with singular tragic intensity. But only a pedant would deny the broad emotional associations of these modalities.

The most common use of this convention, in both vocal and instrumental music, involves large sonic areas. That is, relatively extended stretches of music are composed in either a major or a minor mode, and one's sonic recollection is of substantial passages, sometimes almost whole works, set in either the one or the other. Think, for example, of the last movement of Beethoven's Fifth Symphony (and ignore, momentarily, the passage before the recapitulation in which Beethoven reverts to material from the scherzo): it remains in the mind's ear as a long, and seemingly unvaried, exercise in the major. Even when a composer constructs a piece around the transition from minor to major (or, less often, from major to minor), we are apt to remember it essentially in terms of two large harmonic blocks. Such, for instance, is the impression left by the first movements of Haydn's late symphonies, with their slow introduction in the minor followed by an allegro in the major.

Like any tonal composer, Schubert is capable of using the major-minor antithesis in this architectural fashion. But what sets him apart is his proclivity for what might be called the "local" deployment of the major-minor antithesis. The unmistakable trademark of a work by Schubert is the precipitate, unannounced, and often evanescent shift (one can hardly call it a modulation, since the word implies a more decorous process) from one of these modalities to the other. Without warning, a song in the major will suddenly find itself in the minor, and just as suddenly it will revert to the major. The effect is of a tiny cloud momentarily blocking out the bright midday sun.

Schubert seems blithely contemptuous of the fact that most composers take this sort of harmonic movement with the greatest seriousness. The transition from major to minor (or vice versa) normally requires a certain amount of preparation; its management may call for alterations in pulse, rhythmic pattern, melodic contour, or other components of the musical fabric; and once established, the new tonality is not usually abandoned after a phrase or two. Schubert violates this convention in almost every respect: preparations are nonexistent; texture, pace, and even melody are little (if at all) affected; and the new tonality is apt to pass as quickly as it came. One might say that Schubert views the movement from major to minor with the same sangfroid with which other composers view the much less radical movement from tonic to dominant. No other composer shows so little respect for this fundamental harmonic distinction.*

In *Die schöne Müllerin* Schubert uses the sudden shift from major to minor to a precise psychological end—namely, to signal the miller's emotional fragility. Over and over again in the cycle a bold articulation in the major is followed by a painful response in the minor: the first phrase tells of the character's openheartedness, the second of his anxiety. A while back I mentioned a particularly memorable phrase from the sixth song to the words, "O Bächlein meiner Liebe" ("O brook of my love"). The phrase is two bars long. It is followed by another two-bar phrase, to the words "Wie bist du heut so stumm!" ("How silent you are today!"), which closely echoes the rhythmic pattern of the first. The first phrase is in B major, the second in B minor. The first begins what promises to be a gloriously expansive romantic declaration: the broad B major tune, we feel, announces a shared confidence, the overflowing of a full heart. But no sooner is it out of the man's mouth than comes the equally beautiful echo in the minor, whose message is exactly the opposite: doubt, fear, a near-tangible anxiety. It is, of course, the exquisite anxiety of being in love and not knowing one's chances. The completely unadorned harmonic juxtaposition tells us emphatically what the words imply only dimly: the miller is vulnerable, his joy cannot be separated from his pain. If

---

*I invite the reader to test this assertion by listening to the famous "Serenade" from *Schwanengesang*. The melody of course is lovely, but what raises the song to the level of greatness is precisely the harmonic technique I have discussed in this paragraph. The frequent movement from minor to major and back again is so swift, unexpected, and willful that, in memory, the song belongs to neither mode, but remains magically suspended between the two.

the *Songs of Innocence* are the literary analogue of the miller's ingenuousness, the *Songs of Experience* are the analogue of his anxiety. He is as fragile as Blake's sick rose.

Hardly a song in the cycle is without one of these lightning shifts from major to minor, and in many of the songs they occur repeatedly. Perhaps the seventeenth song, "Die böse Farbe" ("The Evil Color"), contains the single most virtuosic example. The song is introduced by four rapid bars in the piano. The first two are arpeggios in the key of B major, the latter two are hammered chords in B minor, after which the song reverts just as violently to its original B major. The opposition is so stark that one wonders how the passage can even sound like music. But the difference between arpeggios in the first two bars and chords in the third and fourth seems to rationalize what would otherwise be an unconscionably abrupt modulation. The two poles of the miller's character—his joyful enthusiasm and his angry pain—are laid before us with such swiftness that they become virtually simultaneous. Music here seems almost to transcend the constraints of linearity to which it, like literature, is condemned. The effect is closer to painting.

The Yearning Self

The miller is a man who yearns. Yearning is not an exclusively Romantic pastime, but it is nonetheless a habit of mind that the Romantics especially cultivated. It is perhaps most intimately associated with the German Romantics, above all with Goethe's Werther. *Sehnsucht*, as it is called in German, is one of the emotional indulgences of the age.

Yearning might be thought of as a desire for things that one can't have. It is distinguished from mere covetousness, however, by the fact that the yearner has no clear notion of what it is he wants. Yearning is thus likely to express itself as an inchoate dissatisfaction with one's lot, an unspecified emotional disquiet. It provides the impetus to action, but since one isn't sure what one is after, a sense of uncertainty hangs about one's undertakings. Figures afflicted with yearning are prone to melancholy. The hero of Wordsworth's *Prelude* is very much given to yearning, although the greatest yearner is Goethe's Faust.

Yearning is fundamental to *Die schöne Müllerin,* much of whose music has an almost palpable ache. The miller begins with the yearner's characteristic vagueness of purpose: why, after all, does he leave his home to go wandering? He is markedly less conscious of his objective than is the tragic protagonist of Schubert's *Winterreise*, who knows exactly what he wants, even though he is unable to find it. The miller simply announces, in his opening song, that no worthwhile miller is without *Wanderlust*—in other words, a wish to move, but toward no particular goal. We suspect, naturally, that his real goal is romance. But the point is that the miller himself doesn't experience his needs in such precise and delimited terms. He doesn't desire; he longs. Moreover, the trait remains with him even after he has found the beautiful miller's daughter. Yearning, since it is unspecific, isn't really satisfied with concrete rewards.

Schubert's way of conveying this trait is again quite simple: he writes music that suggests reaching. The harmonic system of Western music provides him with an ideal device for this: the avoidance of the tonic, with its implication of resolution. Throughout the cycle he composes melodies with sustained tones on the third, fourth, fifth, and seventh notes of the scale, notes that are arrived at by a leap from below. This avoidance of melodic resolution exactly captures the miller's sense of amorphous and unfulfilled desire: he is forever reaching and not finding. When one plays the cycle over in one's head, these are the phrases that are apt to remain in the mind's ear. The prominence of this device also explains why the cycle is most effectively sung by a tenor. It is not merely that the tenor voice better suggests the miller's youthfulness. More important, a tenor can produce these crucial "yearning" notes with appropriate vocal poise. Taken by a baritone, the notes lie dangerously near the top of the singer's range, and they threaten to assume a strenuousness that is alien to the miller's gentle character. A lyric tenor can produce these D's, E's, and F's with an ease that conveys the young man's wistful agony.

Practically every song in the cycle employs this convention at one point or another. In "Das Wandern," it appears in the seventeenth and nineteenth bars—the two most evocative moments in the song— where the singer dwells on E flat above middle C as he sings the first syllable of the word "Wandern." E flat is the fourth of the key in which the song is set (B flat major), it lies fairly high, and it is approached from a note seven tones below (F). Thus the word "wandering" is invested with that peculiar sense of reaching; through Schubert's music it achieves striking psychological precision.

Similarly, the second song, "Wohin?" ("Where To?"), which describes the outset of the miller's ramblings, ends with the singer holding a D above middle C, the fifth or dominant of the song's G major tonality. This relatively high-lying note frustrates the expected resolution (the return to the home tone: "home" is now behind the miller, both textually and harmonically), and it sustains, in musical fashion, the sense of longing.

The third song, "Halt!" ("Stop!"), marking the appearance of the mill, offers a particularly brilliant illustration of the device. The piece sounds typically artless, with its bouncy triplet rhythms and straightforward C major melody. But the score shows that Schubert has taken every opportunity to avoid the home tone of C in the vocal writing. The song is full of upward leaps in which the singer moves from below middle C to above it, the most spectacular being a repeated octave jump (from g to g′) on the word "Himmel" ("heaven") in the fortieth and forty-fourth bars. And perhaps most touching of all, the last line of the song—a question addressed to the brook, "War es also gemeint?" ("Was it so intended?")—is repeated four times, with the "al-" of "also" sustained first on upper D (the second), then on F (the fourth), and finally twice again on D. The effect is superbly heady, in both vocal and emotional terms.

A nearly identical pattern can be found in the eighth song, "Morgengruss" ("Morning Greeting"), which is also in C major and also in triple meter. The melodic line moves skillfully about its home tone and, as in "Wohin?," declines to return to it even at the end. There the word "gehen" ("go"—like "wandering," one of the cycle's emotional codewords) is set unforgettably on two high sustained notes, F and E, the fourth and third, respectively. The F, moreover, is both the longest and the highest note in the song.

One could continue from song to song in this fashion, but I will content myself with a final example. It is doubly interesting in that it illustrates both the "reaching" device used to convey yearning and the major-minor antithesis whose principal function, I've argued, is to portray the miller's anxiety. It occurs in the sixteenth song, entitled "Die liebe Farbe" ("The Beloved Color"), and the narrative context is pertinent. This is the second song after the appearance of the hunter. With his appearance one of the things that has been associated with the miller's happiness suddenly and unexpectedly becomes a source of grief—namely, the color green. Green, of course, is the basic color of nature, with which the miller is intimately associated, and, more specifically, in the song just before the hunter's arrival, the miller had soliloquized dreamily about a green ribbon he has given his mistress. This in turn had led to many happy recollections about how much she loved the color green.

Unfortunately, the hunter's green outfit and the green forest from which he emerges transform this partiality into a nightmare. And in "Die liebe Farbe" the miller ponders the awful fact of his beloved's fatal attraction. Over and over he sings, "Mein Schatz hat's Grün so gern" ("My darling likes green so much"). Schubert makes the man's hurt almost tangible by setting the line to one of those phrases that reach achingly above the home tone. The word "gern" is sustained on an extremely high F sharp, the fifth of the B major tonality in which the two-bar phrase is set. All the man's innocence, vulnerability, and desire seem condensed into this single note.

Schubert achieves this impression, in part, by contradicting our harmonic expectations. That is, when the voice arrives at this high-lying note, the harmonic support in the piano does not shift to the dominant, as we anticipate it will and as it certainly would have in the hands of a less inspired composer or one less intent on a specific emotional effect. Because the harmony remains stubbornly in the tonic, the singer's pronounced avoidance of the home tone—his refusal to return from that precariously high F sharp to the security and relief of the B natural five notes below, despite the clear harmonic invitation—makes us feel all the more intensely his painfully unrealized desire, his yearning.

Schubert is not yet through with us, however. The yearning phrase is followed directly by another with exactly the same note values and to which the identical words are repeated. But where the first phrase reaches uncomprehendingly toward the dominant in the uppermost register of the voice, the second moves gravely, fatefully, to the tonic—the home B natural—in the lower-middle part of the voice. Even more important, the first phrase is in B major, the second in B minor. In other words, we have here another instance of that juxtaposition of major and minor that Schubert uses throughout the cycle to express the miller's pain. The wistful sadness of the first phrase gives way without explanation to the unambiguous tragedy of the second. In this brief passage Romantic yearning and Romantic agony express themselves to the same text. Only Schubert's music distinguishes between these gestures.

The Self and Nature

Virtually no student of Western culture has failed to note the special importance that nature assumed for the artists and thinkers of the early nineteenth century. It is not just that the Romantics thought more—or more enthusiastically—about nature than had earlier generations. Rather, they conceived of nature in a peculiar relation to the self. It became for them the medium through which the self achieved an essential wholeness, or—to express the matter in the philosophical language of the day—it became the means through which the self realized itself. In this respect, nature might be said to displace both God and society in the Romantic cosmology; it is the principal "other" through which we make our way in the world.

The therapeutic or redemptive function of nature is a recurrent theme of Romantic poetry, where it is explored in a fashion categorically more emphatic than all earlier celebrations of nature's beauty. An especially instructive example of Romantic naturalism is provided by Wordsworth's poem "Tintern Abbey," which appeared in the first edition of *Lyrical Ballads*, in 1798. It bears comparison with Schubert's song cycle in a number of respects, not least in its unrelenting subjectivity: as in *Die schöne Müllerin*, the action of "Tintern Abbey" takes place largely in the poet's head. Its subject is a state of mind, or, rather, a spiritual evolution. An account of the poem's "external" events might run as follows: Wordsworth, on a ramble with his sister, stops near the River Wye above Tintern Abbey at a spot he had first visited five years earlier. The spot inspires him to a series of reflections, which in the poem all take place while he stands on the banks of the river. (Later, Wordsworth was to say that he composed the poem in his head over the next few days, as he completed his tour, and then wrote it down, without correction, after reaching town.) On the basis of his reflections, he may or may not have said something to his sister.

At the very least, this brief exposition should explain why "Tintern Abbey" has never been made into an opera: nothing happens. The poem is an internal dialogue, in which Wordsworth considers the history of his relationship with nature and the significance of that history for his sister, who might be said to stand here for the rest of humanity. In the course of his life, he reports, his sense of self has been reflected in his changing responses to the natural world. As a boy he experienced nature in the direct and unselfconscious manner of an animal. Later—by the time of his first visit to the Wye—nature had evolved from a source of physical pleasure into one of emotional solace, in which "the burden of the mystery" was lightened. But now, in his adulthood, it has assumed a yet profounder significance, an intellectual significance: it has become the agency through which he comprehends the larger order of things, uniting his own experience to that of his species. His thoughts here might be patronized (though not by me) for their orotund pantheism, but they perfectly convey the high Romantic vision of the self in its relation with the world of nature:

> I have learned
> To look on nature, not as in the hour
> Of thoughtless youth; but hearing oftentimes
> The still, sad music of humanity,
> Nor harsh, nor grating, though of ample power
> To chasten and subdue. And I have felt
> A presence that disturbs me with the joy
> Of elevated thoughts; a sense sublime
> Of something far more deeply interfused,
> Whose dwelling is the light of setting suns,
> And the round ocean and the living air,
> And the blue sky, and in the mind of man;
> A motion and a spirit, that impels
> All thinking things, all objects of all thought,
> And rolls through all things.

In a characteristic Romantic poem like "Tintern Abbey" we learn a great deal about nature and about the poet's mind, but very little about society. To the extent that it appears in the poem at all, it is pictured as a hostile reality: Wordsworth speaks disparagingly of "the din / Of towns and cities," from which he has been rescued by his memories of the Wye. The two poles of his universe, then, are nature and the self.

Schubert inhabits precisely the same universe. More than any technical limitations, I believe, this explains why he failed as an operatic composer. Even in the most stylized and symbolic of operas, the essential subject matter remains the relations between persons. Operas may occasionally characterize nature in a suitably dramatic fashion (as Weber does in the Wolf's Glen scene of *Der Freischütz*, or as Berlioz does in the "Royal Hunt and Storm" from *The Trojans*), and natural phenomena can provide an appropriate backdrop for human transactions in opera (as do the sea storms in *The Flying Dutchman, Otello,* and *Peter Grimes*), but nature can never become an operatic protagonist, for the simple reason that it can't speak. The song cycle, one might say, is the ideal recourse for a vocal composer whose conception of reality is Wordsworthian. The song cycle releases the composer from the need to portray a social order. It allows him to concentrate on a single center of consciousness—as represented by the singer—in its relationship to nature—as represented, I hope to show, by the piano.

In the songs of *Die schöne Müllerin*, virtually the whole of the sociable world that Mozart and Rossini describe in their operas has been eliminated. Indeed, Schubert barely invests his characters with even a physical reality. In all twenty songs exactly three details of physical appearance are mentioned: we learn that the miller's daughter has blond hair and blue eyes and that the hunter has a beard. Nor do we hear much about the characters in other respects. The miller's father and mother (or perhaps just his previous employers) are designated as "Herr Meister and Frau Meisterin" in the opening song, but nothing more is revealed. Of his new employer and would-be father-in-law, we know only that he is a man who can compliment his staff: "Your work has pleased me," he says to the assembled apprentices. His daughter speaks just three times: in the fifth song she says (in indirect discourse), "Good night"; in the tenth she opines, "It's going to rain. Goodbye, I'm going home"; and in the thirteenth she says (meaningfully, it turns out), "A pity about the pretty green ribbon, that it is fading here on the wall; I like green so much!" From these we deduce that she is modest, a little shallow, and perhaps irresolute.

If one tries to reconstruct the social and economic milieu of the cycle the pickings are equally slim. It is, we recognize, a preindustrial society, perhaps even a medieval one, in which owning a mill makes one an important man, and where labor is organized along traditional lines. Other than millers and their women, the only social category represented is hunters.

So persons, personal relationships (except for the central one), and social forms are hardly mentioned in the songs. In their stead Schubert and his poet offer an elaborate description of nature. Or, to be more precise, they offer an elaborate account of the relationship between the protagonist and nature. Flowers, stars, and streams are the principal characters of the drama, and the miller works out his ambitions, his doubts, his happiness, and finally his despair by way of a protracted discourse with these entities.

One of them, the brook, serves almost as the miller's alter ego. It is the brook with which he converses most often and with which he shares his deepest confidences; and it is the brook that ultimately claims him for its own. The brook seems as fully present as the miller himself, or, for that matter, as any character in an opera might be, and it is immeasurably more vivid than the cycle's eponymous subject, the beautiful miller's daughter. Indeed, in the most immediate sense one experiences the cycle as a love affair between the miller and the brook, so that their ultimate union has about it something of the appropriateness of the long-delayed but inevitable marriage at the end of a Jane Austen novel. The brook sings:

Gute Ruh, gute Ruh!
tu die Augen zu!
Wandrer, du müder, du bist zu Haus.
Die Treu ist hier,
sollst liegen bei mir,
bis das Meer will trinken die Bächlein aus.

Good rest, good rest!
close your eyes!
Weary wanderer, you are at home.
Faithfulness is here,
you shall stay with me,
until the sea has drunk up the streams.

They will remain united, in other words, until the brook, like the miller himself, ceases to exist. The song promises an eternal happiness of shared nonbeing. Thus while we don't forget the miller's pain, we also sense his newfound bliss, which Schubert conveys through the song's serene major tonality and its comforting lilt.

The brook doesn't wait until the last two songs—when it suddenly becomes articulate—to establish its presence. On the contrary, its newly discovered garrulousness hardly even seems startling, since it has in fact been with us from the start in the piano accompaniment. It is no exaggeration to say that through much of the cycle the piano *is* the brook—that sole other with which the miller is in true harmony, and which accompanies him faithfully throughout his journey. Schubert creates the brook for us largely by means of a single musical device: the arpeggio. These broken chords in the piano aurally reproduce the brook's characteristic movements: of water either rippling down from the heights, or (at a slower tempo) eddying gently but inevitably toward the sea. Schubert's use of this metaphor is often remarkably pointed. Thus when in the twenty-third bar of the sixth song the miller turns to the brook and addresses it ("O brook of my love"), arpeggios are introduced into the piano accompaniment for the first time, and the stream materializes before our very ears. Of course, not every song is accompanied by arpeggios, and arpeggios are a standard accompanying device in classical music even when no specific allusion is intended. But they are so prevalent in the accompaniment to *Die schöne Müllerin* that they register as a fixed element in the cycle's sonic universe. They are the outstanding feature in twelve of the accompaniments, whereas they figure prominently in only four of the twenty-four songs of *Winterreise*. Thus the arpeggio joins the regular four-bar phrase, the local modulation from major to minor, and the avoidance of the tonic as one of the cycle's identification marks. This simple and instantly recognizable convention accounts, I believe, for our sense that the brook is present throughout the cycle. Even when there are no arpeggios, we feel that the brook cannot be far away, that it may come into view at any moment. It is one of Schubert's most striking achievements.

Schubert's preoccupation with nature in the cycle is Romantic in that it is essentially psychological. He has very little interest in nature painting after the manner of Haydn in *The Seasons* or Beethoven in the *Pastoral* Symphony. Like other Romantics, his attitude toward nature is exploitative: it concerns him only as a reflection of the self, as a vehicle of biography. The subjects of his cycle are love, joy, anxiety, and despondency. He seizes on nature as a suitable means through which to express these emotions. Hence my insistence that his conception of nature is at bottom Wordsworthian.

WINTERREISE

If *Die schöne Müllerin* is Wordsworthian, *Winterreise* is Byronic. It is the musical expression of the Romantics' irony, associated not only with Byron himself but with such other figures of the age as Coleridge, Heine, and Kierkegaard. *Winterreise* and *Die schöne Müllerin* share a common preoccupation with death. But where the earlier cycle leads toward the peace of death, the later one seeks death in vain and ends instead in madness. Schubert tailors his music to portray this very different fate.

In certain of its externals, *Winterreise* seems almost a carbon copy of *Die schöne Müllerin*. Once again we have a sequence of musically independent songs—twenty-four rather than twenty—accompanied by the piano and relating a story of romantic misadventure. As before, the tale is told by a man, and, also as before, it is essentially a tale of female inconstancy.

Yet judged even as a narrative, the cycle is strikingly unlike its predecessor. In *Die schöne Müllerin* the romantic betrayal occurs midway through the cycle (in the fourteenth song, to be exact), but in *Winterreise* it has already taken place before the cycle begins. This, in turn, reflects a profounder difference between the two stories: in the later work the narrative has become even more radically psychological. The events of *Die schöne Müllerin,* although seen from inside the narrator's head, still constitute a more or less traditional story, with beginning, middle, and end. Things occur in a particular order: the miller leaves home, finds the mill, falls in love, wins the girl, loses her, despairs, and commits suicide. If they are not presented in this order, the cycle becomes nonsense. By way of contrast, the external occurrences of *Winterreise* have no clear narrative logic. The cycle's events are largely random occasions for the protagonist's ruminations. And while the work might be said to chart a psychological course from disappointment to insanity, that course is not tied with any precision to the sights and experiences of the journey. As in a nightmare, the traveler is constantly on the move, but gets nowhere. Thus the physical progression through a winter landscape gives way to a mental progression through memory, dream, fantasy, and finally to madness. Each of the cycle's outward events has a symbolic rather than a narrative function.

Without a clear story to follow, Schubert cannot have recourse to the broad symmetrical patterning by which he unified *Die schöne Müllerin.* The journey in question is in no way circular. Quite the contrary: it is a journey without end. The cycle's principal theme is the unhappy traveler's inability to escape from life, his imprisonment in a world of misery. This is made explicit in the most famous of the songs, "Der Lindenbaum" ("The Linden Tree"), the "lovely song of homesickness" that Hans Castorp sings as he marches to his death in the final chapter of *The Magic Mountain.* Here the traveler passes a linden tree under which he once shared happy hours with his sweetheart. But now the tree has become a cruel emissary of death—cruel because the death the man would so gladly embrace in fact eludes him. The tree whispers, "Du fändest Ruhe dort" ("You would find peace here"), and Schubert sets the subjunctive "fändest" on a soft high note of unparalleled seductiveness. The promise of death was never more invitingly represented. But our man trudges on. Though without hope, he must endure his pain until the end of his natural days. "Der Lindenbaum," like the cycle as a whole, is a frustrated death wish, one of the leitmotifs of Romanticism. The song is a close cousin to Keats's "Ode to a Nightingale," whose sixth stanza expresses the same hopeless infatuation:

> Darkling I listen; and, for many a time
> I have been half in love with easeful Death,
> Call'd him soft names in many a mused rhyme,
> To take into the air my quiet breath;
> Now more than ever seems it rich to die,
> To cease upon the midnight with no pain,
> While thou art pouring forth thy soul abroad
> In such an ecstasy!
> Still wouldst thou sing, and I have ears in vain—
> To thy high requiem become a sod.

Keats can take solace in beauty's immortality, a sentiment unfamiliar to Schubert's more black-minded (and less poetic) traveler. But both conduct an unrequited love affair with death.

Therefore, instead of a circular journey, *Winterreise* charts a journey into infinity. We feel none of the musical symmetry through which the earlier cycle conveyed a sense of going out and coming back. There is no pivotal song like "Mein," just as there is no pivotal event. Under these circumstances the songs of *Winterreise* depend for their artistic unity on certain shared melodic and harmonic conventions. Each of the conventions is associated with a particular image of the self, and each distinguishes the musical and psychological world of *Winterreise* from that of *Die schöne Müllerin*. Taken together, the two cycles provide an index of Romanticism's intellectual and affective range.

Complexity

In music, as in psychology, complexity is a relative matter. The protagonist of *Winterreise* is a fairly simple fellow if put up against a character out of James or Proust. But compared with the young miller of *Die schöne Müllerin* he is a thoroughgoing sophisticate, quite without his predecessor's unselfconsciousness. He is in fact something of an intellectual, the sort of person one can imagine going mad (which would be beyond the miller's psychological ken). Befitting a philosopher manqué, he can even be downright obscure. Consider, for example, his utterances in "Die Nebensonnen" ("The Phantom Suns"), which is the penultimate song of the cycle:

> *Drei Sonnen sah ich am Himmel stehn,*
> *Hab lang und fest sie angesehn,*

Und sie auch standen da so stier,
Als wollten sie nicht weg von mir.
Ach, meine Sonnen seid ihr nicht!
Schaut andern doch ins Angesicht!
Ja, neulich hatt' ich auch wohl drei;
Nun sind hinab die besten zwei.
Ging nur die dritt' erst hinterdrein!
Im Dunkel wird mir wohler sein.

I saw three suns stand in the sky,
Gazed at them long and steadily.
And they, too, stood so fixedly
As though they'd not depart from me.
Alas, but you are not my suns!
Why don't you stare at other men?
Not long ago, I, too, had three,
But now the best two have gone down.
If but the third would follow them!
I'd feel much better in the dark.

The metaphor, in which his mistress's eyes become two suns and the now familiar death wish is equated with the sunset, lacks consistency as well as pith—no one would mistake it for the work of John Donne. But apt or not, so arch a conceit would never have found its way into the mouth of the young miller.

Schubert underlines the winter traveler's psychological complexity by writing—relatively speaking—complex music. One of the striking differences between the two cycles, in this respect, is the absence of strophic songs in *Winterreise*. None of the songs repeats itself note for note, and only four of them contain verses that are musically identical. By way of contrast, as mentioned, nine of the twenty songs in *Die schöne Müllerin* are strophic, and several of them have three, four, and even five verses. The protagonist of *Winterreise* resembles a nineteenth-century opera composer: he is disinclined to sing the same tune more than once. The young miller has no such qualms.

This relative dearth of repetitions is the clearest musical evidence of the winter traveler's sophistication. No less important, however, is the more supple construction of the cycle's tunes. As will increasingly be the case with Schubert's successors, the songs of *Winterreise* abandon set melodic, rhythmic, and harmonic patterns in order to mold themselves to the text of the poem. One might say that they are more plastic than the tunes of *Die schöne Müllerin*. The difference is similar to that between early and late Verdi. In Verdi's early operas the melodies are fixed, and they carry the words before them, sometimes to jarring effect. In the late operas they are carefully shaped to the libretto. But where in Verdi's case this transformation reflects half a century of experience (as well as the general course of musical history during his creative lifetime), Schubert's two cycles are separated by a mere four years. Thus we are dealing here not with two stages in an artist's evolution but with two different compositional choices, each suited to its subject. The young miller is the sort of fellow who sets his mind on an idea and sticks to it for the duration of a song. The winter traveler, on the other hand, displays an agile and nuanced intelligence: his is the more verbal nature, and his tunes, accordingly, are more respectful of their lyrics. In his garrulousness he sometimes seems almost modern, where the laconic miller is unmistakably medieval. The winter traveler's music, with its constant shifts, reveals the volatility, even imbalance, of his mind.

A noteworthy example of that volatility is provided by the eleventh song, "Frühlingstraum" ("Spring Dream"). Although not unusually long, it contains three changes of meter, five marked changes of tempo, and seven changes of tonality. In the first stanza, set in the major and in a leisurely 6/8, the traveler imagines seeing blossoms outside his window. This is followed by a faster passage in the minor, as he wakes to crowing cocks and remembers that it is not spring but winter. Then comes a return to the major, at a slower pace, and, most radical of all, a shift in meter from 6/8 to 2/4 as the fantasy of the opening stanza is interpreted as a simple mistake: the flowers, the traveler now recognizes, had merely been painted on the window. Thereafter the three-part sequence is repeated, with the symbolic blossoms of the first stanza transformed, as in a sonnet, into their real object, the man's foolhardy dream of true love. All of these fluctuations—of meter, tempo, and tonality—take place in little more than four minutes, and they leave a strong impression of emotional instability.

The traveler's complexity is further conveyed by the irregular phrasing of the songs. The melodies don't breathe in the easy four-bar symmetrical units of *Die schöne Müllerin.* Instead there is an angularity about the music, just as there is an obliqueness about the character. Its unexpected contours inform us that the man is moody and unpredictable. After listening to him for a while, we are apt to recall what an open book the miller had been. One always knew what the miller was up to, just as one could anticipate, musically, where his songs were going. Indeed, among the unexpected effects of listening to *Winterreise* is our becoming even more conscious of the earlier cycle's emotional and musical primitiveness. We can with difficulty comprehend how an artist so at home with this existential traveler could also compose music that in no way patronizes the elemental responses of the heartbroken miller.

Dreams

The Romantics were great depressives, coming to grief in love, strung out on dope, and dying young. Even when they didn't die young, they often exhausted their artistic capital early in life—Wordsworth being the prime example. But just as they were great depressives they were also great dreamers. Schubert is a representative Romantic in his early death (at thirty-one, still four years younger than Mozart at the latter's death), his sexual frustrations, and his ability to give both depression and dreams incomparable expression. In *Winterreise* he finds exactly the right music to portray not only the black despair but also the hyperactive fantasy of his winter traveler. He does so by way of an ingenious variation on the musical device that had served him so well to convey the anxiety and yearning of his young miller.

As one would expect, the preponderance of songs in this woeful tale are set in the minor. But Schubert would not be Schubert if he failed to exploit his singular ability to move back and forth between minor and major. In the earlier cycle, this harmonic facility suggested the miller's anxiety: in the predominantly major tonality of the songs, brief phrases in the minor—generally only a couple of bars—made us instantly aware of the man's vulnerability. In *Winterreise* these modulations are just as sudden, but because of the minor tonality of the cycle, they usually move from minor to major. More important, however, they convey a different emotional message. In the earlier cycle the shifts tended to be languid and fearful: a phrase sung in the major would be varied haltingly in the minor, as if the young man had a sudden premonition of the danger lying ahead. In *Winterreise* the process is reversed: a neutral or dispassionate phrase in the major ("I have thought of you," "At my sweetheart's house") is repeated almost violently, at full voice and often to an ascending melodic line, in the minor. The effect is invariably retrospective and ironic: something once experienced as beautiful is suddenly revealed to be ugly in the harsh glare of hindsight.

Many of the harmonic shifts in *Winterreise* also differ in format from those in *Die schöne Müllerin:* on the whole they are more stable.

The new tonality makes its appearance with the same unexpectedness as before, but once introduced, it tends to stick—for twelve or eighteen bars, say, instead of two. This technical difference makes a precise point about the songs' protagonist: his emotions have achieved a certain solidity. He may be protean, but he's not skittish. His changes of mood, though frequent, are resolute, whereas the miller's were impulsive and evanescent. Through his manipulation of this compositional device, Schubert informs us that the one man is young, the other mature.

The same modulations are also used in an ingenious manner to heighten our sense of the traveler's despair. Considered in the abstract, his situation would seem to offer a composer scant opportunity to employ the major, with its subliminal association of happiness. Unlike *Die schöne Müllerin,* which contains moments of hope and joy, *Winterreise* is gloomy from start to finish. Yet it is a simple fact of musical life that twenty-four songs composed in minor keys would be a crashing bore. The challenge for a composer under these circumstances is to introduce the major in such a fashion as not to disturb the emotional integrity of the cycle.

Schubert does this brilliantly by recourse to a characteristic Romantic conception: he identifies the major with the imaginary. Throughout *Winterreise,* the major tonality denotes the world of memory, dream, fantasy, and illusion. For Schubert, as for the Romantics in general, this is a blissful, even voluptuous, realm, set against the austerity and ugliness of our waking lives. The ironic antithesis between beatific dream and painful reality is, one might say, the fundamental conceit of the cycle, and its musical representation is the rude antithesis of major and minor.

Schubert introduces the conceit in the very first song, "Gute Nacht" ("Good Night"). The traveler is leaving town, and he sings his sad goodbyes to a lovely D minor melody. In all its verses the major is heard exactly four times, and in each case it is associated with dreams or memories—with that illusory mental realm in which the misery of our lives is forgotten. Its first appearance is an eight-measure passage in which the traveler, plodding through the snow, reminisces about the happy beginnings of his love affair:

> *Das Mädchen sprach von Liebe,*
> *Die Mutter gar von Eh'.*

> The maiden spoke of love,
> Her mother even of marriage.

When he comes to the same musical spot in the second verse, the singer calls attention to the one feature of the winter landscape from which he can draw comfort—namely, the shadowy moon. The moon of course is real, but in contrast to the snow-covered objects in his immediate environment, its reality is distant and idealized; it, too, belongs to the realm of romantic imagination and is properly designated by the major. When the same major passage, slightly modified, makes a third appearance, it evokes a wistful and forgiving recollection of his mistress's infidelity. She's not really to be blamed, he sings, for "Love loves to wander, / God made it so." Finally, in the last verse, the song's full melody—twenty-eight bars in all—shifts unexpectedly from D minor to D major, and the traveler reveals that he departed in the night without saying farewell to his beloved because he didn't want to disturb her dreams. The shift is breathtaking—one of the unforgettable moments in the cycle—and it makes the association of the major mode with the world of dreams fully explicit. It tells us, with a precision unique to music, that dreams—in this case, the dreams of his mistress—belong to a privileged realm of bliss against which the real world seems all the more impoverished. In this splendid moment, Schubert's distinctive harmonic facility lends the opposition of sleeping and waking—of dreaming and suffering— an almost excruciating vividness. At the same time he invests his protagonist with a typical Romantic sensibility: the winter traveler, we see, is alienated from his surroundings, but possessed of a dangerously rich interior life of memories and fantasies.

Over the course of the cycle, the major returns repeatedly, and nearly always to bracket the world of the imagination. Indeed, it acquires almost the function of a code. The first song actually set in the major is "Der Lindenbaum." Appropriately, it is a reverie, first of lost love and then of death: by the fountain outside the town gates stands a linden tree in whose shadows the traveler "has dreamed many a sweet dream." Now he passes the tree at night, and the song's melody shifts to the minor, as reality displaces fantasy:

> *Ich musst' auch heute wandern*
> *Vorbei in tiefer Nacht,*
> *Da hab ich noch im Dunkeln*
> *Die Augen zugemacht.*

> Today my journey took me
> Past it at dead of night,

And even in the darkness
I closed my eyes.

But in the very middle of this verse, when the ear expects the melody will remain in the minor throughout, reality again gives way to fantasy, and the original major returns, to magical effect: the traveler hears the tree's branches calling, "Here you will find your rest!" It is a classic Schubertian moment. The eighth song, "Rückblick" ("Looking Back"), inverts the formula of "Der Lindenbaum": it begins in the real world of ice and snow (G minor) into which a reverie of past happiness (G major) intrudes. As the memory fades and the winter reality reasserts itself, the original minor returns. The thirteenth song, "Die Post" ("The Postman"), mocks the traveler's hopes that he might receive a letter from his beloved. The song is a tissue of self-deception and wishful thinking, and Schubert sets it to a lilting tune in an illusory E flat major. Another song in the major, "Im Dorfe" ("In the Village"), recounts the dreams of the village's inhabitants, as the traveler passes through in the middle of the night. He takes an ironic, even cynical, view of those dreams, but the villagers themselves (and Schubert's beautiful phrases) find nothing but pleasure in them:

> *Träumen sich manches, was sie nicht haben*
> *Tun sich im Guten und Argen erlaben.*

They dream of things they don't have,
Finding refreshment in both good and ill.

As the cycle progresses, the traveler's alienation becomes more extreme, and the daydreams and reminiscences of the earlier songs give way to increasingly extravagant and destructive fantasies. Yet even under these more trying circumstances Schubert sticks to his code: the purely mental world, no matter how deranged, is always indicated by the major, the real world of places and things by the minor.

The first clear evidence that the traveler has fallen victim to a neurotic delusion appears in the fourteenth song, "Der greise Kopf" ("The Gray Head"). Its opening phrase describes the snow that has fallen on the traveler's head. The snow is real, and the phrase is in a "realistic" E flat minor. But when he mistakes the snow for his own hair suddenly turned gray, the song shifts to an ironic G major: the exhausted man seizes on this transformation as a promise of impending death. As the snow melts he finds that his hair is still black, and the minor returns to remind him that he has many years to go before he can escape this vale of tears. The next song, "Die Krähe" ("The Crow"), tells of a crow that flies over the traveler's head. It is a real crow, and its tune is set in an appropriate minor mode—until, that is, the man starts to converse with the bird. Unlike the young miller's frequent conversations with the brook—which never cause us to doubt his sanity—the winter traveler here brings to mind the garrulous lunatics who patrol downtown streets. Again, Schubert shifts to the illusory major for this mad discourse. The nineteenth song—entitled, significantly, "Täuschung" ("Illusion")—describes "a dancing friendly light" that the traveler follows hither and thither. The song's gently rocking A major melody contains but a single phrase in the minor, and it marks the only moment in which the man sees things as they are: "Anyone as wretched as I," he groans, only to complete his thought in the "illusory" major: "would gladly yield to this bright deceit."

In the last three songs the traveler moves rapidly through a series of contradictory emotions: exaggerated self-assertion, spent misery, and finally an insane calm, reminiscent of the terminal stage of King Lear's delirium. In "Mut" ("Courage") he is seized with an almost Nietzschean bravura; the A minor tune ends in an A major flourish and a manifestly bogus proclamation of self-sufficiency:

> *Will kein Gott auf Erden sein*
> *Sind wir selber Götter!*

> If there's no God on earth,
> We ourselves are gods!

That the boast is illusory we know from the major key and from the completely broken mind we meet in the twenty-third and twenty-fourth songs. The text of "The Phantom Suns," set in A major, I have already quoted in its entirety, and its deranged metaphor speaks for itself. In "Der Leiermann" ("The Organ Grinder") the distinction between dream and reality is effectively abolished, marking the traveler's unqualified abandonment of his senses and therewith his release from the obsessions that have made his existence a living hell. He proposes to accompany a hurdy-gurdy man on his rounds:

> *Wunderlicher Alter!*
> *Soll ich mit dir gehn?*
> *Willst zu meinen Liedern*
> *Deine Leier drehn?*

> O you strange old fellow,
> Shall I walk with you?

> Do you want to grind your organ
> Playing to my songs?

"Der Leiermann" is the only song in the cycle to remain in a single mode from start to finish. Schubert composes it in A minor, and in terms of the cycle's harmonic code (minor = reality; major = illusion) one might expect it to signify a return to reality. But it is a very curious A minor, in which the piano plays open fifths, largely omitting the flatted third that would affirm the song's tonality unambiguously. The immediate reason for this is Schubert's wish to imitate the "open" harmonies of a primitive hand organ. But there is a psychological reason as well, I believe: the open fifths (which are constituents of both the major and the minor triads) suggest a realm beyond the familiar major-minor antithesis, a novel harmonic arena where the traveler is liberated, symbolically, from the fixations that have ruined his life. Schubert here forgoes his most distinctive and powerful compositional tool—the juxtaposition of major and minor—in order to convey the ironic transcendence that his traveler achieves in his final delirium.

Schubert's identification of the imaginary with the major throughout *Winterreise* reflects the peculiar charm that dreams held for the Romantics. The beauty of Romantic dreams indeed seems almost aggressive, reducing waking life to emptiness. In this respect they differ from the dreams of both earlier and later generations. Before the Romantics, dreams were often symbols of error or, more commonly, agents of suffering—one thinks of the dreams of Hamlet, Lady Macbeth, and Richard III. Even the benign dreams of *A Midsummer Night's Dream* symbolize confusion, as against the ecstasy of the Romantics. Since Freud's *Traumdeutung*, dreams have become the object of dispassionate interpretation, and it takes no great expertise as a cultural historian to see the categorical difference between the dream of "Irma's Injection"—Freud's first in that epoch-making book—and, say, Coleridge's dream poem "Kubla Khan," composed (or so he claimed) in his opium-induced sleep. Richard Strauss's Klytemnestra is a representative modern dreamer: "Ich habe keine guten Nächte" ("I have no good nights"), she complains to her unsympathetic daughter. In the famous "Snow" chapter of *The Magic Mountain*, the difference between Romantic and modern dreaming is powerfully delineated: the sleeping Hans Castorp finds himself in a pastoral landscape of frolicking children and animals, only to have the vision suddenly transformed into images of a hideous blood sacrifice.

Of course, not all Romantic dreams are idyllic. Byron, De Quincey, and Poe, for instance, had nightmares of impeccable modernity. Still, the typical Romantic dream is pleasurable. The greatest Romantic dreamer is Keats, whose *Endymion,* "Sleep and Poetry," "Sonnet to Sleep," and above all "Eve of St. Agnes" are glorious celebrations of a nighttime world innocent of quotidian tensions. Similarly, Wordsworth's child in the "Immortality" Ode basks in "the dream of infancy," and there is a comparable rapture in Coleridge's dream of stately pleasure domes on the river Alph, though their spell is threatened by "Ancestral voices prophesying war." Wagner's Elsa, in *Lohengrin,* and his Walther, in *Die Meistersinger,* also dream in the Romantic mode, Elsa of a knight in shining armor, Walther of a garden and a maiden on a summer morning. The dreams recounted in *Winterreise* share this same enchantment, which Schubert's music makes more immediate than words ever can. With the shift to the major, the voluptuous realm of sleep is brought instantly before us. But the shift is also punishing, both because the traveler's dreams give way to delusions and because they heighten, by contrast, our awareness of the "minor" reality to which he is condemned.

Depression

The stark juxtaposition of major and minor—symbolizing dream and reality—is, then, the primary means by which Schubert portrays the traveler's despondency. This device is seconded by a distinctive melodic procedure. Unlike the tunes in *Die schöne Müllerin,* which are characterized by upward leaps—conveying, I've argued, a sense of reaching or yearning—those of *Winterreise* typically have a downward melodic trajectory. At the same time, Schubert makes no effort, as he had in the earlier cycle, to avoid the tonic; instead the tunes are permitted to follow their natural pathway to the home tone. Whether consciously or not, we come to associate the typical downward melodic pattern ending on the tonic with the state of the traveler's spirits. Our most vivid recollections are of phrases that move from higher to lower pitches, and just as the emphasis on sustained notes in the upper part of the voice in *Die schöne Müllerin* becomes linked to the miller's yearning, so the prominence of sustained low notes in *Winterreise* reminds us of the winter traveler's depression. No wonder, then, that the cycle seems most suited to the baritone or bass voice, just as the earlier cycle is suited to the tenor voice. Only a baritone or bass can sit comfortably on the crucial low-lying notes that give the cycle its peculiar emotional flavor. This is not a matter that can be resolved by transposition, which is freely practiced by lieder singers. Rather, it is a question of tessitura: the songs of *Winterreise,* because of their melodic construction, draw on the strengths of a voice with a low center of gravity, just as those of *Die schöne Müllerin* show to best advantage in a voice pitched three or four tones higher. The distinction also corresponds to our sense of the difference in age between the two protagonists.

The typical depressive melodic line of *Winterreise* is already on display in the cycle's opening phrase, which moves downward in two sweeps over an octave and a third to rest solidly on a low D natural, the tonic. The song's gait-like pulse and minor tonality announce a sorrowful utterance, but only the descending melodic arc, heard first in the piano and then in the voice, informs us that our traveler is a man without hope. The phrase should be compared with the miller's opening phrase in *Die schöne Müllerin.* There, too, the pulse and tonality (brisk arpeggios in the major) set the general mood, but it is above all the upward curve of the miller's first line, ascending an arc that traces a full octave (from f to f'), that introduces a character every bit as sanguine as the winter traveler is demoralized.

Needless to say, not all the phrases in *Winterreise* move in a downward direction, and not all its sustained notes are on low pitches. That would be musically impossible. It is, rather, a matter of degree, of strategic location, and of melodic inspiration. The mind's ear lingers on these descending phrases and low-lying pitches; they are the most beguiling notes in the cycle. Thus in the third song, "Gefrorne Tränen" ("Frozen Tears"), we remember the line "Ei Tränen, meine Tränen" ("O tears, my tears"), set to a descending minor second in the bottommost reaches of the voice and wonderfully appropriate to the stale mood in which the man's tears are shed. The fourth song, "Erstarrung" ("Numbness"), exhibits the characteristic declension in the prominent bass line of the piano's opening and closing bars: seven measures winding tortuously downward from low C to a cavernous tone an octave below. This device of a downwardly meandering bass line occurs in several other songs as well (notably "Die Wetterfahne" and "Der greise Kopf") and to similar effect. The grand opening phrase of the ninth song, "Irrlicht" ("Will o' the Wisp"), again takes the singer from the tonic note in the middle of the voice to the same note an octave lower, as he tells of the "deep and rocky chasms" he has passed. Likewise, in the fourteenth song, the haunting complaint "Wie weit noch bis zur Bahre" ("So far yet to the grave") takes the voice down seven tones (from c′ to d).

Perhaps the most memorable use of the device comes in "Die Krähe," a song, as we've seen, in which Schubert also deploys his special "illusory" antithesis of major and minor. The man describes a crow that has followed him out of the town and hovers menacingly overhead. This circumstance is turned to ironic effect when the traveler expresses the bitter hope that the crow, unlike his mistress, will remain faithful to the grave. The account begins on a long phrase that seems to wander endlessly downward, traversing the melodic space from the tonic in the middle of the staff to the tonic an octave below. The phrase contains thirteen intervals, ten of which are from higher to lower pitches, suggesting a heart sinking to the depths. Indeed, the melody is like a physical weight on the singer's shoulders, dragging him ever deeper into hopelessness. But at the concluding line,

> *Krähe, lass mich endlich sehn*
> *Treue bis zum Grabe!*

> Crow, let me finally behold
> Fidelity to the grave!

Schubert composes one of the few phrases in the cycle with an uninterrupted upward movement, taking the singer to a thrillingly sustained high G natural on the word "Grabe." The depressive syndrome is thus illuminated by the music: the despairing voice can soar upward only in moments of lacerating irony. It is the melodic counterpart, one might say, to Schubert's ironic use of the major, throughout the cycle, to signify illusion.

Nature

For all their radical differences in psychology, *Die schöne Müllerin* and *Winterreise* both describe the same world in one respect: in each, the essential components are the self and nature. If anything, the sociology of *Winterreise* is even sketchier than that of *Die schöne Müllerin*. For instance, we never find out what the traveler does for a living. We know only that he is a person of modest means, since the girl's family has passed him over in favor of a son-in-law with more money. As in *Die schöne Müllerin*, we still picture the civilization through which he travels as a rural one: he is in a town but once, and the only persons he meets are a postman and an organ grinder.

Even the minimal physical descriptions of *Die schöne Müllerin* are dispensed with, and no direct discourse (unless it be imaginary or obsessed, as with the crow or the organ grinder) is reported. God is mentioned twice, but in an entirely perfunctory way. In sum, there has been an even more uncompromising reduction of reality to self and nature.

But here the similarities, important though they are, end. The natural world of *Winterreise* is not that of *Die schöne Müllerin,* and the protagonist relates to it in a correspondingly different way. The earlier cycle takes place in spring and summer, the later, obviously, in winter. Nature symbolizes life and love in *Die schöne Müllerin;* in *Winterreise* it symbolizes death. In both, the aquatic part of nature is the most prominent; both, as it were, are cycles about water. But, of course, where the dominant image of the first cycle is moving water— namely, the brook—the dominant image of the second is frozen water: ice, snow, petrified rivers, and even frozen tears. This antithesis, as well as the psychological antithesis it implies, is so obvious that it hardly requires comment. Indeed, it is almost too pat, and again only Schubert's unqualified confidence in his texts prevents the metaphor from cloying. That confidence is entirely a musical matter. Each song addresses the metaphor as if it were freshly minted.

As in the earlier cycle, the piano performs a crucial role in establishing the cycle's atmosphere, but that role cannot be exactly compared to the piano's function in *Die schöne Müllerin.* In the earlier cycle, the piano often seemed to represent nature, especially the brook. Occasionally it retains that function in *Winterreise:* in "Der Lindenbaum," as in "Die Wetterfahne" ("The Weathervane"), it becomes the wind that blows the traveler's hat from his head; in "Frühlingstraum" it seems to imitate the crowing cocks that interrupt his springtime fantasy; in the accompaniment to "Die Post" one hears the galloping of the postman's horse; in "Letzte Hoffnung" ("Last Hope") there is a brilliant pianistic re-creation of falling leaves; and watchdogs growl (though they don't bark) in the low trills of "Im Dorfe." But these are isolated moments, and the piano never threatens to become the embodiment of nature as it does in *Die schöne Müllerin.*

Rather, its primary function is to convey a sense of walking, of movement at the deliberate pace of a man on foot. Arpeggios, so common in *Die schöne Müllerin,* are extremely rare, primarily because they suggest the fast, undifferentiated movement of a stream. Instead Schubert uses a variety of accompanying procedures that make one think of ambulation. They give us an almost physical sense of the traveler's weary movement through the winter landscape. Where *Die schöne Müllerin* flows, *Winterreise* slogs.

The simplest way in which Schubert achieves this effect can be observed in the first song: the melody is supported by steadily repeated chords, each of which designates a step. Schubert leaves no doubt as to his intent here: the song is marked "Mässig, in gehender Bewegung" ("Moderate, in a walking movement"). The accompaniment of the seventh song, "Auf dem Flusse" ("On the River"), displays the same tired saunter, while the twelfth, "Einsamkeit" ("Loneliness"), finds the piano beating a somewhat slower tread, as the traveler "walks his street with leaden feet." The walking pulse first heard in the opening song is felt again in the twentieth, "Der Wegweiser" ("The Signpost"), and its heavy tramp is all the more poignant here coming directly after the lilting 6/8 of the nineteenth song, "Täuschung." The cycle is reaching its close now, and the pedestrian rhythm reminds us that nothing has changed—nothing outward, at least. Our traveler still trudges along.

Two other devices that contribute to the sense of gait-like movement are dotted rhythms and triplets. Composers of marches, like John Philip Sousa, have often exploited the peculiar "walking" effect of these rhythmic conceits. Such classic Sousa marches as "Washington Post" and "King Cotton," for example, combine them to irresistible effect, as, on a more exalted plane, does Verdi's "Triumphal March" from *Aida*. Schubert, of course, avoids Sousa's snappiness or Verdi's pomp, but he extracts a similar ambulatory pulse from dotted rhythms and triplets. The sixth song, "Wasserflut" ("The Water's Flow"), would seem, by its text, to invite the "flowing" arpeggios so common in *Die schöne Müllerin,* but Schubert maintains the image of walking before our ears by combining dotted figures in the piano with triplets in the voice. The result might be described as a musical version of plodding. In "Auf dem Flusse" the man tramps across a frozen river, and the strong walking beat suggested by the dotted rhythms of the vocal melody is further intensified when triplets are introduced into the accompaniment in the thirty-first bar. The same combination—triplets in the piano, dotted rhythms in the voice—gives the seventeenth song, "Im Dorfe," its slow but steady ambulatory pulse.

The examples could be multiplied. The important point is that the piano does not become, as in *Die schöne Müllerin,* the objective Other with whom the winter traveler can eventually converse. Rather, it remains an extension of the traveler himself—his feet, as it were.

The emotional atmosphere of the cycle is thus more claustrophobic than that of *Die schöne Müllerin*. Nature is dead, and the piano can't become its mouthpiece, although it may try from time to time. One might argue that the cycle's subjectivity is more completely realized than its predecessor's, where nature, though a mirror of the self, continued to enjoy an independent existence. In *Winterreise* it has been absorbed into the voracious Romantic ego. Appropriately, therefore, the listener ceases to be conscious of an antithesis between voice and piano: the musical dialogue of *Die schöne Müllerin* gives way to a musical monologue, in which the piano discreetly supports and often imitates the movements of the voice. The cycle is among the most utterly self-absorbed of all works of art, the quintessential expression of the Romantics' subjectivity.

CONCLUSION

Perhaps my assertion, in the previous chapter, that Schubert is Rossini's opposite among early-nineteenth-century vocal composers will now be more readily comprehended. Schubert and Rossini mark the breakdown of the Mozartean compromise, the delicate balance of musical interest between private emotion and public order. At one extreme stands Schubert's unprecedented exploration of the self, at the other Rossini's arch stylization of the human comedy. Schubert the Romantic ignores society and history to probe biography, while Rossini the Neoclassicist banishes all subjectivity that might dull his bright social spectacle.

I have no doubt that Schubert is the greater of the two artists. Indeed, at the risk of exceeding the limits of even decent opinionatedness, I would contend that his is the finest vocal music written in the first half of the nineteenth century. There are moments in Schubert when it seems that nothing more beautiful has ever been conceived. The song "Nacht and Träume" ("Night and Dreams"), composed in 1825 and belonging to neither of the cycles discussed here, is one among dozens of examples, many of them far from familiar. "Return, holy night! Soothing dreams, return!" writes the poet, and Schubert spins out a melody of unearthly serenity and loveliness. A more sober judgment—which can be arrived at only after the music has stopped—forces one to acknowledge the limits of this art. Whether for technical reasons or (more likely, I think) because of the essential intimacy of his sensibility, Schubert was never fully at home with the larger musical forms that permit Mozart, Beethoven, and Wagner, among others, to negotiate the most complex artistic subjects. And insofar as the very greatest art is complex—just as the human reality it mirrors and illuminates is complex—Schubert's accomplishment must be reckoned lesser. The same liability—a failure to master larger forms—makes Keats a lesser poet than Chaucer, Shakespeare, or Milton. *King Lear* and *Paradise Lost* are not more beautiful than "The Eve of St. Agnes" or "Ode on a Grecian Urn," but they are longer and richer. When Keats and Schubert strive for larger effects, the results are *Otho the Great* (Keats's five-act tragedy in verse) or *Alfonso und Estrella* (the best known of Schubert's largely forgettable operas).

In describing the peculiar character of Schubert's exploration of the self, I have sometimes borrowed M. H. Abrams's notion of a "circuitous journey." Strictly construed, that archetypal Romantic image applies only to *Die schöne Müllerin:* the cycle's outgoing arc traces a movement from home into the world, its conclusion a retreat back to the ancestral home of death. But the image is also pertinent to the emotional and musical logic of *Winterreise,* which might be called a failed circuitous journey. It is precisely the winter traveler's inability to follow the itinerary of the young miller that gives his songs their distinctive pathos, as if the earlier cycle lingered in the back of his mind. But the circle has been wrenched straight and stretches now into infinity: the movement of the songs is centrifugal, forever away from the town in which the traveler had hoped to find his home. In the last song we are made to feel that the journey will continue indefinitely, as the traveler sings his songs again and again to the accompaniment of the hurdy-gurdy man. The different narrative paths of the two cycles are also reflected in their music: *Winterreise* is not only more somber than its predecessor, it also forgoes the symmetrical patterning that lends *Die schöne Müllerin* a musical circularity to match its story.

There is yet another variation on the Romantic journey, which Schubert, because of his inability to control larger forms, did not address. It provides the central motif of Berlioz's Romantic opera *The Trojans*—the story of Aeneas's travels from Troy to Carthage, and thence to Rome. Aeneas's journey is, properly speaking, neither circular nor endless, but linear and purposive—a journey toward a goal. It further differs from the Romantic itineraries of Schubert's two protagonists in that it is a public journey: Aeneas sails under the aegis of destiny to found a civilization, and he does so with all the clamor and rhetorical gesturing appropriate to a great historical calling. To represent his journey, Berlioz requires the full musical arsenal of grand opera: huge performing forces and the most extended and complex of compositional structures. The work would seem to be the exact antithesis of the Schubertian song cycle, where all is private, indeed introverted, and economical—a single voice, a piano, and the shortest, simplest formal structure known to classical music, the lied.

But, as we shall see, at the center of Berlioz's massive historical drama lies the same intense subjectivity that one finds in Schubert's song cycles. Berlioz's traveler, like those of Schubert, is also a victim. His public mission is accomplished only at the expense of private happiness. He, too, would gladly find his way home, but he is driven on by forces beyond his control to seek an unknown future. Indeed, one suspects that beneath Aeneas's splendid armor and historical persona is a man not so very unlike Schubert's young miller or his winter traveler. Schubert and Berlioz represent, as it were, two sides of the same Romantic coin, Schubert the miniaturist, the ally of the Romantic poets, best compared, as I've suggested, to Keats; Berlioz the epic designer, the musical counterpart of the Romantic philosophers and historians of the age, above all of Hegel. The drama of the self stands at the heart of both artists' very different musical creations.

3

The Idea of History

Hector Berlioz's *The Trojans*

Hector Berlioz's *The Trojans* is one of the great operas of the nineteenth century, comparable to Verdi's *Otello* or Wagner's *Tristan und Isolde.* Unlike the latter works, however, it is an opera that many (including myself) know only from recordings. The reasons for this are not far to seek: in the end they come down to questions of performing forces and expense. *The Trojans* is constructed on a monumental scale. In particular, it makes exceptional demands on the chorus—far greater demands than any of the operas of Verdi or Wagner. Over a third of its numbers require the participation of the chorus, and many of those numbers are long and intricate. Today most opera companies simply lack the resources for this gigantic assignment. And if that weren't enough, the central role of Aeneas is almost impossible to cast. It calls for a dramatic tenor of the sort that can sing Otello or Tristan—a voice, in other words, able to contend with large orchestral and choral forces. But unlike Otello or Tristan, the role also requires a singer able to produce sustained and exposed tones in the region of high B flat, B natural, and even high C, notes that Verdi and Wagner almost never asked of the heavier (and hence lower) tenor voices for which they wrote their heroic roles. In this generation only one tenor, Jon Vickers, has been able to do the role justice, and not even Vickers has found its tessitura comfortable.

The libretto for *The Trojans,* written by Berlioz himself, is based

on Books I, II, and IV of the *Aeneid*. The first part of the opera—
given the title *La Prise de Troie (The Capture of Troy)* when the score
was published in 1863—tells of the final days of the Trojan War.
Berlioz alters Virgil's story by showing its events from the perspective
of Cassandra, the Trojan prophetess and daughter of King Priam and
Queen Hecuba. (In the *Aeneid* the story is recounted by Aeneas, and
Cassandra is mentioned only in passing.) The opera's opening scene
finds Cassandra bewailing the stupidity of the Trojans, who assemble
in the fields outside Troy to celebrate their victory. They are convinced
that the Greeks have finally abandoned the war, leaving behind only
a giant wooden horse as an offering to Minerva. Cassandra tells her
fiancé, Corebus, that not wedded bliss but death awaits them, and she
urges him to flee the city. After the Trojan dignitaries—Priam,
Hecuba, and Hector's widow, Andromache—make their formal entrance, Cassandra joins in the general horror as Aeneas relates the
gruesome story of Laocoön, who threw his sword into the flank of
the horse, only to be devoured by two sea monsters. She then brings
the first act to a close with her terrified commentary on the procession
that leads the deadly horse within the city's walls.

Cassandra remains the center of attention in the next act as well,
which takes place during the destruction of Troy by the Greeks. The
act begins with the only scene in *La Prise de Troie* in which she does
not appear: Aeneas's vision of the ghost of Hector, from whom he
receives the charge to "seek Italy." This is followed by a long set
piece for soprano and chorus, in which Cassandra exhorts the Trojan
women to join her in death rather than submit to being ravished by
the conquering Greeks. She promises them that under Aeneas's
generalship their sons will raise a new Troy in Italy, and on this note
of heroic anticipation the curtain falls.

The last three acts of *The Trojans* are entitled *Les Troyens à
Carthage (The Trojans in Carthage)*. Based largely on Book IV of the
Aeneid, they recount the story of Dido and Aeneas. At the opening
of the third act we are introduced to Queen Dido, who has come to
Carthage from Tyre, fleeing her husband's murderer. In seven years
under her stewardship, the city has grown to prosperity, and she is
greatly beloved by its citizens. She confides to her sister, Anna,
however, that she is disturbed by a vague melancholy, which Anna
promptly diagnoses. She is also disturbed by a Numidian chieftain,
Iarbas, who is threatening her borders and hopes to force her into
marriage. At this point the Trojans arrive, and the act ends with
Aeneas leading the combined forces of Carthage and Troy off to

"exterminer la noire armée" ("exterminate the black army").

Act IV is devoted entirely to the love of Dido and Aeneas. It is an act in which astonishingly little transpires—an hour-long celebration of romantic passion. Its essential languor stands in marked contrast to all that has preceded. It ends when the god Mercury appears to awaken Aeneas from his reverie and recall him to his mission.

The last act consists of two parts. The first depicts Aeneas's resolve to leave Carthage in order to fulfill his destiny in Italy. Berlioz shows us not merely Aeneas's great moment of decision but its profound effect on the lives of his followers as well. The closing scenes of the opera are then given over to Dido—first remonstrating, then resigning herself, and finally committing suicide.

La Prise de Troie and *Les Troyens à Carthage* might seem to be two separate operas, loosely tied together by the figure of Aeneas. The only other characters to appear in both parts of the work are Aeneas's son, Ascanius, and his follower Panthus, neither of whom has a significant role. Moreover, Aeneas himself is a relatively secondary figure in *La Prise de Troie.* He sings only a few dozen lines, although, admittedly, they are memorable ones. Even in the scene with Hector's ghost, his part is overshadowed by a huge orchestral introduction (in which Berlioz represents the distant sounds of battle, as the Greeks destroy the city) and by the ghost's awesome pronouncements. Nevertheless, the two halves of the opera are musically and conceptually so closely linked that the impact of either is considerably lessened when heard in isolation. The two define a single intellectual and emotional landscape. Cassandra, the protagonist of *La Prise de Troie,* embodies the ideal that haunts Aeneas throughout *Les Troyens à Carthage;* she is his conscience, much as Brünnhilde is Wotan's conscience in the operas of the *Ring.* Thus Part One of *The Trojans* shows the birth of a concept that inspires the heroic—as well as tragic—events of Part Two. In musical terms, the two halves of the opera are linked in many ways, most obviously by the Trojan March, which accompanies the entrance of the horse at the end of Act I and recurs no less than four times at crucial moments in the second half of the opera, including its glorious conclusion.

Much of the pleasure to be derived from *The Trojans* is of the sort one expects from any good opera: beautiful melodies, passages of great excitement, and powerful situations. What lends the work its distinctive flavor—and raises it to the level of special greatness—is its single-minded devotion to an idea. More than any other opera I can think of, *The Trojans* reflects a unique intellectual inspiration. This is not to say that Berlioz composed his opera with a view to illustrating that idea, or even that he was conscious of being in its grip. But his creation is inconceivable outside the intellectual atmosphere that made the idea available to him—indeed, that all but forced it on his attention. To ignore the opera's intellectual affinities is to fall victim to the most myopic form of the intentional fallacy.

The idea in question is the idea of history. Arguably it is the most pervasive assumption of European intellectual life in the nineteenth century, finding expression in the philosophy, science, political theory, literature, art, and—as I hope to show—music of the age. Many students of nineteenth-century culture have drawn attention to this peculiar historical consciousness. It is, for example, the object of a blistering attack by Friedrich Nietzsche in one of his earliest writings, *The Use and Abuse of History,* where Nietzsche complains that his century is besotted with history. Later it became the principal theme in the historiographical writings of Wilhelm Dilthey, Friedrich Meinecke, and Ernst Troeltsch. More recently it has provided the leitmotif in one of the few synoptic treatments of nineteenth-century thought, Maurice Mandelbaum's *History, Man, and Reason.* For all these writers, the idea of history is the underlying assumption that lends the nineteenth century its intellectual unity.

Perhaps the best way to grasp the distinctiveness of this idea is by way of comparison with the historical consciousness of the eighteenth-century Enlightenment. Edmund Burke was among the first to argue that the Enlightenment was fundamentally unhistorical. By that, Burke meant that the thinkers of the Enlightenment failed to appreciate the organic nature of the historical process. In their enthusiasm to correct the abuses of their time, they assumed that institutions and customs could be transformed almost at will to conform to some abstract conception of the good society. Against that assumption, Burke insisted that history transcends individual volition. It has its own inherent logic, and any attempt to interfere with that logic is not only presumptuous but an invitation to disaster.

Since Burke's time, the friends of the Enlightenment—in our own century such scholars as Ernst Cassirer and Peter Gay—have shown that the eighteenth century was more attuned to history than its critics have allowed. But even when all correctives have been taken into account—even when it is recognized, for example, that the *philosophes* wrote a good deal of very fine history themselves, and that they made important contributions to the modern practice and conception of history—it remains true that the thinkers of the

Enlightenment lacked a *sense* of history such as was to become the common property of thinkers in the nineteenth century. Their ideas about the past tended to be atomistic, stressing individual actors and events rather than impersonal forces or organic developments. This was so, I believe, not because the *philosophes* were somehow more moralistic than their successors, but because the central categories of Enlightenment thought were at bottom unhistorical. The great battle cries of the age were Reason and Nature. Ideas and institutions were to be judged good or bad according to whether they were reasonable or natural. No reader of a characteristic Enlightenment tract such as Voltaire's *Philosophical Letters* can fail to note that Voltaire assessed the practices of his civilization according to timeless and universal canons: things were either reasonable or they were not, and if they were not, they should be changed. To be sure, neither he nor his fellow *philosophes* were entirely insensitive to cultural and historical differences. Their rationalism was not uninflected. But their essential cast of mind remained universalizing. Those who thought in different terms—who valued historical and particularistic knowledge above rational and categorical knowledge—did not belong to the mainstream of the age, and it remained for subsequent generations to resurrect a figure like Giambattista Vico (1668–1744), who, as Isaiah Berlin has shown, anticipated the profoundly historical consciousness of the post-Enlightenment era.

By way of contrast, nineteenth-century thought is saturated with history. One might even say that history performs the same function for nineteenth-century intellectuals that reason and nature performed for the Enlightenment. This new historical consciousness originated in Germany within the confines of the eighteenth century itself, in thinkers like Herder and Fichte. After the French Revolution, it becomes the key to virtually every major intellectual development, even to the ideas of such adversarial figures as Kierkegaard, Dostoevsky, and Nietzsche. The German Idealists of the early nineteenth century introduced this historical consciousness into philosophical thought. In the middle years of the century Karl Marx introduced it into political economy, and very soon thereafter Charles Darwin introduced it into biology. Nothing, not even God, remained immune to the historical onslaught: John Henry Newman's *Essay on the Development of Christian Doctrine* marks the insinuation of a historicizing imagination into the realm of theology, and the same process can be observed in the growth of Liberal Protestantism from Friedrich Schleiermacher to Adolf von Harnack. History was the century's *idée fixe,* and no important thinker of the age could fail to come to terms with it. Perhaps the most striking illustration of this is provided by John Stuart Mill, whose *Autobiography* charts the process by which the young Mill, heir to the unhistorical ideas of Benthamism, entered upon a personal and intellectual crisis that was resolved only when he incorporated the new historical ethos into his thinking.

The central figure in the emergence of this ethos was the German philosopher Georg Wilhelm Friedrich Hegel. Hegel's philosophical system transfixed the century's intellectuals, who sought to embody its principles in a variety of conceptual and aesthetic projects. Hegel's single most important contribution was the notion of history as a suprapersonal process with its own immanent dynamic. Independent of the actions of individual men and women, according to Hegel, history evolved in a particular direction, its content unfolding like the will of God. It did so in what Hegel called a dialectical fashion—that is, through a process in which the forward movement of events was regularly interrupted by what might be described as creative reversals. This conception was sufficiently imprecise (and subject to enough contingencies) to leave the interpretation of individual historical episodes just as ambiguous as ever. Yet for all its imprecision, the conception worked a powerful effect on the nineteenth-century imagination. No longer was history a sequence of random occurrences dictated by accident or individual initiative. Instead it came to be seen as the working out of a universal drama with a logic entirely its own.

Two further aspects of the Hegelian theory of history need to be noted. First, Hegel insisted that modern Western civilization was the highest product of this inexorable historical dialectic. The modern West was not necessarily the end point of the historical process, but it unquestionably marked its finest accomplishment to date. The theory, in short, was Europocentric, and partly as a result of Hegel's influence, nineteenth-century Europeans came to entertain a thoroughly complacent image of themselves. Toward the end of the century they even presumed to take over large areas of the non-Western world. Thus the historical consciousness of the nineteenth century was also a kind of celebration of the European achievement, a celebration whose intellectual pedigree is to be found in Hegel's *Lectures on the Philosophy of History* (1822–1823).

Second, Hegel believed that the historical process, though ultimately impersonal, worked itself out through human agencies. He drew attention in particular to two such agencies: historical heroes (or "World-Historical Individuals") and historical victims. Both were vehicles of what he termed the "cunning of Reason," the process by which private ideals and struggles were put to work for transcendent public ends. Even historical heroes were in a sense victims, but they differed from victims proper in that their experience was one of achievement; for heroes the discrepancy between personal and public objectives was never extreme. Authentic victims, by way of contrast, lived not for greatness but for happiness, and when events frustrated their happiness, they necessarily had to consider their lives a failure. They were utterly used—and abused—by history. A good deal of nineteenth-century social thought represented an elaboration of these two Hegelian categories: the cult of the historical hero, such as one finds in Carlyle, reflected one side of the Hegelian legacy, while the effort to reclaim the rights of history's victims became a central strain in nineteenth-century radicalism, above all in Marx.

This great nineteenth-century conceit, I believe, provided the implicit inspiration for Berlioz's opera. To state the matter baldly, *The Trojans* is a musical embodiment of the Hegelian idea of history. Such, at least, will be the burden of my argument in the following pages. The opera is constructed according to a grand dialectical pattern. The Trojan acts plant the opera's thesis: a new civilization is to arise out of the ashes of the old, with Cassandra as its prophet and Aeneas as its agent. But that idea cannot be realized before it passes through an antithetical testing, a creative setback, in which the idea comes into mortal combat with its opposite. Thus Aeneas does not proceed directly to Italy, but goes instead to Carthage, where his mission is all but forgotten as he loses himself in a great romance. Only thus burdened with the memory of Dido's tragedy does he set sail to found his civilization, and that civilization, one feels, will be morally and psychologically enriched for having emerged from its Carthaginian antithesis. The geographical trajectory of the opera— from Troy to Carthage and thence to Rome—charts a historical course from discredited homeland, through exotic alienation, to the true homeland of the future.

The opera's affinities with this major intellectual preoccupation of the age—whether or not intended by Berlioz—serve to account for the work's unique atmosphere. At the same time, they also explain why Berlioz's treatment of the Virgilian theme is so utterly unlike that of his predecessor Henry Purcell. Purcell's *Dido and Aeneas* was composed more than a century and a half before *The Trojans,* and it is quite without the later opera's historical pathos. Where Berlioz's Aeneas is the hero of a great and inexorable historical drama, Purcell's

Aeneas is merely a romantic dupe. Moreover, the drama in question is nothing less than the founding of Western civilization, a civilization that for Berlioz, no less than for Hegel, marks the culmination of history. Over and over again in the opera, one hears the call to Italy, which, after all, is the call to our own beginnings. Because he has music at his disposal, Berlioz can invest this great historical moment with unparalleled evocativeness. And for the same reason he can also record its costs—the story of history's victims—with a poignancy that emerges but feebly from the pages of Hegel's lectures. Thus the tale of Dido and her "immortal love" assumes an emotional resonance unsurpassed even in Virgil. Just as Aeneas is the musical realization of the historical hero, Dido is the Hegelian victim. Her tragedy results neither from a failure of character nor from an unfortunate turn of events, but from the simple fact that she stands between Aeneas and his historical destiny. She is one of those who would sacrifice greatness to happiness.

THE PUBLIC REALM

The historical pathos of *The Trojans* is a complex achievement. Certainly among its most important preconditions is Berlioz's ability to create and sustain the sense of a public drama, one whose outcome affects, if not all humanity, at least a large and significant portion of it. This public atmosphere of *The Trojans* is diametrically opposed to the radical privacy of Schubert's song cycles, where but a single consciousness exists. And it is hardly less remote from the narrow social worlds of Mozart and Rossini, where, except on those occasions when a few townspeople, peasants, or soldiers gather about, the action touches the lives of only a small number of persons—the members of one or two households.

Of course, *The Trojans* is a public opera almost by definition. Even when we observe its characters in private, we know that their actions have epochal consequences. But Berlioz has devised a variety of means to intensify our sense of the public and historical nature of the drama. To a certain extent this "publicness" is conveyed quite simply by the opera's dimensions. The public realm is, naturally, the larger realm; private life is associated with intimacy. Thus one way to designate actions as public is to set them in the largest of all possible spaces—namely, outdoors. Berlioz does this throughout the opera, not only in those scenes that by their nature must be outdoors, but also in some that could just as well take place inside. The most striking example is the fourth act of the opera, the great love scene, which could easily transpire in some palatial interior. Berlioz, however, locates it in Dido's gardens by the sea. Similarly, the lovers' rancorous separation takes place on the seashore, near the harbor from which the Trojan ships are about to depart. Even the opera's indoor settings seem to partake of the outside world and its vastness. From the room of Aeneas's vision in Act II we hear "noise of distant fighting." The palatial chamber in which the Trojan women resolve to kill themselves opens out onto a prospect of Mount Ida. In Act III the Carthaginian ceremonies transpire in "a vast hall of greenery." The setting for the most completely private scene in the opera, Dido's famous lament in the last act, is simply "a room" in the Queen's palace. But Berlioz adds, "Le jour se lève" ("Day breaks"), and once again we are in mind of the opera's cosmic dimensions. The vastness of the opera's space, one might say, corresponds to the vastness of its subject.

Die schöne Müllerin and *Winterreise* also take place outdoors, but in a very different outdoors. Schubert's exteriors are limited by dark forests and steep mountains, and his vistas are contracted by sleet and snow. They are the exteriors one sees in certain paintings of Caspar David Friedrich. Berlioz's opera, on the other hand, opens upon a limitless and unclouded sky. Its imagined boundaries are those of the horizon. The space of the opera is that of the globe, as in Shakespeare's *Antony and Cleopatra.* By way of contrast, the highly socialized and intimate bedrooms and sitting rooms of *The Marriage of Figaro* and *The Barber of Seville* define not a public but a domestic space. We are briefly on the street outside Dr. Bartolo's house at the start of *The Barber of Seville,* and the last act of *The Marriage of Figaro* takes place in Count Almaviva's garden. But to move from the Count's provincial orchard to Queen Dido's "gardens by the sea" is to move from the world of private relationships to that of history.

One also obtains a subliminal sense of the opera's essentially public character from the musical dimensions of *The Trojans.* The work is large in a number of ways. Most obviously, it is a very long opera: with its five acts (in ten scenes) a performance lasts well over four hours—which puts it in the select company of *Die Meistersinger, Götterdämmerung,* and *Parsifal.* But this protraction is not achieved, as one sometimes feels with Wagner, by allowing the opera's music to unfold at an unusually grave pace. On the contrary, much of *The Trojans* is quite brisk. Thus one rarely has the sense of a normal-sized opera being stretched out simply by slowing down the tempo. If anything, the effect is just the opposite: vast amounts of material seem to have been packed into a narrow compass. It's almost too much to absorb: too many characters, too many events—above all, too much music. There is a kind of extravagance that one associates with highly public gestures.

The largeness of the whole is reflected in the largeness of the parts. The numbers in an opera by Mozart or Rossini run to three or four minutes, and those in a typical mid-nineteenth-century opera are not a great deal longer. But the numbers in *The Trojans* commonly last between six and ten minutes. The duet in the first act between Cassandra and Corebus, for example, takes up a full quarter hour. The effect of this monumentality is once again to suggest figures whose utterances and actions have a public—and hence historic—character. Even when alone, they speak on a grand scale.

In a similar fashion the sheer size of the opera's performing forces contributes to its aura of publicness. Most important in this respect are the seventeen formal choruses. Some of these are brief and relatively inconsequential, but at least half a dozen are extraordinarily complex—magnificent sonic friezes of overpowering effect. In *La Prise de Troie* the entrance of Priam and Hecuba is marked by such a chorus—a long, sonorous, march-like hymn, "Dieux protecteurs de la ville éternelle" ("Gods who watch our eternal city"). Soon after follows an even more elaborate Octet and Chorus, in which the Trojans react to the news of Laocoön's death. It might be considered the serious counterpart of Rossini's famous "picture of stupefaction," "Fredda ed immobile," in *The Barber of Seville:* in both, the characters are frozen with terror and sing of their predicament at great length. The first part of the opera ends in what is virtually a choral scene, as the Trojan maidens resolve to share Cassandra's suicide. *Les Troyens à Carthage* opens with yet another elaborate choral number, the Carthaginian national anthem, "Gloire à Didon" ("Glory to Dido"). The chorus then absents itself from the opera's fourth act (save for the discreet support it lends to the beautiful septet), but in the last act one hears it again before Dido's sacrifice in a massive "Chorus of the Priests of Pluto." Each of these episodes is comparable in scale and complexity to the large choral scenes in *Aida* or *Don Carlo,* but where Verdi writes two or three such numbers for his opera, Berlioz writes six. In no other important opera, except perhaps *Boris Godunov,* is the balance between individual and communal expression so heavily weighted in favor of the latter.

Just as there is a surfeit of choruses, there is a surprising dearth of arias—the aria being the prime vehicle of private, introspective expression, comparable to the soliloquy in drama. A solitary figure is on stage only five times during the whole of *The Trojans,* and of the opera's fifty-two numbers, only four are full-scale arias—one for Cassandra, one for Aeneas, and two for Dido. Even many of the work's seemingly private moments are publicly observed. Dido and Aeneas may ultimately sing their love duet alone, but that supreme romantic moment is preceded by nearly half an hour of music in which their attachment is watched and commented on by members of the court. Their duet should be contrasted with that of the lovers in *Tristan und Isolde,* the essence of which is privacy—indeed, secrecy. Although Isolde's maid, Brangäne, is present, she is there only as a watch, and when she fails to alert the lovers, the public realm, in the person of King Marke, breaks in on their secret world, with tragic consequences.

Large numbers of performing forces and elaborate musical construction do not, of course, always convey a sense of publicness. In some operas they can be used primarily to suggest variety and multiplicity. Verdi's *Forza del destino* is a case in point. Its many scenes take one across a wide swath of Spanish and Italian geography, in which one sees soldiers, peasants, townspeople, gypsies, and monks. The opera conveys a feeling for the texture of society, but little sense of the public order. If anything, just the opposite is the case: *Forza,* Verdi's most sprawling and loosely constructed opera, hints at a world in which the public order has dissolved. The "destiny" that is the opera's subject is a purely private matter, the impulse—perhaps unconscious—that leads men and women to act against their own best interests.

The element missing in *Forza,* which would bring the public order to mind, is ceremony. Not religious ceremony (of which there is a good deal in *Forza*), but civil ceremony, with its pomp and circumstance. By way of contrast, *The Trojans* abounds in ceremony. Among great operas it is surely the most stately—a word whose etymology should be taken in earnest here. Its elaborate formalities are not gratuitous scenic and musical exhibitions, but an essential part of its argument. Ceremony betokens the public arena, an arena of stylized speech and action. The opera's ceremoniousness thus reminds us that the actions we observe are not merely those of private individuals. They bear upon the state, and ultimately upon the history of mankind.

Accordingly, entrances and exits in the opera tend to become processions. The entrance of the Trojan King and Queen with their court in the first act is set to a grand march. When Andromache presents her child to Priam, Berlioz composes a magnificent orchestral pantomime—some seven minutes long—which lends the moment great public dignity. Dido's entrance in Act III receives equally weighty musical representation. These and similar ceremonial devices raise the opera's rhetorical temperature. They might be considered the operatic counterparts of the slightly pompous band music that often prefaces large public gatherings in our own day.

Ceremony is also implied by Berlioz's frequent reliance on the proposition that we are listening to music within music—a device exactly comparable to the dramatist's play within a play. Thus several of the opera's numbers are meant to be viewed as performances, not merely by the audience but by the participants in the drama as well. In the first act, for example, the Trojan people sing a hymn to their deities, and Berlioz composes it in wide intervals and open harmonies, supported by a battery of drums, triangles, and timbrels, all of which lend it a distinctly antique flavor. In a similar fashion the Carthaginians intone their national anthem at the opening of the African acts. Indeed, they sing it no less than four times, and it reappears twice later on in the opera. There are also two ecclesiastical scenes—the prayer of the Trojan women and the Ritual for the Dead conducted by the priests of Pluto—in which the choral incantations suggest liturgical utterances that might well have been sung "in real life."

Then there is a whole series of official entertainments, also involving music within music, and also contributing to the aura of ceremony and publicness. In Act IV Dido's court poet, Iopas, is called on to sing his "poem of the fields," "O blonde Cérès" ("O golden Ceres"), a number that is sometimes cut in performance, perhaps because of the difficult high C in its third refrain. It is an intoxicating piece of music, marking the beginning of Berlioz's campaign, in Act IV, to create an atmosphere of perfect erotic serenity. Yet for all its evocativeness, we do not forget that it is, after all, a song—that is, an official entertainment—and that we are therefore in the presence of public figures. A similar effect is created by the opera's ballets, of which there are no fewer than three. These also are "performances" not merely for us but for the characters on stage. Thus for the assembled Trojan royalty in the first act there is a "Wrestlers' Dance," which precedes Andromache's pantomime. In Act III there are balletic entrances—each with its own music—for "Builders," "Sailors," and "Farmworkers." In the fourth act, the love duet is preceded by ballets for "Oriental Dancing Girls," "Slaves," and "Nubian Slave Girls"—

again, each with its own music. Finally, the opera's two great pantomimes—that for Andromache in Part One and the splendid "Royal Hunt and Storm" in Part Two—are, in effect, ballets with vocal commentary, and they, too, contribute to the opera's stateliness. Berlioz thus cleverly exploits the often meretricious devices of grand opera to establish an essential premise of his great theme.

The opera also receives the stamp of officialdom from its distinctive orchestration, above all through the frequent and effective use of brass and percussion. The brass are the traditional instruments of ceremony, their characteristic expression being the fanfare. And Berlioz is perhaps the greatest modern composer for brass. Anyone who has heard the *Symphonie fantastique* or the "Roman Carnival" Overture will be familiar with his love for and mastery of this orchestral choir. Of all the great operas, *The Trojans* is the most brilliant in orchestral color. Its surface shines like polished armor. Trumpets sound out thrillingly even in its opening bars, where they are soon joined by horns and trombones. For the next five hours the brass return over and over, lending a pervasive metallic tonality not only to the opera's martial events but to many of its less agitated moments as well. The brass are especially associated with Aeneas and his historical mission. But they appear in other contexts to establish a subliminal consciousness of the public order. Thus at the moment when King Priam blesses Andromache's son, Berlioz interrupts the woodwind and string music of the pantomime to introduce a sonorous chorale of low trombones. Similarly, when Dido's political adviser, Narbal, frets about the consequences of the love affair with Aeneas, the low brass accompaniment reminds us of the state and its reasons.

In much the same fashion, Berlioz associates the public realm with the percussion, especially the cymbals, whose metallic ring has obvious affinities with the brass. I have already mentioned the exotic percussion accompaniment for the entrance of Priam and Hecuba. Similarly, King Priam's trombone chorale in the pantomime is launched with a quietly authoritative sounding of the cymbals. Brass and percussion are notably silent in the fourth act, which celebrates Dido and Aeneas's love. But they return spectacularly at its end when Mercury appears to wake Aeneas from his romantic torpor. Mercury's three calls of "Italie!" are punctuated by nasty commentary from trumpets, horns, trombones, tuba, and heavy percussion (timpani, bass drum, and tam-tam). Here and elsewhere Berlioz's orchestration contributes, as do the opera's monumentality and ceremoniousness, to inform us of its public nature.

Two further procedures should be mentioned in this context, although they are perhaps more equivocal than the matters I've discussed so far. Surely, however, Berlioz intensifies our sense of the opera's publicness by showing us its opposite, the private realm, and by doing so through sharp contrasts. Our awareness of the public order is thus heightened, one might say, retrospectively and by relief. This sort of juxtaposition is common to many operas with political themes. One thinks, for example, of Verdi's skillful alternation between the public and private arenas in *Aida* or in *Don Carlo*. The public assembly of the Egyptians in the first act of *Aida* gives way to the private agony of Aida's "Ritorna vincitor"; the *auto-da-fé* in *Don Carlo* gives way to King Philip's monologue in his study. A somewhat clumsier instance of the same procedure is provided by Bellini's *Norma,* where Druids march on and off stage, interrupting the private drama of Norma, Adalgisa, and Pollione. But, as is not the case in Verdi's and Bellini's operas, the public realm is overwhelmingly the dominant one in *The Trojans.* It is not merely the noisy background against which the opera's more serious private events are set. If measured only in terms of sheer stage time, it always remains the center of our attention. Thus where in Verdi or Bellini the contrast of public and private tends to suggest the emptiness and hypocrisy of the former, the same contrast in Berlioz has no such invidious effect. It merely intensifies our awareness of the drama's historic import.

Private moments that "heighten" one's sense of the public order occur in each of the opera's five acts. In Act I the Trojan celebrations and the entrance of the horse are set against Cassandra's solo lament, "Malheureux Roi!" ("Ill-fated King!"), and her duet with Corebus. In the second act the public sacrifice of the Trojan women follows upon the nocturnal appearance of the Shade of Hector in Aeneas's palace. Between the ceremonial entrances of the third act and the arrival of the Trojans comes Dido's private dialogue with her sister, Anna. Another duet, this time between Anna and Narbal, serves a similar purpose in the fourth act: it, too, is a kind of tête-à-tête, setting off the public love feast that ensues. The fifth act boasts the richest interplay of public and private. It begins with the solitary miseries of the lower orders: a young Phrygian sailor, Hylas, sings of his lost homeland, and two Trojan sentries grumble about leaving their Carthaginian mistresses for some harebrained venture in Italy. But Aeneas then arrives, and the scene ends with the Trojans' exalted departure en masse. In the opera's final scenes, Dido's elaborate public suicide is preceded by the most affecting private moment of all, her monologue "Je vais mourir" ("I am going to die") and the exquisite farewell to her adopted city.

There is, I believe, one last means whereby we are made to feel the essentially public nature of the opera. It is related to the work's musical complexity and its vast dimensions, yet is not identical with them. I have in mind the sense one gets from *The Trojans* of observing a whole society, a kind of cross-section of the social order, from the humblest to the most powerful. Berlioz consciously broadens the canvas so that we develop a rounded sense of many characters whose roles in the drama are secondary, or even tertiary. The true principals are exactly three in number: Cassandra, Dido, and Aeneas, and they are drawn with appropriately broad musical strokes. But extensive and superb music is also lavished on Cassandra's fiancé, Corebus, Dido's sister, Anna, and her minister, Narbal. All of these roles— which might well have been assigned to comprimarii in a less ambitious work—are substantial enough to require major artists. In this way the world of advisers and confidants is lent unusual texture and vividness. Similarly, the world of servants and entertainers takes on unexpected richness when court dancers perform not just a few steps but extensive ballets and when court singers are given the leisure for songs with three verses. Most important of all, the world of society at large is repeatedly brought to life by the many embodiments of the chorus—as warriors, priests, citizens, virgins—just as it is by the substantial scenes for what might be called representative figures— the melancholy sailor Hylas, the complaining sentries. Only one other opera I know achieves this kind of social inclusiveness: Musorgsky's *Boris Godunov,* which moves from the public squares of the Kremlin to the isolated monastery of Pimen and the pretender Grigori, thence to the popular environs of Varlaam and the innkeeper on the Lithuanian frontier, back to the chambers of the Tsar and his adviser Shuisky, and finally, after a sojourn among the Polish aristocracy, to the marginal world of the abused but prescient simpleton. Indeed, of all the operas in the standard repertory, *Boris*—with its grand historical theme, its episodic structure, and above all its extraordinary use of the chorus—is most like *The Trojans.*

Berlioz also seeks to give musical expression to this social inclusiveness. The spectrum of society is reflected in the spectrum of the opera's formal musical devices, from the strophic artlessness of Hylas's song, through the intricacy and extension of the arias, duets, and ensembles for the principals, to the imposing contrapuntal complexity of the great choruses. Finally, something of that inclusiveness is suggested, I believe, by the unusual variety of the work's orchestral coloring, rhythmic patterns, and dynamic range. In its musical heterogeneity—now dignified, now martial, now simple, now gruff—we hear the artistic reflection of the social whole.

THE MOVEMENT OF HISTORY

The public atmosphere of *The Trojans,* as I've suggested, is a necessary precondition for establishing that aura of historical pathos that I take to be the opera's most distinctive feature. But it is only a precondition. An opera can be public without being historical, at least in the nineteenth-century, Hegelian sense I have in mind. Indeed, many public operas are without discernible historical interest and are hence relatively static. In such operas there are, of course, historical occurrences, but we are not made to care about them or feel that they bear on some larger issue. The public events in *Aida,* for example—the defeat of an Ethiopian army by an Egyptian one, the capture of the Ethiopian king and his subsequent escape—matter very little in our response to the opera; instead our concern is taken up with the private tragedy that they occasion. Even in an opera like *Boris Godunov,* where public events have genuine weight, we are left mainly with a sense of historical futility: the cycle of power and corruption repeats itself eternally, as the masses entertain the same false hopes and suffer the same disillusionments time and again. Along with the author of Ecclesiastes, we are led to conclude that there is nothing new under the sun.

The Trojans, by way of contrast, is historically in earnest. The most profound emotion it elicits is of being gathered up in the sweep of great events. Berlioz's singular achievement in the opera is to have composed music that evokes a sense of the historical process. Needless to say, much of the opera's power depends simply on our response to Virgil's epic. But I wish to consider the strictly musical means Berlioz uses to heighten the story's theme to a Hegelian pitch.

The common effect of all these musical procedures is to create a sense of irresistible forward movement. Of course, virtually all music suggests movement, simply because music is a temporal medium, and rhythm—the measure of movement—is one of its essential ingredients. But certain rhythmic and melodic procedures convey a more intense feeling of unbroken forward motion. Perhaps the most striking instance of this is provided by the march, which suggests movement that is steady, directional, and purposive. In part these associations are extramusical: they depend on the sight or experience of marching, whether in a parade, at a football game, or in a military exercise. But the actual musical construction of a march also strongly implies movement of this sort. The most salient feature of a march is its beat, which is both prominent (a prominence emphasized by the percussion) and absolutely regular. A march neither speeds up nor slows down; it is utterly without rhythmic flexibility. At the same time, its melodic and harmonic construction tends to be relatively simple, so that the listener easily anticipates what lies ahead in the music. The element of surprise is at a minimum, and we know, musically speaking, that certain things simply have to occur. These qualities of emphatic regularity and predictability contribute to an overall sense of inexorable movement, which makes the march an ideal musical representation of that endless unfolding of events that we call the historical process. Hence the appropriateness of such expressions as "the march of time," "the march of events," or simply "the march of history."

Berlioz seized on this obvious affinity and made it the musical crux of *The Trojans*. He himself felt that the Trojan March was the musical centerpiece of his opera, embodying its deepest truth. When, in 1863, *Les Troyens à Carthage* was given a separate performance (it was the only time Berlioz saw any part of his work staged), he arranged to have the story of the deleted first two acts recited by a speaker in Greek costume, followed by a performance of the march. This single musical excerpt, he believed, would convey the dramatic essence of the missing acts.

I would not argue that the Trojan March is uniquely designed to suggest the movement of history, since the same might be said of other marches of similar grandeur and élan. In common with many marches it emphasizes the notes of the major triad, they being the "natural" fanfare-like tones of the brass instruments in which the march is usually heard. Like the Triumphal March from *Aida*, it relies heavily on dotted rhythms and triplets, although where Verdi's march is stately, Berlioz's is headlong. As a piece of music, the march's most notable features are its brilliance and exuberance. But more important than its melodic or harmonic construction is its artful deployment over the course of the opera's development. It appears repeatedly, in different guises, and always at crucial moments in the drama's unfolding, so that by its final triumphant sounding as the Trojan ships depart for Italy, no listener can fail to sense its historic import. It has become the sonic metaphor of Aeneas's calling.

Somewhat surprisingly, the march is heard only once during the

Trojan acts of the opera. Moreover, its introduction does not come, as one might have expected, at the grand processional entrance of the Trojan court, for which, instead, Berlioz composed the antique hymn, "Dieux protecteurs de la ville éternelle," to which I have already alluded. Rather, the march is first heard at a supremely ironic moment—namely, as the Greek horse is brought within the city walls. Here it forms the musical basis of the Act I finale, and it sounds out ever more grandly as the Trojans bring on their own destruction. I am tempted to say that Berlioz introduces the march in a dialectical fashion, for the very tune that will later be associated with the triumphant mission of the Trojans in Italy makes its debut to mark the end of their former glory. It is as if the Trojan disaster were necessary to the birth of the new civilization. The musical logic resembles that dialectical conception of history according to which future triumphs grow out of past tragedies. Or, in terms of an older intellectual tradition, it is a musical illustration of the *felix culpa*.

Although the full march is sounded only once in the Trojan acts, Berlioz borrows from its harmonic and rhythmic components at a significant moment in Cassandra's final scene. As she addresses the Trojan maidens, she plants the idea of Aeneas's mission:

> *Bientôt en Italie, où le sort les appelle,*
> *Ils verront s'élever, plus puissante et plus belle,*
> *Une nouvelle Troie.*

> Soon, in Italy, where destiny calls them,
> They will see a new Troy rise, stronger
> And more beautiful.

Berlioz marks this short passage "tempo di marcia," and he sets Cassandra's prophetic words to the rising melodic line that one has come to associate with the opening phrase of the march. If the tempo and melodic resemblance were not enough, the passage is also characterized by the energetic dotted rhythms that are a prominent feature of the march. It is a brief gesture, but sufficiently precise in its musical allusions to make Berlioz's point. The march is the symbol of destiny.

In the Carthaginian acts of the opera the march is heard three times. Its thunderous appearance at the opera's close resembles a symphonic recapitulation: by now we fully expect it, and indeed one can't imagine the opera ending with any other music. It has the effect of summing up, of rehearsing an argument that by this time has achieved the inevitability of a geometric proof. But in its earlier appearances it serves more genuinely dramatic or expository purposes.

The first of these occurs when the Trojans arrive in Carthage. If the march's sounding in *La Prise de Troie* had been ironic, here it is pathetic. The Trojans are a straggling remnant, abused by the Greeks and the elements alike. They come in defeat and disarray. Although they still represent the vanguard of history, they are at that stage in the historical drama where their fortunes have reached the lowest ebb. Appropriately, therefore, they enter to the march "dans le mode triste." That is, Berlioz transposes the melody from major to minor, strips it of its jaunty triplets, and scores it for two cornets playing *mezzo forte* instead of the usual *fortissimo* trumpets. The transformation perfectly reflects the Trojans' dispirited condition, while reminding us of their historical continuity with the heroic warriors of the first two acts.

The march's other appearance in *Les Troyens à Carthage* comes at the turning point of the opera: Aeneas's resolve to depart for Italy. This occurs at the end of the first scene of Act V and terminates a long sequence of events in which Berlioz explores, with mounting tension, the implications of Aeneas's decision. Dramatically, the decision is shown to touch on an ever greater number of lives. Musically, the scene builds in waves of increasing excitement—heightenings and relaxations—until it is capped by the sounding of the march in the full orchestra. The march thus has the effect of gathering up all that has come before it.

This powerful scene is constructed like the gradual ascent of a mountain: one climbs a series of lesser peaks, each followed by a valley, but always with the final goal—in this case the departure—before one's inner eye. Just as each peak surpasses the preceding one, the level of musical excitement rises stepwise as the departure grows nearer. The march, which the listener begins to anticipate in his mind's ear, is the inevitable fulfillment of the scene's ascending musical and dramatic arc.

We begin in the private world of the sailor Hylas, who, to a gentle rocking melody, sings of his homesickness. There is a hint of anxiety in the air, but the music is essentially quiet and intimate. As Hylas falls asleep the Trojan chieftains enter, and the musical temperature is immediately raised several degrees. To an agitated melodic line, interrupted by nervous syncopations, we hear the first intimation of what's about to happen:

Quittons sans plus tarder ce rivage funeste!
A demain! à demain!
Préparons tout, il faut partir enfin.

Let us leave this ill-omened coast without more delay.
Tomorrow! tomorrow!
Get everything ready, we must leave.

As the soldiers retire to their tents, Berlioz introduces the first of the scene's strategic musical retreats—or, if you prefer, the first of those musical valleys of which I just spoke: the almost lighthearted duet of the two Trojan sentries, which, though more energetic than Hylas's song, undeniably comes as a relief after the chorus of chieftains. When Aeneas appears, however, the tension is notched up again. In a bracing allegro he swears not to depart without taking proper leave of his "beloved queen." It is a tremendous piece for the tenor, and it would be more than adequate to bring a conventional operatic "scene of decision" (such as that in which Verdi's Manrico sings "Di quella pira") to a resonant and satisfying conclusion.

Berlioz, however, is not yet through with us. We are, so to speak, only halfway to the summit. Aeneas's aria is followed by another momentary relaxation: to a somber andante, his dead compatriots—Hector, Priam, Corebus, and Cassandra—appear and urge departure:

Plus de retards!
Pas un jour!
Pas une heure!
Il faut vivre et partir!
Il faut partir et vaincre!
Il faut vaincre et fonder!

No more delay!
Not a day!
Not an hour!
You must live and depart!
You must depart and conquer!
You must conquer and found!

The effect of these apparitions on Aeneas is nothing less than terrific. He seems now a man possessed. "To sea!" he shouts, and his chieftains, scurrying from their tents, echo his sentiments. This is set to music of thrilling élan, with all the earmarks of a finale: rushing dotted rhythms in the strings and huge brass fanfares that seem to promise the imminent launching of the march, and with it the fleet.

By all logic the act should end right here, with the Trojans setting sail. But once more—and for the last time—Berlioz delays the inevitable. As he had done after the entrance of the Trojan chieftains and at the end of Aeneas's aria, he relaxes the musical tension just slightly in order to introduce Dido for an angry farewell. It is a painful moment, not merely because of what transpires, but also because we experience it as an interruption in what had seemed like a musical avalanche. Aeneas is immune to Dido's blandishments—a "monster of piety," she calls him—and he takes leave on a beautiful phrase that exactly captures his agony and resolve: "Je pars et je vous aime!" ("I am leaving and I love you!"). Now—and only now—when the decision is irrevocable and properly memorialized, does the Trojan March sound out in its full glory. Aeneas soars to an exultant high B flat in a final shout of "Italie!" Everything in our better nature—our sense of decency, our partiality for sweetness and light, our romanticism, even our attenuated liberalism—sides with Dido, but Berlioz's music, and especially his great march, carries all objections before it. Scruples are useless in the face of this musical onslaught and the inexorable historical process it depicts.

The enormous musical energy of this scene also illustrates a more general procedure that Berlioz uses throughout *The Trojans* to lend his opera a unique sense of historical movement. The work contains a great many passages, beyond those in which the Trojan March appears, that convey a powerful impression of forward impetus. What all these passages have in common, at the most rudimentary level, is their speed. Perhaps this association is largely subjective, but I find it striking that an opera of such length should contain so much fast music. There is, of course, much slow music as well, especially in the fourth act. But unusually large portions of *The Trojans* have a fleetness that one more readily associates with comic opera. There is nothing comparable to it, for example, in the longer operas of Wagner or Meyerbeer—or even Verdi, who can seem almost ponderous by comparison. The cumulative effect of these many rapid passages, I believe, is to intensify that sense of historical momentum of which the Trojan March is the more explicit expression.

The very opening number of *The Trojans* offers an excellent illustration. Anyone expecting something like the sonorous cadences of the *Meistersinger* Prelude, or—to take an example Berlioz would have known—the noble cello solo of the *William Tell* Overture, is in for a surprise. Berlioz dispenses with any orchestral introduction and launches immediately into the action. From the first upward rush of the trumpets, the music surges forward at a headlong pace. Soldiers, citizens, women, and children virtually tumble onto the stage, shouting and cavorting on the plain outside their city. There are games and dances, as well as a sudden moment of terror (though no slackening of the pace) when someone identifies the spot of Achilles' tent. The entire chorus is on and off the stage in a mere four minutes ("They rush out in tumult," Berlioz indicates), leaving the viewer slightly disoriented. By this point in *Parsifal* Gurnemanz has yet to open his mouth, and the Norns in *Götterdämmerung* have uttered only a couple of lines. Time seems a boundless commodity in Wagner's mythological world, but here it is in short supply. The pace of the scene makes us vividly aware of its passing.

Many passages in the opera share this remarkable urgency. Naturally, Berlioz screws up the excitement to the most feverish pitch in the work's several finales. The Act I finale, as noted, is set to the Trojan March (as the Greek horse is brought within the city), and although certainly brisk, it depends for its musical energy less on speed than on an increase in performing forces and volume. But the second finale—the chorus of Trojan maidens—is taken at a fearsome pace. It begins "allegro con fuoco" and gets even faster. One has the impression of women veritably racing to their deaths. The finale to Act III rivals the scene of Aeneas's departure for speed and energy. It begins with the news that the Numidian Iarbas is advancing on Carthage and ends with Aeneas taking command of the combined Trojan and Carthaginian armies. Its approximately eight minutes are composed in a violent allegro, which is broken only for Aeneas's short farewell to his son. The sequence of announcements, arrivals, responses, revelations, imprecations, and departures—all of them commented on, at appropriate moments, by the chorus—is a musical whirlwind, held together by a blazing quarter-note sequence in the strings and punctuated by hair-raising outbursts from the brass.

Other examples might be cited—Cassandra's breathless arioso, "Non, je ne verrai pas la déplorable fête" ("No, I cannot watch their pitiful rejoicing"), or Dido's anxious recollection of her own voyage to Carthage, "Errante sur les mers" ("Wandering on the seas")—all of which illustrate the opera's characteristic celerity. I hardly need say that not every opera containing fast music is an opera about history. By that criterion, Verdi's *Falstaff* would be the historical opera par excellence. My claim is more modest and, I hope, more precise: given a drama with a historical theme, Berlioz exploits fast tempos and their suggestion of forward momentum to translate that theme into musical terms. Above all, the swiftness of *The Trojans* is a relative phenomenon: it must be measured against the pace of operas of comparable format and ambition—the later works of Wagner, the grand operas of Rossini, Meyerbeer, and Verdi, or the historical operas of Musorgsky. None of these contains anywhere near so much fast music as *The Trojans,* and, consequently, none has its sense of urgency.

Berlioz uses one further device in *The Trojans* to suggest the movement of history. For want of a better phrase I will call it "the historical bass." It is among the opera's most distinctive features, and it consists of a prominent musical line assigned to the cellos and contrabasses of the orchestra. In most nineteenth-century orchestral writing, the bass line is part of the musical support system: it supplies the discreet, virtually inaudible, grounding for the more insistent melodic and harmonic activities of the higher voices. If you try to recall how a particular piece of music "goes," you will in all likelihood have those upper voices in your mind's ear, and, conversely, if you were to listen only to the bass line from even a very familiar piece, you might well not recognize it. Anyone who has played one of those instruments belonging to the lower choirs will know the musical anonymity of which I speak.

The historical bass, however, involves a striking violation of this general musical rule. It is not simply an inversion, where the melody is given to the lower instruments and the accompaniment to the higher ones. Rather, the bass is released from its supporting role and takes on a life of its own; it assumes a kind of subversive musical independence. The result is to create an impression of forces at work—and on the move—beneath the explicit musical gestures of the characters. In *The Trojans* those forces, I believe, are the impersonal laws of history, which carry the characters toward a destiny that they don't fully understand.

I cannot of course prove that this musical procedure—a more or less independently moving bass line—has exactly the subliminal connotation I've here assigned it. After all, it could be no more than a compositional idiosyncrasy on Berlioz's part, without any bearing on the argument of his opera. Or it might as easily have a quite different extramusical association, such as with the unconscious or anxiety. Nevertheless, one salient fact about Berlioz's use of the device persuades me that it can legitimately be related to the historical ethos of the opera: he employs it only when he is treating characters or situations connected with Aeneas and his historical mission. One almost never hears the historical bass, for example, when Dido or the representatives of the Carthaginian court are on stage. Dido stands between Aeneas and his calling. She and the love she evokes in him threaten to subvert the historical process. And when she is in the ascendency—notably in the third and fourth acts—the historical bass is largely silent. It comes vigorously to life, however, when Berlioz deals with Aeneas alone, with his insistent forebears, or with his spiritual mentor, Cassandra.

Its association with Cassandra is particularly striking. Berlioz introduces it whenever she speaks in her prophetic mode—in other words, whenever she articulates the opera's historic theme—and he abandons it just as quickly when her thoughts turn to romance. As with Dido in the second part of the opera, love stands in opposition to history. These musical associations can be neatly illustrated in her opening aria and the subsequent duet with Corebus.

The subject of the aria, naturally, is Cassandra's sense of impending doom. From her first appearance, we are more conscious of the bass line than is normally the case in nineteenth-century music. But it has not yet worked itself free from the other string voices, all of which play in unison. When, however, she comes to the words

> *Tu ne m'écoutes pas, tu ne veux rien comprendre,*
> *Malheureux peuple, à l'horreur qui me suit!*

> You heed me not, nor wish to understand,
> Ill-fated race, the terror that haunts me!

the bass surges into prominence in a series of upward runs and dotted figures. It plants itself in the ear as an independent and ominous musical force—a power behind the scenes—as Cassandra bewails her unhappy knowledge of the future. In the middle of the aria, her meditations turn to her fiancé, Corebus, and exactly at this point the bass line dissolves into innocuous pizzicati. The listener has the impression of a great weight being lifted. But when Cassandra reverts to her original subject, the Trojans and their fate, the imperious voice of the unison cellos and contrabasses materializes once again, and their low groans haunt her thoughts to the end.

Berlioz carries the same formula over into the succeeding duet. Cassandra urges Corebus to flee from Troy, while the latter insists that she should rejoice over their imminent wedding. Corebus, in other words, expounds romance, while Cassandra continues to harp on fate. For Corebus Berlioz writes broad flowing melodies in three-quarter time, and the bass retreats into its wonted accompanying role. But when Cassandra speaks, the bass rumbles into the musical foreground, spectacularly so as she envisions the destruction of the city and Corebus's murder. Corebus reiterates his complacent assurances, and again the bass withdraws, although Cassandra's every interjection is underlined by its nervous figurations. The association is so consistent and precise that the independent bass becomes a musical symbol of Cassandra's anxious historical consciousness, of which the romantic Corebus is innocent. Appropriately, the same sort of bass line figures prominently in the final scene of Part One, as Cassandra leads the Trojan women to their collective suicide.

Throughout the course of the opera one finds examples of this musical association: an energetic bass line that surges up unexpectedly when the issue at hand is the Trojans' mission. One hears it, for example, as the Shade of Hector invests Aeneas with his charge, or at the entrance of Mercury after the love duet, or, finally, beneath the excited orchestral rustlings as Aeneas calls his men from their tents for the departure in Act V. It combines with the Trojan March and the generally precipitous pace of the opera to lend the work its distinctive sense of historical momentum.

THE HISTORICAL HERO

"The History of the World," wrote Thomas Carlyle in 1840, "is the Biography of Great Men." *The Trojans,* one might say, is the history of the world at a particularly critical moment in its unfolding, and Aeneas is its Carlylean protagonist. He is the work's most extraordinary creation and arguably the most exciting tenor in opera. In Aeneas, Berlioz fashions a character large enough to fill the dimensions of his historical epic. Dido's greatness, though indisputable, is a reflective greatness. She is an accomplished and liberal monarch in her own right—this Berlioz establishes in the opening scene of Act III—but she is raised to an epic plane by the love that she inspires in Aeneas. We are made to feel about her as we do about Wagner's Isolde: she is a grand and tragic figure, but some element of her glory is borrowed from the Promethean figure to whom her destiny is linked. Appropriately, her final scene shares the retrospective mood of Isolde's "Liebestod."

What distinguishes Aeneas from other operatic heroes is his

consciousness of a great historical mission. The issue is often addressed in the opera, not only by Aeneas himself but by the other characters as well. Berlioz permits us to watch the idea grow, planting it firmly but unobtrusively in the Trojan acts, insinuating it into the early scenes of *Les Troyens à Carthage,* and then allowing it to overwhelm every other consideration in Act V. He is astonishingly resourceful in finding different means—even comic ones—of pressing the idea upon us. By the end of the opera, Aeneas and his mission have become identified in our minds.

Aeneas receives his historical charge at the beginning of Act II, after the Greek horse has been admitted and Troy is in flames. The ghost of Hector appears to him in his tent:

> *Va, cherche l'Italie,*
> *Où pour ton peuple renaissant,*
> *Après avoir longtemps erré sur l'onde*
> *Tu dois fonder un empire puissant,*
> *Dans l'avenir, dominateur du monde,*
> *Où la mort des héros t'attend.*

> Go, seek Italy,
> Where for your people reborn,
> After long wanderings over the sea,
> You are to found a mighty empire,
> Destined in the future to rule the world,
> And where a hero's death awaits you.

Aeneas seems mainly dazed by this imperative, and his immediate reaction is not to set sail but to order his troops to a last defense of the city. His sense of mission must be allowed to mature over the course of the opera. Cassandra, one might say, accepts the charge in his stead. Addressing the Trojan women—and in a most un-Cassandra-like burst of optimism—she foresees Aeneas's historical achievement. Her last words, echoed by the other women, are "Sauve nos fils, Enée! Italie! Italie!" ("Save our sons, Aeneas! Italy! Italy!")

In the second part of *The Trojans* the allusions to Italy grow more urgent. By now Aeneas's own consciousness has become saturated with the idea. Naturally, if he were unambiguously faithful to it, there would be no story and no opera. But we never doubt—from both the musical and the textual evidence—that Berlioz takes the mission with complete seriousness. Nowhere does he suggest that he disapproves of what might appear Aeneas's unadorned egotism—his desire for a heroic death "to crown my glory on the Ausonian fields." In this respect Berlioz's attitude is exactly the same as Hegel's: the hero's ambition is ultimately impersonal, because it stands in the service of something beyond itself.

The process through which the hero and his historical mission become identified begins even before Aeneas makes his appearance. When Dido is told of his arrival in Carthage, the first thing she learns about him is his calling:

> *Obéissant au souverain des dieux*
> *Ce héros cherche l'Italie,*
> *Où le sort lui promet un trépas glorieux*
> *Et le bonheur de rendre aux siens une patrie.*

> Obedient to the king of the gods
> The hero seeks Italy,
> Where fate holds out for him a glorious end,
> And the happiness of giving his own a homeland.

These are the words of Aeneas's chieftain Panthus. "Happiness," however, is not what Aeneas seeks. Like the protagonist of Hegel's *Lectures on the Philosophy of History,* he chooses greatness over happiness. Preparing to leave his son, Ascanius, in Dido's care, he effectively corrects Panthus by drawing this distinction himself:

> *D'autres t'enseigneront, enfant, l'art d'être heureux;*
> *Je ne t'apprendrai, moi, que la vertu guerrière*
> *Et le respect des dieux;*
> *Mais révère en ton coeur et garde en ta mémoire*
> *Et d'Enée et d'Hector les exemples de gloire.*

> Others, my child, will teach you how to be happy;
> I myself will teach you only the courage of a fighting
>   man,
> And respect for the gods.
> But honor in your heart and keep fast in your memory
> The example of the glory of Aeneas and Hector.

That "glory" rings out on a sustained high B flat, banishing any doubts one might have entertained about Berlioz's enthusiasm for his hero.

In the fourth act, as Aeneas drifts precariously into romance, we are reminded three times of his unfulfilled mission, first by the disheveled nymphs in the "Royal Hunt and Storm" pantomime, then by Dido's minister, Narbal, and finally by the god Mercury, who terminates the love duet with his calls of "Italie!" History may be in retreat in this act, but its shadow still hangs over the erotic paradise that Dido and Aeneas seek to construct for themselves. In the last act, of course, history returns with a vengeance, and we are made witness to an excruciating renaissance of Aeneas's sense of mission. Suddenly the matter is on everyone's lips. As Panthus and the chieftains begin their anxious preparations, they hear a chorus of Trojan ghosts chanting "Italie! Italie! Italie!" Thereafter the two Trojan sentries try to make a joke of the issue: "Par Bacchus," they grouse, "ils sont fous avec leur Italie!" ("By Bacchus, they're mad, with their Italy!") When Aeneas arrives, he has become the fully conscious vessel of his calling, and he agonizes over Dido's failure to understand what for him is now a simple inevitability. He thinks to see her one last time, but the Trojan ghosts are unrelenting: "Il faut vaincre et fonder!" ("You must conquer and found!") This, their last, apparition serves to close whatever gap may have remained between Aeneas the private man and Aeneas the vehicle of history: "Ma tâche, jusqu'au bout, grands dieux, sera remplie" ("My task, great gods, will be accomplished to the end"). In this mood he then turns to salute farewell to Dido's palace, almost as if he were addressing a former self:

> *A toi mon âme! Adieu! digne de ton pardon,*
> *Je pars, noble Didon!*
> *L'impatient destin m'appelle;*
> *Pour la mort des héros, je te suis infidèle.*

> To you, my soul, farewell! Deserving of your forgiveness,
> I go, noble Dido!
> An impatient destiny summons me;
> For a hero's death I must forsake you.

At the opera's close, with Aeneas gone, Dido finally recognizes the truth of his calling. She envisions the destruction of Carthage and the rise of the Capitol, and her last words are "Rome . . . Rome . . . immortelle!"

Berlioz's Aeneas, of course, is above all a musical creation, for which the libretto supplies only the raw material. More than is usually the case with operatic characters, one needs to hear this role performed in order to appreciate its singular nature. Berlioz's music succeeds in conjuring up a figure of stupendous assertiveness. It is the sort of music to make one believe in heroes—figures grand enough to alter the course of human history.

One can identify at least some elements in the musical formula Berlioz uses to bring his Aeneas to operatic life. The qualities he seems most set on conveying are energy and exaltation. Aeneas is presented as if he were a force of nature, a figure of seemingly inexhaustible vitality. At the same time he is infused with a towering sense of purpose. To convey this dual impression, Berlioz relies especially on two musical devices: speed and altitude. That is, he writes music that is either exceptionally fast or exceptionally high, and often he combines both, to sensational effect. He does other things as well, but speed and altitude are the distinctive ingredients in Aeneas's musical profile.

In any opera, a crucial moment in establishing a character is his entrance. Music can lend moments of arrival an intensity unapproachable in drama, thereby fixing the character in our aural memory. In part this is managed through orchestral preparation and commentary, but above all it is a function of the unique powers of the singing voice. When words are sung instead of spoken, they can be intensified in at least three ways: they may be sustained over an unusually long period of time (whether on one note or several); they may be pitched well up into the vocalist's register (thus drawing attention to themselves by their unnatural height); or they may be emitted with the exceptional volume of which only operatic voices are capable. A good example of such intensification, in which all three of these means are employed, is the entrance music that Verdi composed for his Otello, whose very first word, "Esultate!" ("Rejoice!"), establishes the character's stature in our minds. The tenor rises majestically to a sustained E sharp, sung *forte,* on the third syllable of the word, and the effect is indelible. Thereafter we never doubt the man's greatness.

In *The Trojans* Aeneas makes not one but three entrances, and all are devised to convey his exceptional energy. The common feature of these entrances is their abruptness: almost without warning, Aeneas is suddenly on stage, as if powered by supernatural forces. He has something of the quality of an apparition—appropriately so, in view of his frequent association with apparitions over the course of the opera. The music of each of these entrances is highly charged, with an underlying nervousness that aptly suggests the character's intensity.

Aeneas's first entrance comes after the pantomime for Andromache, which, as one would expect, ends in the most hushed tones.

There is a commotion in the brass, and he bursts upon the scene and launches into a furious recital of the disaster that has befallen Laocoön. Rarely are dramatic tenors asked to sing music of this speed, least of all in their first moment on stage. Complementing the passage's brutal tempo is its punishing tessitura: the first two notes alone are on G sharp and A above the staff—very near the upper limit of the dramatic tenor's range—and virtually all of the recitative lies in the upper half of the voice, culminating in a stupendous high B natural. Simply from the musical contours of the passage, we know that Aeneas is an elemental force.

He makes a second entrance in Act III, when he presents himself to Dido. The impression of bursting upon the scene is here realized even more perfectly, because he has already come on the stage disguised as a sailor and has only to step forward and announce himself. This revelation occurs after the news of the Numidian attack has sent the court into an uproar. Aeneas's words have the godlike effect of bringing order out of chaos. "Reine," he interrupts, "je suis Enée!" ("Queen, I am Aeneas!") The egotism of the announcement would seem monomaniacal if Berlioz's music weren't so exalted. The first word, "Reine," is sustained for two measures on E natural near the top of the staff. It silences everyone on stage, and the entire orchestra as well. The other three words (also unaccompanied) proceed down through a perfect E major triad with the inexorability of a law of nature, carrying the voice in a majestic swoop to E natural an octave below. It is one of those moments that press themselves into the memory even on first hearing—like Otello's "Esultate!"—and it perfectly represents Aeneas's heroic self-consciousness. Having thus broken on the scene with characteristic éclat, he plunges into a stretch of tenorizing that, in terms of tempo, pitch, and volume, surpasses even the frenetic manner of his entrance in Act I. Measured against this dynamo, all other operatic heroes are apt to seem slightly limp.

The same precipitousness marks his entrance in the last act, where he breaks in on the complaining sentries. Again, there is a suggestion of the whirling dervish, as the duet of the two basses is simply broken off by the hero's unannounced arrival. The interruption is musical as well as dramatic: without even a gesture toward bringing the duet to a proper close, the tempo is suddenly increased and the orchestration thickened. Presently Aeneas is before us, singing breathlessly of his "useless regrets." This frenzied recitative introduces his longest scene in the opera, and its concluding "allegro agitato" creates an effect of overwhelming exhilaration.

Sheer energy, then, is the primary quality that Berlioz confers on Aeneas. But it is energy to a purpose, and Berlioz also seeks to convey something of Aeneas's intentions. Music is not equipped to tell us the precise nature of a character's intentions, but one can argue that Berlioz nevertheless has found means to suggest Aeneas's exalted sense of mission. The music, not just the text, informs us that his is a high calling.

Berlioz achieves this effect through the manipulation of pitch. Pitch is the vertical component in music, and it carries obvious metaphorical associations of spiritual elevation or debasement. There is, in other words, an affinity between high purposes and high notes, just as there is between low purposes and low notes. This association is not mechanical or automatic. After all, noble Sarastro sings some of the lowest notes in opera, while the Queen of the Night sings some of the highest. Mozart, however, was working against form in *The Magic Flute,* and the natural association of high notes with light and low notes with darkness remains strongly felt by both composer and listener. It is analogous to the affinity one senses between physical and spiritual elevation in the architecture of the Gothic cathedral.

Berlioz exploits this association in several ways. He does so, perhaps most subtly, by setting the general level of Aeneas's music somewhat higher than usual. The role's tessitura—that is, the average level at which it is pitched—is a tone or more above that of the other roles assumed by tenor voices of comparable format. This elevation is made to seem more extreme by placing Aeneas opposite female roles of unusually low tessitura: the part of Dido is written for mezzo-soprano (most operatic heroines, of course, are sopranos), and that of Cassandra, while written for "dramatic soprano," also lies relatively low and is frequently sung by a mezzo. Thus just as Aeneas's vocal line tends to run a note or so higher than, say, Otello's or Tristan's, Dido's and Cassandra's run a note lower than Desdemona's or Isolde's. The result is a kind of perspectival heightening of Aeneas's music. Finally and most strikingly, Berlioz asks his tenor to sing exposed individual phrases that soar well above the territory to which the heroic tenor is generally assigned. These passages work a crucial influence on our sonic picture of Aeneas. They startle us because they take the voice into a region where our ears (if they have any sensitivity to voices) expect the singer to fail. They are, one might say, impossible phrases that, by the normal laws of physiology, should terminate in self-strangulation. When, however, a tenor succeeds in reaching them, the effect is almost superhuman. Their impossible height, one feels, reflects the impossible height of Aeneas's ideals.*

I have already made passing reference to one of these moments of vocal elevation—namely, the final phrase of Aeneas's opening monologue, in which he describes the serpents that have devoured Laocoön. On the word "devoured" the voice rises to a high B natural, which is followed by a sustained high A. The listener is still in a state of disorientation from the violence of Aeneas's entrance and the hectic pace of his recital. Then, as it were, out of nowhere come these two notes that seem impossibly high. The voice we have been listening to, and whose measure we have begun to take, simply shouldn't be able to sing them. Yet there they are, right in front of our ears, as unexpected as Aeneas himself. One doesn't know whether to be more shocked at Berlioz for writing them or at the tenor for producing them. In the succeeding ensemble, the Trojans express their astonishment at the news about Laocoön, but they could as well be expressing astonishment at the piece of singing that they have just heard.

Later in the opera, toward the end of the love duet (and again with characteristic unexpectedness), Aeneas is sent up after a high C flat, which he must sustain for a full measure. The note is painfully exposed, and it alone, I suspect, has driven many a tenor to retire the role from his repertory. Moreover, there is no reasonable musical excuse for it. Yet if it can be sung, it is unforgettable. Then in the closing measures of Aeneas's aria in Act V, Berlioz makes the ultimate demand of his tenor: Aeneas must reach and sustain a high C, leaping to it from the uncomfortable distance of a sixth below. Nothing in the preceding musical line prepares us for this note. It is gratuitous, arbitrary, willful. But in its unreal extension, it is a perfect musical reflection of Aeneas's vaulting idealism.

Speed and elevation, then, combine to make Aeneas—as I suggested—the most exciting tenor in opera and an appropriate

---

* Berlioz may not have been aware of the contradictory demands he was making on his lead tenor. The role's altitude was not in itself unprecedented, as one finds high C's in the tenor role of Arnold in Rossini's *William Tell* (1829), an opera Berlioz knew and admired. Moreover, during Berlioz's lifetime the French tenor Gilbert-Louis Duprez had revolutionized the opera world by singing Arnold's high C's from the chest, and there can be no doubt that Berlioz also intended Aeneas to be sung in this same manner. Arnold, however, didn't have to compete with the massive orchestral and choral forces one finds in *The Trojans*. It is thus difficult to escape the conclusion that Berlioz had unwittingly sabotaged his own opera by planting a near-unsingable role at its center: the role combines the altitude of earlier (and lighter) tenor roles with the demand for volume and weight associated with lower voices.

musical vehicle for Berlioz's conception. His music creates a figure large enough to shoulder the burdens of a nineteenth-century historical hero.

LOVE AND TIMELESSNESS

The Trojans is a dialectical opera. It is organized as an argument between two great nineteenth-century themes: love and history. History, I've suggested, is its dominant idea, absorbing the larger part of its attention and, of course, triumphing in the end. But history's great antagonist, love, is also presented on the grand scale. It is the subject of the opera's fourth act, where it achieves a spaciousness and intensity worthy of its historical adversary. Moreover, the historical theme itself gains in stature by being shown in mortal, and ultimately victorious, combat with so formidable an opponent.

The conflict is anticipated throughout the earlier parts of the opera. It is, for example, the theme of Cassandra's opening aria, in which she appears divided between historical forebodings on the one hand and romantic fantasies on the other. That division is then externalized in her duet with Corebus, where she takes the side of history and he that of love. These two numbers occupy all but the opening moments of Act I and thus firmly establish the opera's major polarity.

The first two scenes of Act III perform a similar function, but on a yet grander musical scale. Scene 1 introduces the public Dido, queen of a large commercial empire. Built around the Carthaginian national anthem ("Gloire à Didon"), the scene celebrates Dido's political genius, which has brought Carthage to greatness in a mere seven years. She responds to this praise with a recital of the nation's accomplishments and a call for further sacrifices. The libretto reads like a speech for the secretary of commerce:

> *Déjà des bords lointains où s'éveille l'aurore*
> *Vous rapportez, laboureurs de la mer,*
> *Le blé, le vin et la laine et le fer,*
> *Et les produits des arts qui nous manquent encore.*
>
> *Chers Tyriens, tant de nobles travaux*
> *Ont enivré mon coeur d'un orgeuil légitime!*

Mais ne vous lassez pas, suivez la voix sublime
Du Dieu qui vous apelle à des efforts nouveaux!

Already from far-off lands where the sun rises
You, toilers on the sea, bring back
Corn, wine, wool, iron,
And the products of skills still unknown to us.

Dear Tyrians, your noble and unstinting toil
Has filled my heart with justifiable pride.
But do not relax your efforts, follow the sovereign voice
Of the god who calls you to fresh endeavors!

One would be hard put to imagine a less operatic discourse, unless it be that between Wotan and the giants Fasolt and Fafner about the terms of their contract to build Valhalla. Berlioz risks it—indeed, he composes a splendid entrance aria for Dido to this unlikely text—in order to establish the first term of his dichotomy: Dido the public figure, the queen whose passions have been sublimated into a great political enterprise. No sooner has her court excused itself, however, than he plants its romantic antithesis. In a colloquy with her sister, Anna, the queen confesses to "a strange sadness, without cause." Both text and music (with its melancholy violin obbligato) inform us that her political sublimation is less than fully successful, as Anna is quick to understand ("Vous aimerez, ma soeur"—"You will love, my sister"). Again we have that dichotomy between politics and romance that was the subject of the Cassandra-Corebus duet in Act I.

Thus the alpha and omega of the opera have been well rehearsed by the time Berlioz comes to his fourth act, which is an extended musical treatise on the subject of romantic love. In a letter to his sister, Berlioz characterized it as "the act of tenderness, of love, of fêtes and hunts, and the starlit African night." A single idea, reflected in the music, dominates this act: the notion that love is beyond time. Love, as Berlioz presents it, is the quintessentially antihistorical force, seeking to bring the forward progression of events to a halt. Love desires changelessness, and by abolishing time it seeks to abolish change. It was Berlioz's genius to recognize that music is uniquely empowered to evoke a sense of temporal suspension. The sequence of musical events in the act gives us a feeling of things grinding to a halt, of the temporal regime being somehow magically frozen in a romantic eternity. We couldn't be further removed from the history-drenched music of Aeneas's calling, associated above all with the

Trojan March and its powerful suggestion of forward momentum.

The act might be said to move from the passionate to the sublime. This order is well calculated to distance us gradually from our normal sense of time. It begins with the "Royal Hunt and Storm," which Ernest Newman calls "the finest and most sustained piece of nature painting in all music." Even more important than nature painting, however, is the musical evocation of sexual bliss. This great orchestral essay is the Gallic counterpart of Wagner's *Tristan* Prelude, a musical representation of physical ecstasy. At its magnificent height, Dido and Aeneas are seen entering a cave. Appropriate to a celebration of sexual rapture, the music grows thunderous and agitated, with the full Berlioz orchestra in high abandon. Yet these very qualities of volume and speed make the pantomime seem more akin in its musical manner to the events that have preceded it, and Berlioz surely judged correctly when he placed it at the beginning of this act, in which slow tempos and hushed sonorities will be the rule. The music of Act IV moves toward entropy, and the sexual frenzy of the "Royal Hunt and Storm" properly stands at the outset, not the end, of its journey into tranquillity.

The much longer second scene of Act IV takes place in Dido's palatial gardens, and, befitting an act whose theme is timelessness, very little transpires. As Dido and Aeneas enter with their court, we know immediately that everything is changed, for the Carthaginian national anthem has undergone a romantic transformation: the grand tune, formerly sung by the entire populace to full orchestral accompaniment, is now reduced to a wistful echo in the harp and woodwinds, with muted violin obbligato. The music tells us that the political starch has been taken out of Dido; no longer the self-possessed monarch of a prosperous state, she is simply a woman in love. With the dramatis personae assembled and elegantly arranged—rather, one imagines, as in Pierre-Narcisse Guérin's early-nineteenth-century painting "Enée racontant à Didon les malheurs de Troie"*—Berlioz now begins his great argument. What follows can be divided into three parts: the entertainments, the public observation and celebration of the lovers, and finally the duet. Each stage marks a further slowing of the clock, a further movement toward stasis.

The entertainments consist of three ballets and a song. The ballets, coming at the start, contain the scene's liveliest music, but if

---

* Mentioned apropos of *The Trojans* in one of Berlioz's letters, dated March 12, 1857.

one compares them with the ballets in the previous act, their relative
languor is apparent. Where the dances of Act III were economic,
those of Act IV are sexual. In the former we observed the entry of
builders, sailors, and farmworkers, and the music was plain and
purposive, rather like the entrance music that Wagner writes for his
cobblers, tailors, and bakers in the final scene of *Die Meistersinger*.
Here, however, we have Oriental dancers, slaves, and Nubian girls.
The music is alternately sultry and exotic. For the last of his pleasure
dances Berlioz even fabricates a "Numidian" dialect:

> Ha! Ha!
> Amaloué
> Midonaé
> Faï caraïmé
> Deï beraïmbé
> Ha! Ha!

The sturdy commercial order of Act III has given way to an indulgent
eroticism, which has boundless time for such diversions. The Dido
who watches these leisurely displays (the three dances last ten minutes)
is hardly the industrious creature who built the Carthaginian empire,
nor is her paramour the Aeneas whom an urgent destiny has called
to found Western civilization. In the grips of their romantic lethargy,
they have been robbed of all responsible sense of time.

With the last of the entertainments, Iopas's "poème des champs,"
Berlioz introduces the specifically musical principle through which
he seeks to effect a sense of temporal suspension. That principle is,
quite simply, repetition. In *Beyond the Pleasure Principle* Freud argues
that the desire to repeat is at bottom a desire for complete inactivity,
for death. Repetition, one might say, is the form of action closest to
entropy: as the same gesture recurs over and over, we eventually lose
all sense of change, and thus of the passage of time. Berlioz draws on
this subliminal association to bring the forward progress of events to
a standstill. An elaborate series of musical repetitions alienates us
from the normal temporal framework.

In Iopas's song, these repetitions are of a fairly obvious variety:
the melody of the song is presented three different times, and although
each verse is more elaborate than the preceding one, the tune is
always recognizably the same. It is a gentle flowing song, spun out at
a leisurely pace. As the identical phrases, indeed the identical words,
return, the audience—both on stage and in the theater—is gradually

tranquilized. The effect is rather like a lullaby. At its end comes a brief snatch from the love duet, where the principle of repetition is integrated even into the melodic structure: the tune's first three notes are set on the same pitch, with unvarying harmony and rhythm. To create a sense of timelessness, Berlioz moves in the direction of music in which all change—whether of pitch, harmony, or rhythm—is minimized, leaving only a kind of pulsating sameness.

The two numbers that follow belong to what I have termed the public observation of the lovers: Dido and Aeneas are on display for the members of the court, who comment on their mutual affection. These large concerted pieces—a quintet and a septet—give the courtiers a sense of vicarious participation in the romance and draw them musically into the temporal suspension that it effects. The quintet contains the only significant piece of action in the scene: Dido asks Aeneas to relate what became of Andromache after the fall of Troy, and she is embarrassed to learn that the unhappy widow ended by marrying her Greek captor, Pyrrhus. The parallel with her own situation is not exactly perfect, but Dido draws it anyway: "Quoi! la veuve d'Hector! Ô pudeur!" ("What! Hector's widow? For shame!") At just this moment Ascanius playfully removes her wedding ring, which in her distraction she leaves on the couch. Her separation from the past is now symbolically complete, and Berlioz here launches his quintet. Anna, Narbal, and Iopas join the lovers in marking Dido's break with her historical identity: "Tout conspire," she sings, "à vaincre mes remords et mon coeur est absous" ("Everything conspires to overcome my remorse, and my heart is absolved"). Her confession is set to a haunting phrase whose most distinctive feature is a repeated descending scale of four notes, followed by other intervals in which one hears yet further repetitions of the descending motif. As the different singers join in, the phrases overlap one another in a reiterated declension. The repetitions are subtle but strongly felt, advancing the hypnotic process begun with Iopas's song. When virtually the whole of the quintet (starting with Dido's "Tout conspire") is then sung for a second time, we are well on our way toward temporal indifference. The principle of sameness is taking hold.

The septet is one of the most extraordinary numbers in the score. It is essentially an atmospheric piece, setting the mood for the love duet that follows. It does so by dramatically intensifying our sense of movement held in suspension. The participants in the quintet are now joined by Ascanius and Panthus, supported discreetly by the chorus. This ensemble occupies itself with only three lines of text:

> *Tout n'est que paix et charme autour de nous!*
> *La nuit étend son voile et la mer endormie*
> *Murmure en sommeillant les accords les plus doux.*

> Peace and enchantment are all around us!
> Night spreads its veil, and the sleeping sea
> Murmurs in its slumbers the softest harmonies.

With so many voices involved, it is perhaps not surprising that the effect Berlioz achieves resembles that of a choir: there is a sustained cushion of homogeneous vocal tone, with overlapping entrances and exits. One's impression is of an uninterrupted block of sound. Its solidity is highlighted by the occasional vocal figurations for Dido—decorative lines whose movement makes one all the more conscious of the virtual immobility of the massed voices beneath. Most striking of all, a solo flute (supported an octave below by clarinet and horn) pulses away unrelentingly above the chorale, playing repeated triplets, nearly all of them on a single note. In forty-six of the septet's fifty-eight measures, the flute plays exactly the same tone: high C. In the remaining twelve measures Berlioz permits what might be described as the smallest conceivable deviation from the reiterated C's: the triplets alternate between C and the D flat lying half a tone above it. In total, high C is sounded 314 times during the four minutes that the septet requires to run its course. This is, one might say, the purest form of repetition: a single tone, which comes to seem like a throbbing vessel in one's head. The reiteration of this high C combines with the sustained vocal harmonies to create a sense of utter stillness. "The enchantment of night by the sea," writes Newman, "truly lies on this exquisite movement," and "enchantment" is precisely the right word. The only other operatic number that approximates its mood of serenity is the trio "Soave sia il vento" from *Così fan tutte,* where again "massed" voices (Don Alfonso and the two sisters) sing against an evenly pulsing orchestral accompaniment. But Berlioz is even more daring than Mozart, and his septet magically evokes the sense of being caught in a timeless romantic trance.

The hypnotizing repetitions of the quintet and septet lull us into absolute calm, almost as if our metabolism had been retarded. We are now at polar opposites from the tense, volatile mood induced by the opera's other acts, all of which move toward ever greater activity. Having so skillfully prepared the way, Berlioz now caps the progression toward stasis with the love duet, "Nuit d'ivresse" ("Night of rapture"). The duet carries us to the musical limits of timelessness, and it does so essentially by the same means Berlioz has used to slow the clock in the previous numbers. Repetition here works at three levels, first at the textual level, then in terms of the duet's larger musical structure, and, finally, at the level of musical detail—the micro level, so to speak.

Berlioz's verses are derived from the dialogue between Jessica and Lorenzo in the last act of *The Merchant of Venice*. Dido and Aeneas sing its refrain in parallel thirds and sixths:

> *Nuit d'ivresse et d'extase infinie!*
> *Blonde Phoebé, grands astres de sa cour,*
> *Versez sur nous votre lueur bénie;*
> *Fleurs des cieux, souriez à l'immortel amour!*

> Night of rapture and boundless ecstasy!
> Golden Phoebe, and you, great stars of her court,
> Pour upon us your enchanted light;
> Flowers of heaven, smile on our immortal love.

These words, with their significant allusions to infinitude, immortality, and the heavenly fixtures, are sung three times by the lovers. Between the refrains come a series of exactly parallel constructions in which, by turns, the lovers compare their night of love to other nights of equal ecstasy and rapture: the night Aeneas's mother, Venus, made love to his father, Anchises; the night Troilus awaited Cressida under the walls of Troy; the night Endymion ravished Diana; and, almost playfully, the first night of their own romance, when, according to Dido, Aeneas was not as ardent as he might have been. Each of these comparisons is introduced by the same phrase: "Par une telle nuit" ("On such a night"), which occurs four times. There are, moreover, repetitions within repetitions: at the word "souriez," for example, the joined voices part momentarily, and the word is allowed to sound twice. As the refrain returns, yet further separations and echoes are introduced, thus heightening the sense of repetition. Finally, the principal phrase, "Nuit d'ivresse et d'extase infinie," is sung by the lovers as a kind of pre-echo before each sounding of the refrain. Altogether the parallels and repetitions are the most elaborate of any number in the opera.

These textual patterns are reflected in the music, which is set to an unvarying accompaniment of rocking strings and pulsating wood-winds. The melody of the refrain, naturally, is heard three times, always with more complex filigree. Likewise, all of the comparisons introduced by "Par une telle nuit," while more varied than the refrain, are audibly parallel structures, especially in the identical musical shape of the introductory phrase itself. No listener, even on first hearing, can fail to detect this emphatic musical patterning. While the duet is far more varied than a simple strophic song (of which it might be considered a distant cousin), the primary impression it leaves is of reiteration. Unlike the love duet in *Tristan*, which moves from stillness to orgastic fullness, or that in *Otello*, which has an almost conversational quality, the piece returns over and over to the same elements, musical as well as textual.

The principle of sameness—of repetition—is also at work on the level of musical detail. The opening phrase of the duet—which sets the pattern for all that follows—is a striking example of this. The first three notes—to which Dido and Aeneas sing the words "Nuit d'ivresse"—are set on exactly the same pitches, giving the momentary impression that Berlioz has abandoned the idea of writing a melody in favor of a single repeated major triad (or sixth). Interestingly, the love duet in *Otello* also begins on a repeated single tone. But where Verdi immediately introduces rhythmic variety—each of the first three soundings of the note has a different rhythmic value—Berlioz's notes are absolutely even. In all respects, they are musically indistinguishable. The next two lines of the refrain—"Blonde Phoebé" and "Versez sur nous"—begin with only the smallest variation on this musical structure, and over the course of the full duet one hears the tiny phrase—three identical intervals—again and again. It performs a function very similar to the repeated flute semiquavers in the septet: by minimizing the element of change in the musical fabric, it effectively undermines our sense of the passage of time.

When Mercury finally interrupts the lovers and shatters the trance, we have been sung into a kind of romantic oblivion by half an hour of slow and predominantly quiet music, from Iopas's song to the end of the duet. Above all, we have been subjected to a systematic campaign of musical repetitions that would blunt the historical consciousness of even the most responsible among us. The argument for love—for a life of private satisfactions—has been mounted with incomparable musical dexterity: the song, the quintet, the septet, and the duet are all masterpieces, any one of which might serve as the musical highlight of a less ambitious work. That Berlioz should have lavished such remarkable effort on what is, in effect, the counterproposition of his opera—its antithesis, as opposed to its thesis—is a measure of the work's richness. And precisely by arguing the romantic antithesis with such fierce musical conviction, he renders the opera's historical theme all the more potent.

THE VICTIMS OF HISTORY

The notion that history has its victims is a common assumption of nineteenth-century thought, signaling a new tough-mindedness in the West's evolving historical consciousness. Against the Enlightenment's doctrine of progress, Hegel and his contemporaries insisted that human advancement—whether material or spiritual—brings with it a considerable burden of suffering. "The History of the World is not the theatre of happiness," wrote Hegel. "Periods of happiness are blank pages in it." Strictly construed, the Hegelian victim is not simply one who suffers, but one who is used as well. Whether great or humble, the victim is a person whose private ambitions are exploited for larger purposes by the "cunning of reason." He seeks to realize his own goals, but in doing so he plays into the hands of forces beyond his understanding.

This idea probably won't allow of operatic translation, because it depends on an invisible fit between a character's motives and certain transcending realities—a social force, a theological imperative—that music is ill-prepared to represent. Ironically, the closest thing to a true Hegelian victim in *The Trojans* is Aeneas, particularly if one stresses the disjunction between his own wish for a hero's death and the ulterior motives of his Trojan demons, who, of course, have the well-being of the nation in mind and are not above using Aeneas's *amour-propre* to advance their cause. But the disjunction is hardly pronounced, since for the most part Aeneas is shown to be of one mind with his spirits. He is not tricked into the Italian venture (as is Purcell's Aeneas), but shares consciously in the historical aspirations of his dead countrymen.

Taken in a more latitudinarian sense, however, victimization is clearly one of the opera's important themes. The idea is perhaps closer to Freud than Hegel, but it reflects the ambivalent historical sensibility that virtually all modern artists and intellectuals have inherited from the early nineteenth century. The notion of victimization holds that culture is achieved only at a price. It may be an internal psychic price, as Freud and Nietzsche argued, or a social one, as Marx argued. In either case, human advancement is a complex phenomenon, in which the accomplishments of some are paid for with the sufferings of others. This bitter truth is strongly felt in *The Trojans*. Like Freud (and Hegel as well), Berlioz is ultimately willing to pay the price. That, indeed, is the very point of his opera. But he refuses to gloss over the discontents that civilization brings in its wake, and the dialectical texture of his score is accordingly enriched.

Dido is the opera's greatest victim. Her victimization is of such heroic proportions that Berlioz devotes his last two scenes to a representation of it. But, as with all the opera's important concerns, the idea is introduced early on and shown in a variety of embodiments before our attention is directed to its fullest realization. In effect, Berlioz proceeds here as he had with the antagonism between love and politics—an idea introduced in the confrontation between Cassandra and Corebus in Act I, elaborated in Dido's and Anna's duet in Act III, and finally represented on a monumental scale in the antithesis between the love music of Act IV and the gathering momentum of Aeneas's departure in Act V. Dido's sacrifice at the opera's close is no less well prepared.

The theme is first foreshadowed in the treatment of Hector's widow, Andromache. She is, in a sense, the most primitive of victims in that she is completely uncomprehending. Her husband has been killed in a great historical battle, and she has been stunned into silence. Berlioz writes a splendid pantomime for her, in which she presents her child to Priam and Hecuba. She is the center of attention for nearly seven minutes—the time required for two normal-sized operatic arias—yet she utters not a single word. Because her incomprehension has left her speechless, Berlioz entrusts her agony to a solo clarinet, whose soft, plaintive timbre (in contrast to the more incisive tones of the other high woodwinds) seems exactly suited to her bewildered condition. The long, arching melody of the clarinet, supported by muted strings, gives voice to a sorrow that is no less intense for being inarticulate. In a strict sense, Andromache is dramatically gratuitous—as, indeed, are all of the opera's victims, except Dido. But by giving her such extensive musical attention, Berlioz fixes the notion of victimization in our minds.

A victim of a different sort is the Phrygian sailor Hylas, who makes his appearance at the beginning of Act V. Hylas, obviously, belongs to the opposite end of the social spectrum from Andromache. For a moment, Berlioz abandons the world of high politics to view the tragedy from the prospect of a man in the ranks. Although Hylas is no less uncomprehending than Andromache, he at least can express his sense of loss: his grief takes the form of a song. The song, which he sings while rocking at the masthead of a Trojan ship, is remarkable mainly because of the distance it reveals between a private and a public consciousness. Like that of most people in his situation, Hylas's view of the world is very limited. For all we know, he may be entirely ignorant of Dido and Aeneas's love and the impending departure, as he makes reference to neither. From his standpoint, the tragedy reduces itself to his having been uprooted from his native Phrygia. He sings of the homeland that is now inconceivably far away: the echoing valleys, the cool branches with their scented shade, the humble cottage where he lived with his mother. The song occurs at the opera's most critical juncture—between the love duet and the departure—and Hylas's very ignorance of those great events is itself a measure of his victimization. The song's ironic placement heightens our sense of the victim's irrelevance.

Appropriate to his station, Hylas's lament is almost mechanically strophic: he inhabits a rudimentary musical universe, comparable to that of Schubert's young miller and utterly remote from the musically sophisticated world of Dido and Aeneas. When, in Act III, Dido's court poet Iopas sings his "poème des champs" (which invites comparison with Hylas's song in that both are slow, strophic tunes composed for a light tenor), the listener detects subtle variations in the vocal figuration and orchestration of the three stanzas. The song is an altogether elegant affair, an aristocratic entertainment. No such subtlety infects Hylas's song, however. He sings like the peasant he is. Each of his three verses is musically identical, and each culminates in an identical apostrophe to the "potent sea." Moreover, the sea for Hylas is not what it is for Aeneas—namely, the highway to his destiny in Italy. Rather, it is a gulf that yawns between the sailor and his lost past. We are made to feel its terror in an unexpected orchestral outburst, a kind of musical shudder, at the end of the second refrain. It is the only violation of the song's strophic order. As the homesick melody completes its final verse, the young sailor falls asleep halfway through his last line. We never see him again, but we know that he stands before an arduous journey that will bring him no closer to home and that he may not even survive. Throughout this elegiac lament, the clarinet—the instrument that had spoken for Andromache—is the most prominent fixture of the orchestral accompaniment.

Hylas is a gentle and innocent youth, who had been destined for a simple life of farming but discovers himself stranded on the coast of an unknown country awaiting yet further senseless adventures on the "potent sea." Both the words and the music of his song convey a strong, if narrow, spirituality. He is a bit like King Lear's fool: guileless, childlike, and melancholy. Not all of history's victims, however, are such attractive figures. Berlioz acknowledges this unsentimental truth in the duet he composes for the two Trojan sentries. The sentries also are victims, but they are made of cruder stuff than Hylas. Overhearing his song, they comment, with unsympathetic obviousness:

> *Il rêve à son pays*
> *Qu'il ne reverra pas.*
>
> He's dreaming of his homeland
> Which he won't see again.

Unlike Hylas, they have adjusted only too well to their new environment. Thus they complain not of a distant and long-lost happiness, but of immediate practical inconveniences. The absurd Italian venture, they note, will deprive them of "la belle vie": good wine, tasty venison, and sex. The sentries are the Papagenos of the opera, and to them also Berlioz extends his musical sympathy. The duet he writes for them is appropriately rough—one might even call it undistinguished—but its predominantly minor tonality betrays an underlying anxiety. The sentries may be hard livers, but they, too, have their worries. Miraculously, one feels no aesthetic inconsistency between their blunt remarks—and slightly bumptious music—and the exalted pronouncements of Aeneas or the tragic ones of Dido. Again, the clarinet—which might almost be thought of as the instrument of the victim—figures as the most prominent element in the duet's accompaniment.

Andromache, Hylas, the sentries—all, in a sense, pave the way for Dido. We have seen her as queen and as lover. Now, in the opera's last two scenes, she appears as the supreme victim. Naturally, her victimization is represented on a much grander scale than that of her predecessors. At the same time, she is also shown to be more conscious of her situation than any of the others: where Andromache, Hylas, and the sentries don't quite grasp why their lives take the course they have, Dido is entirely disabused about the forces at work in her tragedy. It would be inconceivable for her to retreat into the mute incomprehension of Andromache or the unspecific alienation of Hylas. On the contrary, she becomes superbly articulate. Above all, however, Dido's victimization is distinctive because of the emblematic quality Berlioz lends it. He presents it not simply as a romantic tragedy—although it is certainly that—but as the tragedy of a whole culture. Dido becomes the representative of all those peoples who lose out in the civilizing process, peoples whose decline and even destruction were, in the view of Europe's nineteenth-century cultural elite, the unavoidable concomitants of mankind's dialectical advance. Hers is the fate of a prosperous but insufficiently bellicose African nation—a nation of "laboureurs de la mer" ("toilers on the sea"), as she says in her opening aria—destined to be crushed by the military empire that Aeneas founds in Europe. Carthage, one might say, is the original third-world country.

In the opera's final scenes, Berlioz carries us skillfully from a private to a public understanding of Dido's tragedy. We observe her romantic misery, but also the miserable destiny of the race she represents. First comes her monologue, "Je vais mourir" ("I am going to die"), the most famous vocal number in the opera. As its opening phrase suggests, it is a piece of intense introspection, which considers the events of the opera from a strictly romantic perspective. The Dido of the monologue is a woman so profoundly in love that, when she is betrayed, her life ceases to be meaningful. Her soul, she sings, is borne down "into everlasting night" ("en l'éternelle nuit"). Berlioz conveys the sense of her decline into death by composing the monologue in a series of primarily downward melodic arcs. The first phrase, "Je vais mourir," descends through the notes of a minor triad, and it is immediately echoed by another descending phrase in the lowermost register of the bass clarinet.* The descent into "everlasting night" carries the voice majestically down a twelve-note scale from F at the top of the staff to E natural more than an octave below. In total, the monologue contains twenty-three distinct musical phrases, all but seven of which move from higher to lower pitches. The sinking effect of this musical construction resembles the descending vocal line of Schubert's song "Die Krähe" in *Winterreise*.

Following the monologue is an aria, whose primary function is to remind us that Dido is not merely an unfortunate lover but also the architect of a flourishing if ill-fated civilization. In a manner similar to Shakespeare's Othello in his final speeches, Dido here conjures up something of her former greatness. For a moment Aeneas is forgotten, and she quietly recalls the dangers she has passed and the triumphs she has won. The aria contains her most beautiful music

---

* Dido's fatal triad is in E flat minor, and it has the same melodic trajectory and rhythmic structure as the splendid E major triad through which Aeneas first presented himself to Dido in Act III ("je suis Enée").

in the opera, a sequence of gentle phrases whose transparent major tonality and easeful pulse contrast sharply with the passionate utterances of the monologue. The effect is wonderfully still and dignified:

> *Adieu, fière cité, qu'un généreux effort*
> *Si promptement éleva florissante;*
> *Ma tendre soeur qui me suivis errante,*
> *Adieu, mon peuple, adieu; adieu, rivage vénéré,*
> *Toi qui jadis m'accueillis suppliante.*

> Farewell, proud city, raised
> By selfless toil so swiftly to prosperity;
> My gentle sister, who shared my wanderings,
> Farewell, my people, farewell; and you, blessed shore,
> Which welcomed me when I begged for refuge.

The passage evokes a moving identification of person and place, such as one associates with Hans Sachs and his "beloved Nuremberg" in *Die Meistersinger*. Berlioz here maintains a delicate balance between psychological and historical perspectives, effecting a synthesis of the two as Dido's thoughts of Carthage and of Aeneas unite in an apostrophe to the African sky:

> *Adieu, beau ciel d'Afrique, astres que j'admirai*
> *Aux nuits d'ivresse et d'extase infinie.*

> Farewell, fair skies of Africa, stars I gazed on in wonder
> On those nights of rapture and boundless ecstasy.

The music of the first line follows the established contours of the aria, since we have as yet no reason to think Dido's farewell to the African sky will differ from her farewell to the city, her sister, or the Mediterranean seashore. After all, she has doubtless "admired" this sky many times in the seven years she has ruled in Carthage. But the next line calls to mind the particular occasion when she gazed on that sky with Aeneas, and the textual reference to the love duet invites, and receives, a musical allusion to the duet's melody. Romantic musical flashbacks of this sort are common in opera—the most famous perhaps coming in the mad scene from *Lucia di Lammermoor*—but the convention was never more effectively used or more seamlessly integrated into the musical fabric: the queen and the lover here seem to coalesce. Dido then brings her reflections to a close on an exquisitely suspended E flat—the fifth of the aria's A flat major tonality—sustained *pianissimo* for two bars as the orchestra dies away into silence. "Ma carrière est finie" ("My career is ended"), she sings, and again we are in mind of Othello—like Dido, a heroic leader undone by romance—who, in one of his great speeches, also bids farewell to his "occupation." The aria reaches back over the intervening acts to our first vision of Dido, "Queen by the love of her happy subjects," evoking through its beauty and quiet resignation a profound historical sympathy for the doomed civilization she represents. Throughout, the orchestral accompaniment has been dominated by two clarinets—one playing in the upper register, the other in the lower—establishing an aural link with the music of Andromache, Hylas, and even the humble sentries.

Although the queen's reflections have moved in an increasingly public direction, the monologue and the aria nevertheless are sung in private. In the final scene of the opera, Berlioz makes certain that we have not misunderstood the broader historical significance of the tragedy. The private realm is left behind, and Dido's grief becomes fully public. Once again the scene is her gardens by the sea, where she has had an enormous pyre constructed; on the platform of the pyre are a bed, a toga, a helmet, a sword, and a bust of Aeneas. There, before her priests, her court, and ultimately all the citizens of Carthage, Dido makes her last speeches and, having thrown Aeneas's toga on the pyre, stabs herself with his sword. As the icon of a civilization destined to fall by the historical wayside, she dwells in her final moments not on her own fate but on that of her people.

Here Berlioz shows the victim of history in two characteristic attitudes. The victim's first response is to dream of retaliation. Thus Dido envisions a great historic reckoning with the Trojans, when one of her descendants will right the wrongs that she and her people have suffered. She even prophesies the name of the imagined vindicator: Hannibal! Only Berlioz's complete faith in the historical ethos of the opera prevents this anticipation of the Punic Wars from seeming ludicrous: Hannibal is separated from Dido by roughly a millennium. (In the *Aeneid* Dido invokes a great "Avenger," but she is not so rash as to propose his name.) Her vision of the triumphant Hannibal is magnificently intoned on a series of rising phrases that take the singer to a sustained G flat above the staff, and the authority of the music forces us to tolerate Berlioz's extravagant historical reach.

But of course, there is no real justice for history's victims. The nineteenth century prided itself on its sober acceptance of this unsavory truth. That, indeed, is the essential point of a dialectical conception of history, which sets out to criticize the notion, inherited from the Enlightenment, that evil is merely a historical accident, an

epiphenomenon. Thus Dido, too, must be made to recognize the
hopelessness of the victim's cause. The notion of historical justice is
a fantasy, and revenge, therefore, must give way to resignation. Before
she dies Dido has a vision of the Capitol, in front of which pass
Roman legions and an emperor surrounded by poets and artists—
civilization in its lowest and highest manifestations. Hannibal, she
now understands, is doomed to fail:

> *Ah! Des destins ennemis ... implacable fureur ...*
> *Carthage périra!*

> Ah! The fates are against us ... their hate unrelenting ...
> Carthage will perish!

Her words introduce the last sounding of the Trojan March, which
blazes out in the orchestra as the Carthaginian people, not blessed
with Dido's historical consciousness, continue to dream of revenge:

> *Haine éternelle à la race d'Enée!*
> *Qu'une guerre acharnée*
> *Précipite à jamais nos fils contre ses fils!*
> *Que par nos vaisseaux assaillis*
> *Leurs vaisseaux dans la mer profonde*
> *Périssent abîmés! que sur la terre et l'onde*
> *Nos derniers descendants, contre eux toujours armés,*
> *De leur massacre, un jour, épouvantent le monde!*

> Undying hatred for the race of Aeneas!
> May our sons be hurled against theirs
> In relentless war for all time!
> May our ships attack theirs
> And send them shattered to the bottom
> Of the sea! By land and water
> May our last descendants, armed against them to the end,
> One day astonish the world with their total destruction.*

Berlioz captures the ambiguity of the historical process by setting
these wild imprecations—the "first Punic war cry," he calls them—
against the triumphant orchestral sounding of the march. The victorious
advance of civilization and the hopeless illusions of its victims ring
simultaneously in our ears. As the opera closes, one is apt to think of
Carthage in our own day: no longer a city but a mere location. While

---

* In the *Aeneid* this "imprecation" is attributed not to the Carthaginian people but
to Dido herself. Virgil's Dido lacks the sense of historical resignation of Berlioz's Dido.

Rome survives as the recognizable center of a once great ancient empire, Carthage has disappeared from the face of the globe no less completely than Troy itself.

POSTSCRIPT: PURCELL'S *DIDO AND AENEAS* (1689)

The story of Dido and Aeneas has been set to music many times. *The Concise Oxford Dictionary of Opera* mentions some ninety versions, nearly half of them based on Metastasio's libretto *Didone abbandonata.* Only two of these works, however, have survived the test of time: Berlioz's *The Trojans* and Henry Purcell's *Dido and Aeneas.* Although it is the best known and most frequently recorded of all seventeenth-century operas, *Dido and Aeneas* is a miniature, a chamber work written to be performed at a girls' school. It lasts well under an hour, making it a fifth as long as Berlioz's full score, and less than a third as long as that part of *The Trojans* treating the Dido and Aeneas legend. Because of this difference in scale, as well as the obvious differences in musical style between the seventeenth and the nineteenth centuries, the two operas, not surprisingly, bear only faint resemblance to one another. But what sets them apart most radically, I believe, is neither the matter of size nor that of musical vocabulary, but the intellectual discrepancy between Berlioz's and Purcell's conceptions of the story that they both took from Virgil.

Purcell's opera is entirely innocent of the historical theme that Berlioz makes the very centerpiece of his drama. There is nothing in either text or music to suggest the pathos of Aeneas's civilizing mission. Indeed, the only way that Purcell can make sense of Aeneas's departure from Carthage is to treat it as a ruse. Aeneas becomes the butt of a joke, planned and executed by a coven of Restoration witches. In place of Berlioz's Cassandra and the other Trojan shades who repeatedly urge Aeneas on to his destiny in *The Trojans,* Purcell writes a brilliant comic scene for a sorceress and her "wayward sisters," who hope to destroy Dido's happiness by tricking Aeneas into leaving. They have no motive for their plot other than malice:

> The Queen of Carthage, whom we hate,
> As we do all in prosperous state,
> Ere sunset shall most wretched prove,
> Deprived of fame, of life and love!

These jangling couplets, sung by a quavering voice in a mock-villainous minor, are superbly funny, all the more so when the tonality shifts pompously to the major and the witches break out into a chorus of "Ho ho ho, ho ho ho!" "Tell us," sing two of them, "how shall this be done?" and their leader reveals her plan:

> The Trojan prince, you know, is bound
> By fate to seek Italian ground;
> The queen and he are now in chace.
> [FIRST WITCH:] Hark! Hark! the cry comes on apace.

> But, when they've done, my trusty elf
> In form of Mercury himself,
> As sent from Jove, shall chide his stay
> And charge him sail tonight with all his fleet away.

There follows a second chorus of cackling laughter, and the witches then finish off their fun by promising to ruin even the hunt. The event that Berlioz transforms into a symphonic poem of sexual ecstasy is in Purcell reduced to a prank:

> But ere we this perform,
> We'll conjure for a storm
> To mar their hunting sport
> And drive them back to court.

This is sung in gleeful contrapuntal coloratura, the vocal equivalent of rubbing one's hands with anticipatory pleasure. In almost every respect, Purcell's and Berlioz's responses to the idea of Aeneas's calling could hardly be more different, and that difference, I believe, is attributable at least in part to the emergence in Berlioz's century of a historical sensibility that simply did not exist in Purcell's.

The same difference governs their respective treatments of Aeneas. For Purcell there is really not very much to be done with this character, who may well be the weakest protagonist in any important opera. Indeed, the role of Dido's "lady-in-waiting" Belinda (an utterly un-Virgilian creation) is vocally more substantial than that of Aeneas, who doesn't even merit a proper aria. Instead he must settle for a few lines of recitative—this in contrast to the extraordinary music that Berlioz lavishes on *his* Aeneas, who is, of course, the dramatic fulcrum of *The Trojans.* In the confrontation with Dido, Purcell's Aeneas does something altogether unthinkable in Berlioz (or in Virgil, for that matter): he changes his mind and decides to remain in Carthage after all:

> In spite of Jove's command I'll stay.
> Offend the gods, and love obey!

This is too much for Dido, and she responds as one would expect her to:

> No, faithless man, thy course pursue;
> I'm now resolved as well as you.
> No repentance shall reclaim
> The injured Dido's slighted flame,
> For 'tis enough, whate'er you now decree,
> That you had once a thought of leaving me.

Her scathing rejection is intoned with all the fire and dignity that Berlioz would later invest in Aeneas himself.

One might be wondering where the greatness of *Dido and Aeneas* lies. The answer is that it lies above all in Purcell's musical portrayal of Dido. Purcell's Dido, unlike Berlioz's, is strictly a romantic figure, and the interest of his opera rests almost entirely in her tragedy. This Purcell responds to magnificently. The music he writes for Dido, as well as for the choral reflections on her plight, is deeply moving. It conjures up a superbly passionate figure, who loves and dies in the grand manner. Especially wonderful is the great lament with which the opera concludes:

> When I am laid in earth,
> May my wrongs create
> No trouble in thy breast;
> Remember me, but ah! forget my fate.

Purcell frames this aria with two beautiful choruses, "Great minds against themselves conspire" and "With drooping wings ye cupids come," which mark it off, both in the score and in memory, as the most significant moment in the opera. Much more than with the closing scenes of Berlioz's opera, one is conscious of the structural weight the composer has lent to this final utterance of his heroine. The lament stands at the heart of his inspiration and, save for the final chorus, is both the longest and the most elaborately composed number in the opera. Over and over, Dido repeats, "Remember me," rising eventually to a sustained high G, while the ground bass on which the aria is built moves steadily downward to earth. And, indeed, remember her we do, long after we have forgotten Purcell's feckless Aeneas. She is the opera's raison d'être, and in the best Baroque fashion Purcell memorializes her tragic passion.

Purcell's opera is called *Dido and Aeneas,* but it is recognizably an Anglicized *Didone abbandonata.* The contrast between it and Berlioz's work is among the most striking examples of two artists finding utterly different material in the same literary source. Many factors, doubtless, influenced the choices they made, but surely one of the most important was the radically dissimilar intellectual worlds inhabited by the two men. Berlioz wrote not *Didone abbandonata* but *The Trojans* in order to weave the story of Dido into a richer intellectual fabric, whose design bears the unmistakable imprint of Europe's historical culture in his own century.

Realpolitik

Giuseppe Verdi's *Don Carlo*

Of all the great opera composers, Verdi is the most political. Issues of power and authority figure more centrally in his operas than they do in those of any of his artistic peers. Moreover, the political ethos of the Verdi operas is not merely a question of subject matter: Verdi also developed a musical vocabulary admirably suited to the expression of political ideas. He not only chose political themes, he also wrote what can fairly be called political music.

Verdi's political concerns follow the course of Italian and European political opinion during his lifetime. His career began in the 1840s, during which thirteen of his twenty-six operas had their premieres. The 1840s were a time of rising political consciousness, as the conservative hegemony of the post-Napoleonic era gave way to a revival of liberalism and nationalism. Verdi was one of many young artists and intellectuals whose work reflected this liberal renaissance (Karl Marx was another). As a frequent victim of political censorship himself, he was readily drawn to the ideals of individual freedom and self-determination, and he was no less ardently committed to delivering Italy from her Hapsburg oppressors. In the mid-1840s he became the intimate of a group of Milanese republicans and literati, and in 1847 he met Giuseppe Mazzini, with whose political ideals he closely identified. There is also reason to believe that, had the republican cause prevailed, Verdi might have taken political office. In 1848, when revolution erupted in Milan, he wrote his friend and librettist Piave: "The hour has sounded—be convinced of it—of [Italy's] liberation. It is the people that wills it, and when the people wills there is no absolute power that can resist.... Italy will yet become the first nation of the world." Appropriately, the operas Verdi wrote during the decade of the 1840s are the most ideological of his career. Several of them are explicitly patriotic operas, but even at their most thoughtful and refined (as in *Luisa Miller*) they are deeply imbued with the liberal spirit of the age.

The failure of the revolution of 1848, and with it the hopes for a united Italy, led to a sudden withdrawal of Verdi's interests from politics. From 1851 to 1853, he composed a series of three operas whose concerns are largely domestic or romantic: *Rigoletto*, *Il trovatore*, and *La traviata*. In *La traviata* politics are banished entirely, while in *Rigoletto* and *Il trovatore* they are relegated very much to the periphery. At the emotional center of these operas is the family, and their most powerful scenes examine, in a manner that sometimes anticipates Freud, the tensions between parents and children. During the immediate postrevolutionary years, then, politics appear to have been driven from Verdi's artistic consciousness.

Over the course of the next two decades, as the cause of Italian nationalism gradually revived (albeit in a new guise), Verdi wrote six operas in which politics again come to the fore: *I vespri siciliani* (1855), *Simon Boccanegra* (1857), *Un ballo in maschera* (1859), *La forza del destino* (1862), *Don Carlo* (1867), and *Aida* (1871). The ideals of liberty and nationhood still remain significant themes in these works, but they are overshadowed by a new sobriety, a darker, less sanguine vision of the political process than one finds in the early operas. In effect, these works mirror the new realism of the era; they both explore and celebrate the spirit of *Realpolitik* that played so critical a role in the history of Europe, and especially of Italy, during the 1850s and 1860s.

The repoliticization of Verdi's art in the operas of his middle period reflects Italy's movement toward unification under the clear-eyed and sometimes heavy-handed leadership of Count Camillo di Cavour, a man whom Verdi greatly admired and whose disabused vision of politics he ultimately adopted as his own. As prime minister to King Victor Emmanuel of the House of Savoy, Cavour was architect of a series of brilliant diplomatic and military demarches (including an unprincipled alliance with Napoleon III) that, in 1859, drove the Austrians from Piedmont and Lombardy. Verdi was so impressed by this achievement that he accepted Cavour's invitation to run for the first national parliament, to which he was in fact elected. Cavour died in 1861, just months after the founding of the Kingdom of Italy, and although the work of unification was not to be completed for another decade, it proceeded under the aegis of Cavour's Piedmont and in the tough-minded style of political maneuvering that he had initiated. Precisely during these years the cry "Viva Verdi!" came to mean "Viva Vittorio Emanuele Re D'Italia!"

Ironically—or perhaps appropriately—the final achievement of Italian unification in 1870 marks the end of Verdi's political concerns as a composer. After *Aida* his art betrays the sort of disillusionment with politics felt by many intellectuals in the closing decades of the nineteenth century. In Italy, especially, national unification failed to bring about the expected cultural and moral renaissance. Instead Italian public life in the years after 1870 was characterized by pettiness, materialism, and corruption. One is therefore not surprised that when he resumed composing in the 1880s and 1890s, after a decade of semiretirement, Verdi abandoned politics for more universal and perennial concerns. In his last two operas, *Otello* (1887) and *Falstaff* (1893), he turned from Schiller (the source for his greatest political operas) to Shakespeare. These final works seem as oblivious of political issues as were the operas he composed in the years immediately after the revolution of 1848, but they focus now not on the family but on marriage and its tribulations. Significantly, his *Falstaff* has no place in it for Prince Hal.

That Verdi's operas are *more* political than those of the other great opera composers is readily established by even the briefest comparison with Mozart, Wagner, and Strauss. In Verdi, operas without a political theme are the exception—one might even argue the rare exception—whereas with Mozart, Wagner, and Strauss they are the rule. While the operas of the latter composers sometimes invite political interpretations (one thinks immediately of G. B. Shaw's *The Perfect Wagnerite*), in Verdi's case no such interpretive ingenuity is necessary. His operas are political in their manifest, not just their latent, content. When the curtain goes up on a Verdi opera, we can expect to find ourselves on a political landscape and often in the midst of a struggle for power. We are made intensely conscious of the state and its reasons. Most often the action transpires on a piece of real political geography, in a real period of history, and with dramatis personae who either enjoy or aspire to political authority. Counts, dukes, kings, emperors, high priests, grand inquisitors, doges, governors, and generals—these are the figures who populate the Verdian universe. *La traviata* and *Falstaff* are the only important Verdi operas without even a nominal representative from the spheres of power. Not a single one of these generalizations could be made about the operas of Mozart, Wagner, or Strauss.

Verdi's affinity for politics also explains why so many of his operas are set in what historians call the early-modern period of European history—that is, the period from the fourteenth to the eighteenth century. This was the great age of European state-building, when the important political entities of Western Europe were fashioned out of the feudal remnants of the Middle Ages. The period gave rise not only to the first modern states but also to the great body of classical European political theory with its emphasis on *raison d'état*, notably in the writings of Machiavelli, Hobbes, and Locke. These centuries represent the most intensely political era in Europe's long history, their achievement epitomized in the absolute monarchy of Louis XIV.

No fewer than fifteen of Verdi's operas are set in this era of European state-building, and among them are some of the most famous: *Ernani* (Spain in 1519), *Luisa Miller* (the Tyrol in the early seventeenth century), *Rigoletto* (sixteenth-century Mantua), *Il trovatore* (Spain in 1409), *Simon Boccanegra* (fourteenth-century Genoa), *Un ballo in maschera* (seventeenth-century Boston or eighteenth-century Stockholm, depending on the version), *La forza del destino* (eighteenth-century Spain and Italy), *Don Carlo* (France and Spain about 1568), *Otello* (fifteenth-century Cyprus), and *Falstaff* (fifteenth-century England). Indeed, the only popular Verdi operas *not* set in the early-modern period are *La traviata* (Paris around 1850) and *Aida* (Egypt in "the age of the Pharaohs"). This proclivity for the epoch of European state-building helps explain why so many of the operas create a subliminal awareness of politics even when their immediate concerns are entirely unpolitical. *Rigoletto*, for example, is essentially a story of familial affection and its abuse, but because it is set in a sixteenth-century Italian court (originally, like Victor Hugo's play, it was set in the France of Francis I), an unmistakably political atmosphere hangs about the piece. Likewise, *Un ballo in maschera* is a drama of romance and infidelity, but politics are very much in the air and even provide some of the characters with their principal motivation. The state is always on the fringes of our consciousness. Just the opposite is the case in Wagner's *Tristan und Isolde* (which, like *Ballo*, dates from 1859), where politics are simply overwhelmed by passion and introspection. Who would think of describing *Tristan* as an opera about a king and his treacherous vassal? In *Un ballo in maschera,* however, Renato's betrayal of Riccardo, although romantically motivated, achieves its tragic dimensions only when it becomes a matter of politics.

Unlike Verdi, Mozart and Wagner rarely set their operas in the state-building era of European history. Of the five most famous Mozart operas, four have contemporary or near-contemporary settings, while one, *The Magic Flute,* takes place in "Ancient Egypt."* Wagner, for his part, prefers the timeless world of myth. Only two of his important operas, *The Flying Dutchman* and *Die Meistersinger,* take place in the early-modern period. For the rest Wagner sets his stories either outside time altogether or in the very early Middle Ages— indeed, so early in the Middle Ages that they often seem indistinguishable from the imaginary world of the *Ring.* The general feeling one gets from Wagner is that it all happened long ago, just as with Mozart the general feeling one gets is that it is happening right now (i.e., in Mozart's own lifetime). Of the three major opera composers, Verdi alone makes us conscious of a drama that is not merely historical but part of a single temporal continuum with the present. Where Mozart's operas, like the Enlightenment, have very little sense of the past, and while the past of Wagner's operas seems timelessly remote, Verdi's past bears upon the present, both because it is more recent and because it is a past in which the political institutions of our own world originated. In a certain sense, the Verdi operas offer a musical portrayal of the rise of the modern state.

Realism was not merely a political phenomenon. It was also the dominant artistic impulse of the nineteenth century. Historians of literature and art have long recognized this fact, to the point that it has become a kind of textbook cliché. Anyone even modestly familiar with the history of the novel, the drama, or painting knows that during the latter half of the century artists grew increasingly preoccupied with an accurate portrayal of reality, especially of social reality. No exact counterpart to this movement exists in music, for the simple reason that music's representational capacities are so severely limited. The symphonies of Brahms can hardly be considered more realistic

---

* *Die Entführung aus dem Serail* and *Così fan tutte* are set in the eighteenth century; *The Marriage of Figaro* is always played as if it, too, transpired in the eighteenth century, although for tactical reasons Beaumarchais put the action back a hundred years; *Don Giovanni* is set, indifferently, in the middle of the seventeenth century.

than those of Beethoven, even though comparable assertions about the relative verisimilitude of Walter Scott and Thomas Hardy, Victor Hugo and Henrik Ibsen, or Théodore Géricault and Gustave Courbet make eminently good sense.

In a bastard genre like opera, of course, music can lean on its literary collaborator and thereby lend a certain plausibility to the notion of "musical realism." That is, operatic librettos seem to be chasing the same demon as nineteenth-century novels, drama, and painting. Particularly in the last two decades of the century they come to focus on characters and situations from "real life," rejecting the elevated romanticism and implausible melodrama that dominate opera from Beethoven to Wagner. So-called verismo opera—the operas of Mascagni, Leoncavallo, and, in a more attenuated form, Puccini—is thus often regarded as the musical counterpart of naturalism in drama and the novel. The parallel, however, is more apparent than real, for when one examines the music of these operas, it turns out to be no more apposite to portraying reality than was the music of earlier operas. In fact, the appeal of verismo opera has very little to do with realism as it was understood by the novelists and dramatists of the era. These works have earned their place in the repertory above all because they are so shamelessly tuneful. Admittedly, their emotions are raw (or at least they seem to be) and their manner highly charged, but ultimately we go to *Cavallerìa rusticana* or *I pagliacci* not to learn the sordid truth about life in an impoverished Italian village (in the sense that we read Zola's *Germinal* to learn the sorbid truth about life in an impoverished French mining town), but to hear beautiful melodies and spectacular singing. In only one significant respect can the music (as opposed to the librettos) of nineteenth-century operas be said to grow more realistic, and that is in the progressive elimination of the distinction between numbers and recitative, with its implicit suggestion that human time comes in two incommensurable varieties. Even this change, of course, is not purely musical, but it does presuppose an evolution in musical technique, in particular the development of structural control over ever longer compositional stretches. The essential musical units in Mozart's operas characteristically last three or four minutes, whereas in Wagner they can encompass almost entire acts. Still, realism does not appear to be a very useful category for making sense of the operatic history of the later nineteenth century.

If, however, we narrow our sights to the notion of *political* realism, or what the Germans call *Realpolitik,* we can, I believe, identify an important affinity between opera and the intellectual history in this period, an affinity that manifests itself most clearly in the operas of Verdi's middle years, and above all in *Don Carlo*. *Realpolitik* meant politics guided by considerations of power rather than ideology. Historians have always associated its emergence in the 1850s with the triumph of Realism over Romanticism in the arts and of natural science over philosophy (especially idealist philosophy) in intellectual life. Its representative statesmen were Bismarck, Cavour, and Napoleon III, and its theoreticians included Auguste Comte, Walter Bagehot, and above all the German historian Heinrich von Treitschke. In a considerably more refined form, it also provided the inspiration for Jacob Burckhardt's *Civilization of the Renaissance in Italy* (1860), which traces the emergence of modern individualism to the ruthless pursuit of political aggrandizement by the princes of fourteenth- and fifteenth-century Italy. For these modernizing despots, Burckhardt wrote, the state was "a work of art," "the outcome of reflection and calculation." Burckhardt's subjects were Lodovico Sforza and Cosimo de' Medici, but his book spoke very much to the sympathies of the age, and his words could as well have been applied to Bismarck and Cavour.

Characteristically, the proponents of *Realpolitik* were disabused liberals. They were men who had embraced the ideological politics of the 1840s, only to find themselves disappointed by the events of 1848. Although their ideas varied in a number of respects, we can identify certain common features of their political creed. All the *Realpolitiker* consciously distanced themselves from the world of political idealism—which was usually the world of their own youth—a world in which political action was guided by relatively abstract and always high-minded principles. "The State is not an Academy of Arts," intoned Treitschke in his lectures on politics at the University of Berlin—lectures that he repeated every year from 1874 until his death in 1896. "If it neglects its strength in order to promote the idealistic aspirations of man, it repudiates its own nature and perishes." Against political ideologues and absolutists, whom they regarded more with condescension than with scorn, the *Realpolitiker* insisted on pragmatism in the conduct of public life. Like Burckhardt's Renaissance tyrants, they advocated "the purely objective treatment of international affairs, as free from prejudice as from moral scruples." Such pragmatism manifested itself in two ways: first, in a willingness to compromise, sometimes even collaborate, with figures, groups, or regimes that one found antipathetic, and, second, in a candid recognition of the need for force in political life. "The appeal to arms," as Treitschke put it, "will be valid until the end of history."

The adepts of *Realpolitik*, be it noted, were often persons of strong private convictions (as was the case, for example, with Otto von Bismarck), but unlike ideological politicians, they made a sharp distinction between the psychic world of conviction and the real world of action. Indeed, the true hero of political realism was the leader who sacrificed his private beliefs and peace of mind for the sake of the common weal. Political greatness lay not in making a public issue of one's deepest commitments, as the political ideologue did, but in the systematic repression of those commitments and the sacrifice of private life to *raison d'état*. *Realpolitik*, in short, brought with it a new appreciation of the leader, especially the absolute monarch, whose task was psychologically ruinous, lonely, and ultimately thankless. His situation was exactly comparable to the ego in Sigmund Freud's famous structural model of the self: he was a slave to the Reality Principle, able to indulge neither his conscience nor his instincts. It is just such a political leader that Verdi conjures up, with extraordinary musical sympathy, in the figure of King Philip II of Spain in *Don Carlo*.

POLITICAL MUSIC

Rhetoric

We do not generally think of music as expressing political ideas. Operas, to be sure, may be political, in the sense that plays are, but their music is only accidentally so. I would like to suggest, however, that certain features of Verdi's music in fact give his operas a distinctly political flavor. These features are not so explicit that one can identify them with precise ideological positions, but they contribute to the overall political atmosphere of his operas. One might say that they establish a musical universe in which political discourse makes some sort of artistic sense. Indeed, they account, I believe, for our feeling that the politics of the Verdi operas are not extrinsic to their artistic logic.

These procedures set Verdi apart from his bel canto predecessors—Rossini, Bellini, and Donizetti—who, although they frequently address political issues, do so in the gentle, ingratiating, and often extraordinarily beautiful manner in which they address all other issues. Political discussions in bel canto opera usually strike us as slightly ludicrous, because of the discrepancy between form and content. This is true even in Rossini's *William Tell,* which, like Verdi's *Don Carlo,* is also based on a drama by Schiller and is an undeniable masterpiece. As Julian Budden has observed, Rossini's attitude toward his opera's political theme is curiously disinterested; he treats the rising of Swiss patriots under Tell with an aesthetic evenhandedness altogether foreign to Verdi.

The main quality of Verdi's music that makes it so suitable for politics, I believe, is what might be called its rhetoricalness. As everyone knows, rhetorical language differs from ordinary language primarily in being intended for public consumption. Unlike the language with which we address a relative or a friend, it aims at broad effects, sacrificing subtlety and nuance for sharp contrasts and unambiguous formulations. It indulges in repetitions, structural parallels, and alliterations that would be unacceptable in private discourse. It is, of course, the characteristic manner of the political platform, where, if skillfully managed, it arouses the passions of the audience.

In his operas, Verdi transforms many of these rhetorical habits into musical terms. His is an entirely unembarrassed musical manner, contemptuous of the good opinion of experts and aiming consciously at the box office. Isaiah Berlin (drawing on a distinction of Schiller's) has called him a "naïve" composer, meaning one whose artistic responses are always direct, never filtered through philosophical or aesthetic abstractions. It is common to hear his music described as vigorous, energetic, powerful, and masculine. He is the musical opposite of Claude Debussy, who must surely be the least political of all great composers.

Perhaps the most obvious component of Verdi's rhetorical style— to put the matter bluntly—is sheer loudness. He is, with Beethoven, among the noisiest of all major composers. This is a difficult assertion to substantiate empirically, since it is not only impressionistic but, in a sense, dubiously quantifiable. Still, I believe that anyone generally familiar with the great composers from Bach to Stravinsky will, on reflection, agree with me. Other composers have written louder music—Mahler for one, and Wagner and Bruckner as well. But these composers earn their loud moments with long stretches of uninterruptedly quiet music that would be unthinkable in Verdi. Like a political orator, Verdi can't remain still for long. Drop the needle at random on a recording of a Verdi opera, and you will usually be rewarded with a substantial racket. This is, of course, especially true of the early operas, which are among the most splendidly noisy in the repertory and in which, appropriately, politics figure more consistently and more explicitly than in the operas written after *Rigoletto*. But even the mature Verdi is among the least reticent of composers, and measure for measure operas like *Il trovatore, La forza del destino, Don Carlo, Aida,* and even *Otello* (whose last act contains perhaps the most sustained quiet music in all of Verdi) are simply louder than the operas of Mozart, Wagner, or even Strauss—to say nothing of those by such recessive composers as Debussy and Britten.

Quintessentially Verdian, for example, is the recitative that precedes Radames's famous aria "Celeste Aida." The tenor's reflections are punctuated by brilliant fanfares in the trumpets and trombones, an effect no bel canto composer could have imagined. Likewise, *La forza del destino* opens unapologetically with three assertive octaves in the brass. These musical gestures have the boldness, even brazenness, of political oratory. They are among the many instances of Verdi's readiness to turn to the brass choir—that ultimate resource of orchestral volume—to achieve a desired rhetorical weight. Verdi's brass do not aim for the sustained, chorale-like effects that one hears so often in Wagner and Bruckner. Rather, they are used to italicize, to add emphasis, to make a point. In the early and middle operas this sometimes takes the form of a single trumpet underscoring the vocal line (as in the "Sì, vendetta" duet from *Rigoletto*). Later his methods become more subtle, but the brass habit is not given up—as witness the ominous solo trumpet that precedes the drawing of names in *Un ballo in maschera,* as well as the opening scene of *Otello,* where trumpets snarl and shriek in opera's most terrifying storm music.

One particular use of the brass in Verdi is quite explicitly political, that being his fondness for the "banda" (as it is called in Italian): a small contingent of mainly brass instruments playing offstage (and occasionally onstage as well). Many commentators have regretted this compositional idiosyncrasy as an unfortunate residue of Verdi's youthful career as a bandmaster in his hometown of Busseto. Like it or not, however, Verdi's banda music seems to me not at all incompatible with his larger musical and dramatic intentions. It merely represents a more explicit distillation of the political impulse that lies just beneath the surface of so many of his operas. Band music, one might say, is unambiguously political, being associated with parades, rallies, and speeches. And when the stage brass of the banda strike up a march in one of Verdi's operas, we can be almost certain that the allusion is political.

A relatively straightforward deployment of the banda to designate a political moment is the evocative march Verdi writes for the entrance of King Duncan in *Macbeth*. The stage band makes a similar point when it is heard accompanying the royal cortege in the *auto-da-fé* scene of *Don Carlo*, or preceding the triumphal march in *Aida*. The same procedure is made to serve ironical purposes when we hear offstage fanfares as Otello falls beneath Iago's heel after the departure of the Venetian ambassadors. Likewise, the brilliant sequence of tunes played by the banda in the opening of *Rigoletto* establishes the tense and acrimonious political atmosphere of the Duke's court in Mantua. No other composer, not even among Verdi's bel canto predecessors, uses this device so frequently or so effectively.

There is also a marked rhetorical effect, I believe, in Verdi's preference for closed musical forms—that is, for musical structures in which repetition and audible patterning figure prominently. Such patterning, of course, was a staple of bel canto opera, and perhaps it gains its rhetorical flavor in Verdi primarily because he stuck to it even as his contemporaries, notably Wagner, were forsaking it. That is, in precisely those years when Wagner was seeking to tailor his music ever more closely to the text, Verdi continued to allow musical structures to have their head. If he has a good tune to display, he finds a textual excuse to repeat it, and, once again, this habit bespeaks a relative lack of musical embarrassment, the same quality that makes him willing to employ the brass with such abandon.

The most notorious instance of his adherence to formulaic methods—as with his banda music, much to the despair of musicologists—is his use, well into maturity, of the cabaletta, that energetic, strutting, and ostentatious conclusion of a two-part aria. This is platform music par excellence, a kind of musical speechifying, exactly analogous to the politician's or preacher's stylized peroration. Characteristically, moreover, Verdi's cabalettas are both louder and faster than those of his immediate predecessors. These set pieces are, along with the large concerted passages, the glory of the early operas, magnificent in their disdain for verisimilitude and their indulgence of the most blatant rhetorical gestures. Moreover, cabalettas still figure prominently in Verdi's musical scheme for *Rigoletto*, *Il trovatore*, and *La traviata*, and one can find residues of them in the later operas as well (for example, in Don Carlo's "Egli è salvo" in *La forza del destino* and in the "Sì: fuggiam" section of the Radames-Aida duet in *Aida*). But even when the full cabaletta proves no longer viable, Verdi's music continues to exhibit a more transparent musical patterning than that of his great contemporaries. The much admired psychological precision and inwardness of King Philip's monologue in *Don Carlo* do not prevent the listener from noticing that the vocal line makes its way back to the wonderful melody with which the aria proper begins: the King may be musing on the emptiness of life, but he is also singing a great tune, and Verdi will not allow him to end the scene until he has sung it at least twice. At so late a stage in his career, Wagner would have repressed such an unabashedly musical impulse.

The rhetorical effect of this kind of musical patterning is supported at the local level by Verdi's addiction to heavily inflected and absolutely regular accompaniments. This is the famous "big guitar" effect, which might be compared to the public speaker's fondness for repetitions and rhetorical parallels. Almost to the end, Verdi loves to set a strong rhythmical pulse in his orchestra, even when such regularity is at odds with syntactical or dramatic logic. For some listeners, one of the frustrations of *Otello* and *Falstaff* is their greater reticence in this respect. In general, however, Verdi is never embarrassed to set his tunes to an emphatic and absolutely unvarying accompaniment, thereby announcing that his characters speak not in everyday language but in the heightened mode of the platform. The cabaletta, which always receives such elaborate orchestral undergirding, is simply the most extreme manifestation of this tendency.

A further, and closely related, rhetorical element in Verdi's music is his weakness—if that's the right word—for relatively square melodies. Verdi possessed one of the most fecund melodic imaginations in the history of music, and characteristically, he used his melodic gift without a hint of diffidence. Over and over he writes tunes that are instantly memorable because they seldom frustrate our expectations. Sometimes these tunes seem so artless that they barely escape banality, and we wonder that anything so inevitable should not have been thought of before. In reality, of course, they are anything but artless, and we know from Verdi's sketches (such as those for "La donna è mobile") how hard he worked to get them right.

A good example is provided by the first-act duet between Leonora and Don Alvaro in *La forza del destino,* an opera of Verdi's full maturity. Its classic sixteen measures are divided into four perfectly equal phrases. The first two, exactly identical, are dominated by a regular quarter-note melody that hardly budges from the home triad. The third phrase maintains the same quarter-note rhythmic pattern and sounds as if it were simply running up and down a three-note scale. The last phrase, which contains the only significant departure from the melody's strict quarter-note regime, is easily heard as an echo of the theme announced in the first two phrases. One could justifiably call the tune corny, but Verdi is so little chagrined by it that he has both his tenor and his soprano sing it separately, after which he permits them to join voices and sing most of it over again. An exactly parallel passage can be found in the "allegro con brio" section (the cabaletta) of Riccardo and Amelia's duet in *Un ballo in maschera,* particularly its first two phrases: again we have the regular four-bar units, again the uninterrupted quarter notes, again the extraordinary harmonic simplicity as the voices travel up and down a major triad, and again the threefold repetition, as the tune is sung through by both tenor and soprano before they join in a slightly varied reprise. In sum, a minimum of subtlety and a maximum of effect—precisely the qualities one associates with the language of politicians.

At his most inspired, Verdi seems able to compose entire scenes in which one such inevitable tune juts up against another. This is the case, for example, in the Radames-Amneris duet from Act IV of *Aida* and throughout most of *Il trovatore,* where the melodic profligacy is almost criminal. The seeming obviousness of these tunes and their endless proliferation create, I would argue, a highly rhetorical effect. Verdi makes little effort to soften their brilliant contours, to mold them to the less articulate, less emphatic forms of ordinary speech, as do composers such as Mussorgsky, Debussy, or Janáček. Instead they retain the exaggerated shapeliness of a well-turned phrase. Moreover, Verdi supports these broad musical gestures with a harmonic system that, while sometimes complex, tends to subordinate structural considerations (so important in German music) to the task of providing his brilliant melodies with the requisite support. Verdi's harmony is not the kind that looks good on paper. Rather, it aims to give visceral satisfaction. It is of a piece with his melodic naïveté.

Also contributing to the rhetorical aura is Verdi's distinctive way with concluding scenes, which tend to be more highly charged and faster-paced than those of any other composer. Verdi dearly loves to whip his singers and orchestra into a frenzy as the action concludes, dispatching the characters with breathtaking élan. Here speed combines with volume to create an effect comparable to the collective madness that a skillful orator can generate in a volatile audience. This characteristic, above all others, leads commentators to speak of the extraordinary energy of Verdi's operas, in contrast to which those of his predecessors seem decorous, even wan. A tendency to "work the crowd," even when it is only a crowd of one, can be noted over and over in the operas. The cabaletta often serves this purpose, as when Manrico rings down the curtain in Act III of *Il trovatore* with his "Di quella pira." Elsewhere Verdi achieves a similarly high level of intensity by composing assertive marches or unusually brisk stretti to cap his large ensembles. The conclusion of the triumphal scene from *Aida* offers perhaps the best-known illustration of his tendency to combine huge performing forces and accelerating tempos to convey a sense of frenzied emotion and activity.

The triumphal scene, of course, is an explicitly political moment, a grand rally for the homecoming Egyptian troops. But Verdi uses speed rhetorically in many concluding scenes that seem to lack any overt political content. The duet between Leonora and the Count di Luna in Act IV of *Il trovatore* is outrageously, indeed inexcusably, fleet, and its fleetness seems entirely unrelated to the issue at hand: a woman agreeing (but not really agreeing) to submit to a man she detests, in order to save the man she loves. When Puccini set an analogous situation in the second act of *Tosca*, he composed music carefully designed to suggest the changing emotions and purposes of his two principals. But Verdi sacrifices all such psychological niceties to the single consideration of maintaining a headlong pace that will bring the scene to a thrilling conclusion. To be sure, this disregard for textual and dramatic considerations was standard practice among his bel canto precursors. But in Verdi's case it calls attention to itself, both because he is writing at a time when other composers, notably Wagner, were moving toward greater textual responsibility and because Verdi himself at other moments (such as the last act of *La traviata*) forsakes this stylized procedure in an effort to give the impression of greater naturalness. Precisely the discrepancy between substance and manner leads me to speak of his exploitation of speed in passages like the Leonora/Di Luna duet as essentially rhetorical and to suggest that this quality—along with loudness and melodic extroversion—makes his music unusually well suited to political purposes. I hardly need add that by rhetorical I don't in any sense mean artistically inferior.

Power Voices

I have spoken of several features of Verdi's music that, in my opinion, contribute to the political atmosphere of his operas. I want now to consider a more specifically operatic device—though still an essentially musical one—that does much the same thing. I have in mind Verdi's creation and exploitation of voice types that convey a sense of power.

Verdi may be said virtually to have brought these voices into existence by writing music that no longer fit the contours of established vocal categories and thus required that singers develop new skills if they were to master their parts. The two most important Verdian creations in this respect are the high baritone and the dramatic mezzo. Both differ from their bel canto predecessors in the greater volume and intensity of the sound they produce, and both convey an unmistakable sense of power.

Verdi's "power voices" emerge from a general deployment of vocal resources that differs interestingly from the practices of other operatic composers. All the great opera composers, from Mozart to Britten, may be said to favor a particular balance (or imbalance) of male and female voices. In this, as in virtually all other matters, Mozart sets a standard for equipoise: in the famous Mozart operas the ratio of male to female voices is remarkably even. If there is a masculine bias in *The Magic Flute,* it is corrected, so to speak, by the female bias of *Così fan tutte,* where, although the number of male and female characters is the same, the women get the lion's share of the music. Against Mozart, two very different forms of vocal imbalance are represented by Wagner and Britten on the one hand and Puccini and Strauss on the other. Wagner and Britten lean heavily to the masculine side. Wagner's *Siegfried,* although a four-hour opera, has only about thirty minutes of singing for its three female voices (one of them representing a bird), while in *Billy Budd* Britten succeeds in writing a full-length opera without a single female sound—if we overlook the brief appearance of four boy sopranos. At the other end of the spectrum, Puccini and Strauss are notoriously partial to the female voice. The second act of *Madame Butterfly* does for female singers what *Siegfried* does for men, and most of the great vocal writing in the famous Strauss operas is likewise reserved for women, especially those that can soar above the staff.

Verdi's place on this male-female spectrum, I would suggest, lies clearly to the masculine side of Mozart, although he is nowhere near as extreme as either Wagner or Britten. Perhaps because he wrote so many famous individual roles for the female voice, we are inclined to overlook the masculine bias of his operas as a whole, especially those of his middle years. In the operas of Verdi's maturity, however, we usually find one or at most two major female parts set against two, three, or even four equally substantial male parts. Gilda, for example, must hold her own (with only the briefest help from Maddalena) against the Duke, Rigoletto, and Sparafucile. In *Il trovatore,* three principal male parts (Manrico, Di Luna, and Ferrando) are set against two females (Leonora and Azucena). Violetta in *La traviata* gets only walk-on support from Flora against Alfredo (a tenor) and Germont (a baritone).

This discrepancy grows much more noticeable in the operas from *I vespri siciliani* to *Don Carlo,* which, as I've remarked, are also the operas in which Verdi's concerns become increasingly political. In the first two of them, *I vespri siciliani* and *Simon Boccanegra,* the imbalance is at its most extreme. *Vespri* pits a single soprano against three large male roles and a host of male comprimarii, while in *Simon Boccanegra* the ratio is four to one—a fact that accounts for the unusually dark atmosphere of these operas and doubtless for their relative unpopularity. Verdi moves toward greater equilibrium in the next two operas (*Un ballo in maschera* and *La forza del destino*), but only by introducing dramatically extraneous characters. Although both of these operas contain only one essential female part (Amelia and Leonora), Verdi relieves the gloom by creating a mezzo-soprano fortuneteller for *Ballo* and an even more superfluous mezzo-soprano gypsy for *Forza,* and by assigning the role of the page in *Ballo* to a coloratura soprano. By way of contrast, *Ballo* has two hefty and dramatically central parts for male voices (along with several important male comprimario roles), while *Forza* has four male principals (Alvaro, Carlo, Guardiano, and Melitone), and even a fifth (the Marchese di Calatrava) who sings enough music to call for an important artist. The imbalance is hardly less extreme in the greatest of the political operas, *Don Carlo.* To be sure, *Don Carlo,* unlike the other middle-period operas, contains two large female roles that are also dramatically essential. But as in *La forza del destino,* these women are set against four imposing men (Philip, Carlo, Rodrigo, and the Grand Inquisitor), and once again there is yet a fifth male part—that of the Monk—that requires major casting. In the great operas of his middle years, then, Verdi comes very close to duplicating the masculine hegemony of the mature Wagner operas.

Of course, Verdi compensates his female singers by giving them long, hushed arias of striking lyric eloquence, thereby lending the characters greater relative weight (and making the roles more desirable) than might otherwise be the case. In particular, he assigns his female characters those soaring phrases above the staff that are the special glory of Verdi's melodic style—sweeping musical lines that rise majestically into the upper register and then descend with equal grandeur. Amelia's "Consentimi, o Signore" in *Un ballo in maschera* might be considered the archetype of such phrases: a perfect sonic arc carrying the soprano from B in the middle of the voice up over top A and then back down again to a tonic low E.

Nonetheless, males predominate. They may not get the best music, but they get more of it, and that needle dropped randomly on a Verdi recording (especially of a middle-period opera) will generally find not only a loud sound but a masculine one as well. This fact, I believe, contributes in significant if subtle ways to the political aura of the operas. Men, after all, have always been the bearers of political culture, while women have inhabited the world of domesticity and romance. Men talk about war and the state, while women—especially Verdi's women—talk about peace. In the late twentieth century we no longer accept this division of labor as inevitable. Yet it was one of the least ambiguous fixtures of the mental universe in which Verdi's operas were composed, enshrined in such representative nineteenth-century documents as John Ruskin's "Of Kings' Treasuries" and "Of Queens' Gardens." Hence the prevailingly masculine sound that one hears in the operas of Verdi's middle period carries at least an implicit political message. It functions as a persistent sonic reminder that the dramas take place in the public arena, and that the players are combatants in a struggle for power.

Out of this dark, predominantly masculine vocal background emerge Verdi's two most important vocal creations: the high baritone and the dramatic mezzo. In purely vocal terms, these two voice types are exactly complementary. In both, Verdi takes an established vocal category and exploits a particular facet of it, a particular part of the singer's range. In the case of the baritone, he writes music that forces the singer to develop the upper third of the normal (or traditional) baritone range, bringing into regular use notes at the very top of the voice (F, F sharp, and G) that baritones singing Mozart, Rossini, Bellini, or Donizetti were rarely if ever called upon to produce. The dramatic mezzo, conversely, is asked to sing a significant portion of her music in the lower third of the voice, with particular emphasis on those notes at the bottom of the staff where the mezzo can sing in chest register. The effect of these two modifications is to draw the baritone and mezzo-soprano into an area of their respective registers where they emit unusually loud and penetrating sounds. The baritone at the top of his range achieves unparalleled forcibleness, perhaps because the basic timbre of the voice remains dark and virile, yet the notes one hears have the brightness more often associated with tenors.

The voice, in other words, offers a unique combination of brilliance and weight. Likewise, the Verdi mezzo singing in chest voice is able to produce sounds of sufficient volume and cutting edge to project over even the heaviest orchestration. The normally heady female voice assumes unexpected, booming assertiveness.

Both of these characteristically Verdian sounds—the trumpeting high baritone and the snarling low mezzo—give an impression of enormous power. Their tones carry an authority that is rarely matched by the other vocal types, for which Verdi wrote music not greatly different—at least in tessitura—from that written by his predecessors. Moreover, the high baritone and the low mezzo serve analogous psychological purposes in the Verdi operas, the one political, the other sexual.

The high baritone is the political voice par excellence. The bearer of such an instrument in a Verdi opera is more often than not an authority figure, sometimes a figure associated with political aspirations. Appropriately, Verdi wrote some of his most extravagant and rhetorical cabalettas—platform music, as I've called it—for just this voice. In the early operas high baritones are almost invariably politicians. Among the most notable of them are the Babylonian king Nabucco (in the opera of the same name); Don Carlo, King of Spain, in *Ernani;* Francesco Foscari, the Doge of Venice, in *I due Foscari;* and, finally, Macbeth, King of Scotland—the best known of the early baritone roles. Verdi combines an extended upper register with fierce rhythmic intensity to render these figures categorically more potent than any of their baritone forebears.

In the operas of his early maturity, with their domestic concerns, the authority of the high baritone becomes familial rather than strictly political. Three of Verdi's most famous baritone roles from this period—Rigoletto, Germont in *La traviata,* and Miller in *Luisa Miller*—are authoritative, even authoritarian, fathers whose power is conveyed by their many soaring phrases at the top of the register. One might say that although they exercise their power within a narrow domestic sphere, they sing with the assertiveness of heads of state. One senses this particularly in the case of Rigoletto, who is in the service of an actual head of state (the Duke of Mantua), and whose exceptionally high-lying baritone part makes him seem incomparably more potent than his nominal boss (a tenor).

The 1850s and 1860s find Verdi creating a string of high baritone roles in which the voice is restored to the political responsibilities for which it was created. The great baritonal politicians of the middle operas are Guido di Monforte, Governor of Sicily, in *I vespri siciliani;* Simon Boccanegra, Doge of Genoa (generally considered the finest of Verdi's baritone roles); Rodrigo, Marquis of Posa and spokesman for Flemish liberty, in *Don Carlo;* and Amonasro, King of Ethiopia, in *Aida.* (Three other high baritone roles from this period exist, as it were, on the fringes of politics: the Count di Luna in *Il trovatore;* Renato, Secretary to the Governor, in *Un ballo in maschera;* and Don Carlo di Vargas, son of the Marchese di Calatrava, in *La forza del destino.*) Although less inclined to hector than the baritone figures in the early operas and conceived with a psychological subtlety appropriate to Verdi's prime years, these figures are easily recognized as the musical descendants of Nabucco and Macbeth. Not surprisingly, the parts are deemed vocally appropriate for exactly the same singers who specialize in Verdi's renowned fathers. Once again they take the baritone voice into those potent upper regions where earlier composers had not dared to invite it and where it resonates with unparalleled authority.

We can measure Verdi's achievement in this regard, and better appreciate its political implications, if we compare the Verdi baritones with the important baritone roles in Mozart. The Mozart parts generally assigned to baritones are Count Almaviva, Guglielmo, Papageno, and (less consistently) Don Giovanni and Figaro. These figures never sing a note higher than F sharp, and the general tessitura of the roles lies as much as a third lower than the Verdi baritones. Indeed, Don Giovanni and Figaro lie low enough that they are often sung by basses. Moreover, none of these characters is given the uniquely energized music that one associates with the Verdi baritones. That this doesn't merely reflect a stylistic difference between Mozart and Verdi is shown by the music Mozart composed for his sopranos, which is every bit as demanding as that composed for the soprano voice by Verdi. Thus a soprano who can sing Fiordiligi (in *Così fan tutte*) has the technical wherewithal for nearly any of the Verdi heroines, while even the most assured Papageno would be swamped by Rigoletto, Simon Boccanegra, or Amonasro, roles for which Mozart's baritones are a note short at the top and woefully underpowered. Interestingly, neither Wagner, nor Puccini, nor Strauss makes the same demands on the baritone voice that Verdi does. Wagner's baritone roles generally lie at least a tone lower that Verdi's, Puccini wrote only one baritone part—Scarpia—considered vocally equal to its Verdian predecessors, while Strauss largely ignored the baritone voice in his operas.

The "Verdi baritone"—a label affixed to singers like Sherrill Milnes in our own day or Robert Merrill and Leonard Warren in the previous generation—is, then, above all a singer who possesses the unique upper extension and volume that Verdi alone expects from this vocal category. As I have suggested, the Verdi baritone is especially suited to sing political music, or to bring issues of politics to mind. Because of its weight and darkness, the baritone voice sounds naturally masculine. It is in fact the normal singing voice of most adult males. It therefore conveys the "natural" authority that adult males have enjoyed in our culture, against which the higher voice of the tenor seems abnormally impassioned (the voice of a young man in love), while the lower voice of the bass suggests the gravity, even the senility, of old age. Baritones, one might say, are born leaders, mature enough not to get sidetracked by romance but not yet so old as to be ready for retirement.

To these familiar psychological associations Verdi adds something extra: this same dark, weighty, masculine voice is forced to sing at or near the top of its range, where it can operate only under tremendous pressure. The tones we hear from the baritone singing from C to top G are abnormally loud and aggressive. The voice rarely sounds conversational (as, for example, Mozart's baritones can) but always seems screwed up to oratorical heights. Even when the singer addresses only one other person, the elevated tessitura gives the impression of someone making a speech. Such a voice and such a vocal manner lend themselves perfectly to the creation of political characters— characters who speak oratorically rather than conversationally.

Verdi's other power voice, the dramatic mezzo, is a more ambiguous entity than her baritone counterpart. In creating this vocal type, Verdi exploits that region of the mezzo-soprano voice that produces the most masculine sounds—namely, its very lowest register, where notes are sung not in the normal head tone but from the chest. The unique quality of the female chest voice is immediately recognizable even to untutored ears. Its sound is altogether unladylike. Indeed, it has an almost baritonal fierceness. One might expect, therefore, that a mezzo singing in the chest register would be a likely candidate for undertaking masculine things, such as politics.

Interestingly, as Verdi began to fashion this vocal type in the

1840s, he seemed to be moving in precisely such a direction: the Verdi mezzo, like the Verdi baritone, appeared destined for a political career. But by the time the true Verdi mezzo emerges in the operas of his middle years—the first proper example is Azucena in *Il trovatore*—the political impulse that gave birth to the voice has been shunted off into something altogether different: sex. The fierceness and the implied masculinity remain, but they have been redirected now toward the private realm—on the one hand toward the family and on the other toward romance. This voice thus becomes Verdi's main vehicle for exploring the tension-ridden, often Oedipal, relations between mothers and children and for portraying the agonies of the spurned woman. I'm inclined to say—somewhat grandly—that the nineteenth century had no secure place in its ideological universe for a fully political female. Hence power in female hands gets translated into sexual terms. At the same time, we can readily detect the political animal beneath its sexual disguise in Verdi's great mezzo roles.

The two characters that most clearly suggest the political possibilities of this voice are Abigaille in *Nabucco* (1842) and Lady Macbeth in *Macbeth* (1847). Technically, these are both soprano roles, and, indeed, they must sing higher than do any of the mezzo figures of the middle years. Abigaille sings up to high C, and Lady Macbeth must even reach a D flat. Nonetheless, virtually all commentators have recognized these roles as vocal precursors of the famous Verdi mezzos, precisely because in them he draws upon the female chest register in ways unknown to his predecessors (although Bellini's Druid priestess Norma—also a political figure—shows a distinct fondness for the chest). Not surprisingly, the singers who have been most successful in these roles have been either mezzos or dramatic sopranos (like Maria Callas) with unusually potent chest voices. The roles do not fit the traditional soprano voice well at all, and they are rarely taken on by those singers who flourish in the soprano repertory of Verdi's maturity.

Vocally, then, Abigaille and Lady Macbeth are closely related to the classic Verdi mezzos of the later operas. Their single most distinctive feature is their aggressiveness, even violence, especially in the lower register. Moreover, both of these roles—unlike the mezzos that follow—are explicitly political. Indeed, Lady Macbeth—in Verdi no less than in Shakespeare—is virtually consumed by politics; she is, after all, the chief inspiration of her husband's murderous ambition. Abigaille in *Nabucco* is likewise an entirely political animal. Verdi gives her a nominal romantic interest, but she comes to vocal life only as the mouthpiece for her conquering father, Nebuchadnezzar, whom she eventually deposes in order to make herself monarch of Babylon.

For both of these women Verdi writes music of unequaled assertiveness, music in which the singer must dip into the masculine-sounding chest register as rarely before in opera. Perhaps the most spectacular example of this comes in the recitative preceding Abigaille's principal aria, where Verdi asks his singer to drop two octaves from high C to low C (sung in chest voice) on a single syllable. The effect is positively curdling. Listening to these two roles, one recognizes that the chest register in female singers could have served Verdi's political interests in a fashion exactly analogous to the upward extension of the baritone voice among males.

As noted, however, something entirely different happens. The great Verdi mezzo roles are Azucena, Princess Eboli (in *Don Carlo*), and Amneris (in *Aida*). (Two other middle-period roles—Ulrica in *Un ballo in maschera* and Preziosilla in *La forza del destino*—are constructed along the same vocal lines, but are shorter and lack the dramatic importance of Azucena, Eboli, and Amneris.) A singer who specializes in these roles is apt to be called, in exact parallel to the singer who essays the high baritone roles, a "Verdi mezzo," a label meant to designate a large, dark voice with, above all, an ability to sing forcibly from the chest in the range from low C to G in the middle of the staff. Much of the most potent music Verdi writes for these characters either lies in or passes through this extremely low-lying vocal territory.

In contrast to Abigaille and Lady Macbeth, Azucena, Eboli, and Amneris care not at all for politics. Instead, they are devoted to the single-minded pursuit of some private goal. Azucena, the half-crazed gypsy in *Il trovatore*, spends much of the opera in a kind of trance, absorbed with thoughts of avenging her mother, or accusing herself of murdering her own son. Eboli and Amneris are essentially thwarted romantic figures. They use their access to power (Eboli is mistress to the King of Spain; Amneris, daughter of the King of Egypt) first to pursue and then, when repulsed, to revenge themselves against their would-be lovers.

These maternal and sexual figures conduct their vocal affairs in exactly the same manner as did their political forebears. That is, they sing with exceptional violence, booming out raw chest tones and emitting unprecedented volumes of sound. Indeed, in the hands of the right interpreters, they are usually the vocal heroines of the evening: a good Azucena, Eboli, or Amneris can repair the deficiencies of an entire cast. As a result of their overpowering vocal authority, they often convey an impression of sexual ambiguity. It would be incorrect to call them mannish, but they are indelicate in the extreme. Both vocally and emotionally, Azucena all but smothers her adopted son, Manrico—who, in classic Oedipal fashion, does the bulk of his singing with her, not with his mistress, Leonora. Eboli and Amneris are menacing, even castrating, figures whose frequent and terrifying dips into the chest register (especially in opposition to the high-lying soprano roles of Elisabeth and Aida) give the impression of dangerously unfeminine forces at work. The vocal evidence tells us that all three figures are too ferocious to be genuinely successful mothers or lovers. Hence my suggestion that they are politicians manqué. In every vocal respect, they have the goods to be in charge of things. They could as easily dominate the affairs of state as they dominate the musical proceedings.

The combined presence of the high baritone and the low mezzo in the operas of Verdi's maturity is the source of a final and yet more subtle political effect that their music suggests. The baritone and the mezzo redefine the tonal area inhabited by all the voices in the Verdi operas. They do so essentially by raising the general level at which everyone is forced to sing. This gives each of the vocal categories a somewhat novel flavor, and more significantly, it results in an overall heightening of pitch in the operas. Along with Verdi's unique rhythmic vitality and his considerable tolerance for noise, this raising of the operas' pitch creates a musical atmosphere uniquely appropriate to the overemphatic, strenuous world of politics.

The technical basis for this effect lies in the happy coincidence that Verdi's high baritone and dramatic mezzo produce their distinctive sounds on exactly the same notes of the scale. That is, the trumpeted notes at the top of the baritone's register are precisely the same notes that the mezzo sings with threatening authority from the chest: the notes from low C to G in the middle of the treble clef. (Baritone parts are written on the bass clef, so these notes for the baritone appear above the staff.) Verdi, as no previous composer, inhabits the area in which these two voices overlap. One might even call this C to G area "Verdiland," so uniquely prominent is it in the vocal profile of his operas.

As already mentioned, this territory lies high for the baritone and low for the mezzo. In general both voices can operate in it only at full throttle. By way of contrast, the same vocal territory

turns out to be extremely accommodating for tenors and sopranos—
the latter singing up an octave. For these two voices, the C to G area
is one in which they can function with relative ease, but also with
considerable force. Perhaps more important, a compositional technique
that regularly locates both voices in this area puts them in immediate
melodic proximity to the range from G to high C, at which strato-
spheric heights tenors and sopranos make perhaps the most piercing
of all operatic sounds. With, so to speak, normal musical operations
being conducted in what I have called Verdiland (instead of somewhat
lower, as in Mozart and Wagner), the tenor and soprano can follow
a smooth melodic course up into these altitudinous regions, and the
very highest notes of the voice are thus incorporated on a more
regular basis into the musical fabric. Hence not only do Verdi's tenors
and sopranos sing at a level that is generally higher than in the works
of Mozart and Wagner, but every Verdi opera can be expected to bring
several of those unforgettable moments when the soprano or tenor
goes right to the top.

The most obvious effect of this heightening of the vocal line in
Mozart and Wagner are unwilling to force their baritones up (or
their mezzos down), and as a result their operas have a lower
tessitura—a lower center of gravity—than do Verdi's. G. B. Shaw
drew attention to this fact in defending Wagner against the charge
that he ruined voices. Shaw rightly noted that it was Verdi, not
Wagner, who asked his singers, particularly the baritone, to sing
beyond their natural range. Of course, experienced operagoers will
know that Puccini and Strauss also write music that typically lies
higher than that of Mozart and Wagner. The difference is that they
do so by sacrificing the lower voices. The tenor and soprano writing
in Puccini and Strauss is indeed just as high-lying as Verdi's, but their
operas sound top-heavy because they contain so few significant parts
for baritone or dramatic mezzo. Verdi alone succeeds in raising the
overall tessitura of his operas while continuing, like Mozart and
Wagner, to make full use of all the traditional vocal categories.

The most obvious effect of this heightening of the vocal line in
Verdi is to make his music seem more exciting than Mozart's or
Wagner's. The singers in a Verdi opera are apt to sound more
pressured, under greater strain, than their counterparts in Mozart or
Wagner. But they are not merely overwrought in the fashion of
Puccini's or Strauss's tenors and sopranos. The continued presence
of the lower vocal categories—of baritones, dramatic mezzos, and, of
course, basses—means that the raised tessitura is more than an

occasion for vocal hysteria. The operas achieve a new intensity, but they retain a certain gravity as well.

In sum, by repositioning the baritone and mezzo voices Verdi raises the pitch of his operas, both literally and metaphorically. We are conscious that the singers are able to express themselves in these lofty regions only with considerable effort. Perhaps unconsciously, we come to associate the physical strength that makes such singing possible with a more abstract manifestation of power in the realm of politics. Verdi's characters speak at a (literally) higher level than their forebears, and their elevated tones, I'm persuaded, carry an implicit political message.

THE POLITICS OF *DON CARLO**

Don Carlo is the most complete artistic realization of Verdi's political concerns, the opera that takes fullest advantage of the political logic implicit in his compositional methods. Although set in sixteenth-century Spain, it actually addresses the important issues of Verdi's own lifetime. It is, in effect, a kind of political autobiography, in which Verdi re-creates his evolution from the idealistic liberalism of the 1840s to the clear-eyed *Realpolitik* of the 1860s.

The realism of *Don Carlo* must not be confused with verisimilitude. I do not mean simply that the opera plays fast and loose with the historical facts on which it is supposedly based (so, of course, does Schiller's drama, the opera's immediate source). Verdi rarely lost an opportunity to deflate the realistic pretensions of late-nineteenth-century art, referring in 1879 to "this age of *Verismo* in which there is not a scrap of verity." Hence his opera traffics comfortably in the familiar improbabilities of melodrama, including such supernatural elements as a ghostly Emperor and a Heavenly Voice. Some writers go so far as to call it mythic and compare it to Wagner's *Ring*, with which it is roughly contemporaneous. It is, however, profoundly concerned with reality, although the reality it seeks to portray is psychological and, above all, political.

---

* *Don Carlo* is a feast for musicologists. It exists in no fewer than five versions, and in two different languages. Julian Budden's chapter on *Don Carlos* (the French title) in *The Operas of Verdi*, Volume 3, contains a thorough discussion of all the versions. Although substantial, none of the differences among them bears significantly upon my argument. Scholars now agree that the French text of the opera is superior to the Italian, but I have continued to use the latter in this chapter because it remains far more familiar.

The opera, like Schiller's drama, develops from a political premise. Its tragic events unfold as the result of a diplomatic marriage between King Philip II of Spain and Elisabeth de Valois, daughter of King Henry II of France. The original version of the opera began with a long chorus of woodcutters and their wives, complaining of the miseries of war.* Moreover, Elisabeth's acceptance of Philip's proposal, in spite of her being in love with his son Carlo, reflects not filial piety but her magnanimous wish to end those miseries by ending the war. Perhaps not incidentally, as Verdi neared completing the opera in 1866, his own mind was very much preoccupied with the war between Italy and Austria over the Veneto.

The opera contains four principal male roles: the title character (who is the Infante of Spain), King Philip II, Rodrigo (the Marquis of Posa), and the Grand Inquisitor. Each of these men is made to stand for a particular attitude toward politics, sometimes even for a particular ideology, and Verdi composes music that suggests the deeper psychological implications of their respective opinions. Each of the four characters, moreover, has a distinctive view of the opera's action. Each, in other words, would be inclined to write a different synopsis of its plot and would offer a different version of what the opera is "about." Among Verdi's great achievements in *Don Carlo* is that he allows us to view its events from the perspective of all four of these men and to enter sympathetically into their respective political worlds.

Rodrigo

Rodrigo is in some respects the opera's most remarkable creation. He believes unflinchingly in idealistic politics. More precisely, he is a political liberal. He is also—save for the Grand Inquisitor—the least psychological character in the opera: his life is conducted largely in terms of externalities. All his actions are guided by a single consideration: winning political autonomy and religious freedom for the people of Flanders, who are groaning under the yoke of Spanish tyranny and Roman Catholic intolerance.

As Rodrigo makes his way through the opera's neurotic characters and treacherous relationships, he keeps the vision of a liberated Flanders always before his inner eye. This does not mean that his friendships (first with Carlo, later with Philip) are inauthentic, only that they are subordinated to higher ends. Significantly, although a

---

* The chorus is restored to the current Metropolitan Opera production.

young man, he has no apparent romantic interests. One suspects that a composer less serious about politics would have had him fall in love with Princess Eboli, thus providing more of those "situations" that bel canto composers thrived on. Directors who can't appreciate Verdi's political seriousness sometimes transform him into a homosexual, whose behavior can be rendered intelligible only by assuming an erotic attachment to Carlo. Whatever his sexual needs, however, they have been thoroughly sublimated. This, indeed, is the principal point in which he differs from Carlo. His asexuality he shares with only one other character in the opera: the Grand Inquisitor, who is, of course, his ideological opposite—and, not incidentally, ninety years old.

Rodrigo represented an extraordinary challenge for Verdi because the ideas that inspire him are so profoundly unmusical. For the dramatist, of course, he poses no difficulties: like any good liberal, he is exceptionally articulate and can always deliver a reasoned and stirring account of his intentions. But how does one write liberal music? How does one bring Rodrigo to operatic (as opposed to dramatic) life? The essential components of the liberal vision—toleration, the sanctity of the individual, freedom, national self-determination—simply have no musical correlates. The challenge, moreover, was not just academic for Verdi. He had enormous sympathy for the principles Rodrigo championed, and he wished to do them musical justice. They were, after all, the principles of his own political youth. We know that Rodrigo's music caused him more grief than that of any other character in the opera.

Verdi "solves" Rodrigo most brilliantly, it seems to me, in the music he writes for his entrance and his death. Admittedly, from a purely textual point of view, Rodrigo's liberal philosophy is best articulated in the long duet with Philip at the end of Act II. But as that duet went through its various revisions, its musical language grew too sophisticated to be an altogether appropriate vehicle for Rodrigo's forthright and unnuanced opinions. Verdi was here up against the impossible task of writing music that would be faithful to two psychologically incompatible characters, and the results, not surprisingly, are indecisive: Rodrigo sounds too subtle, Philip too blunt. For his entrance and his death, by way of contrast, Verdi managed to compose something that, at least in the context of the opera as a whole, conveys a sense of Rodrigo's distinctive political vision. I say "in the context of the opera as a whole" because the procedures Verdi hit upon depend for their effect entirely on the readily heard difference between Rodrigo's music and that of the other characters. In some of Verdi's earlier operas, this music would not single itself out. Only when set against the melodic and harmonic texture of *Don Carlo* in its entirety does Rodrigo's music legitimately qualify as "liberal."

Expressed in the most general fashion, Rodrigo's music is distinguished by its simplicity. This can be measured in several different ways. First, it is melodically simple. When Rodrigo is on stage, Verdi is inclined to compose old-fashioned, regular tunes— tunes like those that proliferate in his earlier operas. In contrast to the melodies written for the opera's other characters, Rodrigo's melodies tend to be constructed out of regular four-bar units, and like most regular tunes, they are easily committed to memory. Put another way, we usually know where Rodrigo's melodies are going. They are by no means more beautiful than the tunes written for the other characters. On the contrary, because of their relative simplicity they are apt to cloy, more so in the subtle melodic context of *Don Carlo* than they would in the company of their near relatives in operas like *Rigoletto, Il trovatore,* and *La traviata.* Critics who complain about them fail to recognize that Verdi is not regressing here so much as he is making an intellectual point. Rodrigo's tunes are intentionally foursquare.

The relative simplicity of Rodrigo's music can also be measured rhythmically and harmonically. It is more apt to be supported by a steady rhythmic undergirding than is the music of the other characters—the sort of heavily inflected and incessant thumping that is such a marked feature of Verdi's earlier operas and that he increasingly gave up after *La traviata.* Similarly, the harmonic structure of Rodrigo's music is relatively immune to the pervasive chromaticism of the opera as a whole. The basic tonic-dominant-tonic pattern of the traditional harmonic system is a good deal closer to the surface, and Verdi indulges Rodrigo with thirds and sixths that, again, are audibly out of keeping with the subtle harmonic scheme of the rest of the opera.

Finally, Rodrigo's straightforward melodies, steady rhythms, and pleasingly familiar harmonies find their counterpart in the orchestral preferences Verdi adopts for his music. The most striking feature of the orchestral music associated with Rodrigo is the prominence given to the brass, especially trumpets and cornets. Here again, I would suggest, the appeal is to simplicity. The brass, along with the percussion, are the most primitive of instruments, descended from archaic military tradition, and they sound ever so slightly out of place in the sophisticated modern symphony orchestra. Rodrigo, too, is ever so slightly out of place in the psychologically sophisticated world of *Don Carlo*.

The cumulative effect of these musical differentiations is to set Rodrigo apart. In one sense, like his music, he is made to seem simpler than the other characters. He does not share in their involuted emotionality. Psychologically speaking, he lives on the surface of things, immune to and, indeed, largely ignorant of the tortuous motives that find Carlo in love with his stepmother and at odds with his father, the Queen herself torn between Carlo and her sense of duty, Princess Eboli mistress to the King yet infatuated with Carlo, and the King in turn preoccupied with his son's disloyalty, his wife's suspected infidelity, and the sinister machinations of the Grand Inquisitor. Moreover, it is part of Verdi's musical intention to distance us from Rodrigo's unpsychological view of the world. Therefore we experience his music—with its broad tunes, regular rhythms, and obvious harmonies—as slightly patronizing. Set against the complex musical texture of the opera as a whole, it seems one-dimensional— just as his liberalism is one-dimensional when measured against the *Realpolitiker*'s richly nuanced understanding of human psychology and the intricacies of power.

But if Rodrigo's music suggests simple-mindedness it also suggests nobility. Its very transparency makes him a credible vehicle for high-minded and altruistic political ideals. It reflects, one might say, the unblemished spirituality of the original liberal creed—before it had become tainted by bourgeois capitalism—the creed enshrined in the treatises of Locke, Rousseau, and Mill. Rodrigo's is a political vision in which self-interest and grubby materialism have been banished in favor of elevated abstractions. Verdi may know that those abstractions are illusory, but they have not lost their charm for him. Nor does he cease to admire the man who is sufficiently unself-regarding to embrace them. This is precisely the figure he creates for us, musically, in Rodrigo. We are made to respect, even envy, his direct and uncomplicated view of things, to appreciate that, however impracticable they may be, the world would be a much poorer place without its Rodrigos.

Nowhere is Verdi's fond ambivalence more clearly registered than in the music with which Rodrigo enters the opera, music that many critics, failing to understand Verdi's purposes, have judged unworthy of the piece. Returning from France, Rodrigo comes on his friend Carlo, who, characteristically, is rehearsing his romantic predicament: the woman to whom he was engaged, and with whom he fell in love on meeting her in Fontainebleau, is now, for political reasons, married to his father. Apprised of the situation, Rodrigo hesitates hardly a moment before prescribing a remedy. Carlo, he urges, should drown his sorrows in the fight to liberate Flanders:

> *Taccia il tuo cor;*
> *degna di te opra farai,*
> *apprendi omai in mezzo*
> *a gente oppressa, a divenir un Re!*

> Silence your heart;
> yours will be work worthy of you,
> now among an oppressed people
> learn to become a king!

In other words, Carlo is urged to sublimate his romantic frustrations in an idealistic political cause, and the Infante—who is among the more impressionable of operatic heroes—immediately agrees.

The "friendship duet" that follows, "Dio, che nell'alma infondere," contains the most famous—and hummable—music in the opera. Tenor and baritone join together in splendidly resonant thirds and sixths. The phrases are perfectly even, and most of them follow an identical pattern: each measure begins with a sustained harmony followed by two sets of triplets. Moreover, these audibly parallel phrases amble through a rudimentary harmonic sequence: tonic (C major) in the first measure, subdominant (F major) in the second, dominant (G major) in the third and fourth, and then back to the tonic—the sort of unsophisticated harmonic progression that gives immediate satisfaction. The whole is supported by a catchy orchestral rhythm that is a not very distant relative of the "big guitar" effect so familiar in the earlier operas. Moreover, as he does nowhere else in the opera, Verdi repeats the full tune three times: Carlo and Rodrigo sing it through twice, and after their final cries of "Libertà!" it is taken up, *fortissimo* and with emphatic brass embellishments, by the entire orchestra. We seem to have been transported back to the Verdi circa 1850.

Audiences, of course, love this moment (Eboli's "O don fatale" is its only serious rival in popularity), and Verdi himself was sufficiently enamored of the tune to use it three more times in the opera: it bursts out in the orchestra after the Carlo-Rodrigo-Eboli trio of Act III, is heard again—softly on two clarinets—when Rodrigo disarms Carlo during the *auto-da-fé,* and then makes a final appearance between the first and second verses of Rodrigo's deathbed aria. Critics, however, regret it as a lapse in taste. "Corn in thirds," I once heard it called; "that miserable tune" was Francis Toye's verdict. "The best that can be said about this tune," writes Spike Hughes, "is that its banality is rather touching." Wagner, one is made to feel, would never have tolerated such a blatant appeal to the gallery—nor, presumably, would the Verdi of *Otello* and *Falstaff* (although the piece bears an obvious resemblance to the vengeance duet between Otello and Iago). Doubtless he was pleased to finish the scene in so rousing a fashion. But irrespective of its appeal, the tune is a perfect musical embodiment of Rodrigo's uncluttered political vision. Rodrigo manages here, however briefly, to drag Carlo out of his morbidly chromatic self-absorption into the bright tonic-dominant world of political idealism. Moreover, like Carlo himself, we in the audience are meant to share in the moment's lofty enthusiasm. It is as authentic as is our visceral response to the duet's bold tune, firm beat, ingratiating harmonies, and brassy scoring. But because this brilliant music emerges out of the opera's pervasively dark and ambiguous tonality, we also sense something artificial—something unreal—in Rodrigo's strenuous convictions. Heard in the context of the opera as a whole, the friendship duet sounds as if it had been placed in musical italics. Verdi thus memorializes a valuable moment from his own past, while at the same time informing us that he no longer sees the world in quite such clear-cut terms. His music here is at once a celebration and a valedictory.

Rodrigo departs the opera as he entered it: in spite of all he has seen, his idealism remains unscathed, and he is, in every significant musical respect, exactly the same creature we met in the friendship duet. Having incriminated himself with the King and aware that his days are numbered, he bids farewell to Carlo in an old-fashioned stand-up aria, "Per me giunto," whose lucid musical structure exactly mirrors the unambiguous contours of his mind. We are made easily aware of the aria's neat four-bar units, each in turn constructed of two audibly parallel phrases. The harmonic system is more complex than that of the duet, but still remarkably simple and tightly linked to the melodic line. A repeated rhythmic figure in the violins, interrupted only once in the entire course of the aria, gives the music a steady forward tread. Rodrigo, one feels, is the only figure in *Don Carlo* who is sufficiently untroubled by doubts to be able to sing in so artless a fashion.

Once again, critics complain of the piece's conventionality. "Even at the height of his greatness," writes Budden, "Verdi can find for him nothing more impressive than a stream of generically noble baritonic melody." But generic nobility is the very essence of Rodrigo. Precisely because he does not succumb to the epidemic introspection of the other characters, his music must remain externalized. Its reliance on convention is a measure of his selflessness.

Rodrigo's final aria—after he has been shot—also relies heavily on unsophisticated musical ingredients. As he dies in Carlo's arms, his thoughts, appropriately, turn to politics:

> *Io morrò, ma lieto in core,*
> *chè potei così serbar*
> *alla Spagna un salvatore!*
> *Ah! di me non ti scordar!*
> *Di me non ti scordar!*
> *Regnare tu dovevi,*
> *ed io morir per te. . . .*
>
> *Ah! salva la Fiandra—*
> *Carlo, addio . . . ah! ah!*

> I shall die, but happily,
> for so I have been able
> to preserve a savior for Spain!
> Ah, do not forget me!
> Do not forget me!
> You were destined to reign,
> and I to die for you. . . .
>
> Oh, save Flanders—
> Carlo, farewell . . . ah! ah!

This potentially ludicrous departure (what credible human being would die with "save Flanders" on his lips?) is rendered not only plausible but moving by music whose transparent textures capture Rodrigo's sublime ideological purity. The tune is introduced by an aching cantilena in thirds played by two cornets. We automatically recognize its harmonic kinship with the friendship duet of Act II. As if the connection were not already obvious, Verdi introduces an elegiac reminiscence of the friendship tune itself, played by a banda-like coalition of woodwinds, trombones, and tuba, between the aria's two verses.

The aria is constructed out of the same elements as its immediate predecessor: clear four-bar units (with each component phrase echoing an identical pattern), a transparent harmonic progression, and a firm guitar-like accompaniment in the orchestra. "The tune," laments Budden, "is plain to the point of cliché." It is indeed. Once again, however, its plainness is true to the man. Verdi has not run out of inspiration here; he simply knows that if Posa were to adopt the sophisticated musical ways of Carlo, Philip, Elisabeth, or even Eboli, he would betray a psychological depth incompatible with his essentially political existence. Hence the apposite rhetorical manner of his farewell.

A final musical point: Rodrigo's two arias in the death scene have a curious way of coalescing in the listener's mind. They seem, in recollection, to have been only different versions of the same piece. An examination of the score reveals that there are excellent grounds for this impression. Both melodies are in 4/4 time, both in major keys (E flat for "Per me giunto," D flat for "Io morrò"), and both marked to be sung at approximately the same tempo. Moreover, a comparison of their four-bar melodic units reveals a yet more striking similarity. In each, the melody of the first four bars moves gracefully downward a fifth or a sixth (from B flat to E flat in the "Per me giunto," from D flat to F in "Io morrò"), while the second four bars begin on the same pitch as the first and return to it after passing over an unusually high note (F in "Per me giunto," G flat in "Io morrò") in the penultimate phrase. In other words, if one were to chart these two melodies, the graphs would look remarkably alike.

I am inclined to say, on the basis of this evidence, that Rodrigo knows only one song. This is, of course, not literally true, but it identifies an important musical and psychological characteristic that distinguishes him from the other figures in *Don Carlo*. We often complain, metaphorically, of politicians that they play the same old tune, that they are like hurdy-gurdy men, forever grinding out their tired refrain. Rodrigo, it might be said, is guilty of this same fault, although in his case there is not even a hint of disingenuousness. He sings only one song because he has only one message, one devotion, one identity. He is an integral consciousness adrift in an ocean of divided selves.

Carlo

In all opera there can be no more improbable friendship than that between Rodrigo and Don Carlo. Just as Rodrigo is the quintessentially political animal, Carlo is one of those people who seem incapable of a coherent political thought. In the course of the opera, admittedly, he gets deeply involved in affairs of state, beginning with the friendship duet I have already discussed. But we are never in doubt that it is all pretend politics, and that he understands virtually nothing of the Flemish cause or the ideological principles that all but define Rodrigo's existence. Carlo's political acts are thinly disguised sublimations: Flanders is an excuse for expressing his hatred of his father. He is, in short, an entirely psychological creature, for whom politics are mere epiphenomena.

Carlo's very imperviousness to authentic political sentiment, however, is itself a political fact, and not merely because he is heir to the Spanish throne. The *Realpolitiker* knows that ideals must be tempered to accommodate the intransigency of human passions. Much of humanity is incapable of rising to the level of abstraction and self-denial that first makes Rodrigo and his ideals possible. Carlo epitomizes what might be called a subpolitical consciousness: a slave to his febrile emotions, sometimes excessively malleable but ultimately intractable, he is the sort of raw human material that must frustrate even the most resolute idealist. Through the strikingly different profiles he draws of Carlo and Rodrigo, Verdi calls attention to the limits of political action. Moreover, because Verdi has devised means to bring Carlo's tortured emotionality to musical life, we experience the contrast between a political and a psychological existence with an intensity unequaled even by so consummate a dramatist as Schiller.

Don Carlo is a long opera, and it contains many different kinds of writing. But I doubt that it offers any more extreme contrast than that between the two second-act duets in which Carlo participates: the first with Rodrigo, the second with Elisabeth. Indeed, only with difficulty can we believe that we are listening to the same character. In the duet with Rodrigo the rhythms are firm, the harmonies unambiguous, the scoring emphatic. In the duet with Elisabeth, by way of contrast, everything is unstable, elusive, and insubstantial. In the former, Rodrigo sets the tune, and Carlo enters momentarily into his musical and ideological world. In the latter, Elisabeth's role is largely reactive, and Carlo himself gives the piece its essential musical character. The duet, in fact, provides us with our fullest portrait of the Infante. It is also a piece of astonishing beauty, rivaled in Verdi's music for tenor and soprano only by the love music in *Otello*.

The Carlo who emerges in the duet is extraordinarily mercurial. To be sure, he is single-minded in his passion for Elisabeth. But Verdi's music reveals that beneath this seeming resoluteness lies an alarming instability. We sense this most subtly perhaps in the duet's rhythmic patterns, which are sometimes halting, sometimes propulsive, but always restless. In its 185 bars, there are eleven formal changes of tempo (where Verdi gives new metronome markings), and each of these sections contains further differentiations. At the heart of the duet is a forty-four bar segment, marked "meno mosso," with no less than ten indicated tempo fluctuations (ritards and *a tempo* marks). This passage, in which the rhythmic pulse is interrupted on the average of every four bars, stands at polar extremes from the music Verdi writes for Rodrigo, with its steady beat and unflagging forward momentum.

There is a comparable instability in the harmonic structure of the duet. Where Rodrigo's music generally sticks to a single tonality and to relatively conservative harmonic choices within that tonality, the music of the duet shifts from major to minor and from key to key, exploring the most exotic provinces in all its varied tonalities. The ear is aware of constant harmonic movement, and the changes are often sudden and unexpected. In spite of oases of stability, the overall harmonic impression is of a nervous chromaticism. Harmonically as much as rhythmically, Carlo's musical world lacks firmness.

Instability is also suggested by a distinctive melodic procedure Verdi adopts in the duet. A great many of its phrases both begin and end on non-tonic notes—generally on fifths, but sometimes on thirds—notes that are sustained for unusual lengths. The pattern is set in the very first phrase: it starts and finishes on a sustained fifth, while the intervening melodic line wanders through a series of eighth notes and triplets that float between the tonic above and the tonic below. Suspensions of this sort are used most hauntingly in the long melodic paragraph before Carlo's trance. Harmonically, this is the most stable portion of the duet, and one might expect its sweeping B flat major phrases (sung first by the tenor, then by the soprano) to set our feet firmly on the ground. But because each phrase comes to rest not on the home tone (B flat) but on a long-held third (D), the sense of being afloat persists. Altogether the duet contains fourteen phrases that end on this kind of suspended pitch, which, because the tones are sustained, have the effect of rhythmic suspensions as well. The music seems as incapable of melodic resolution as it is of rhythmic consistency, and it is thus an accurate reflection of Carlo's psychic fragility. By way of contrast, the music Verdi writes for Rodrigo has no trouble finding its home tone: "Per me giunto" scurries to its tonic E flat in both of its opening phrases, and "Io morrò" is launched from a confidently sustained tonic D flat.

Underlying Carlo's instability is his imperfect hold on reality. I have already suggested that Rodrigo is unable to see the world for what it really is (or for what Verdi thinks it really is). But Carlo's case is much more severe. If Rodrigo distorts reality, Carlo has simply lost touch with it. In the course of the duet he enters ever more deeply into the realm of fantasy, a progress Verdi charts with great musical precision.

Things begin realistically enough: Carlo asks Elisabeth to intercede on his behalf with the King to send him to Flanders. Her response couldn't be better chosen to trigger his Oedipal repressions and send him on his way, not to Flanders, but to oblivion. Her first words to him are "My son!" After a moment of shock, he settles into the first stage of his retreat from the world, a nostalgic recollection of former happiness:

> *Perduto ben, mio sol tesor,*
> *ah! tu splendor di mia vita!*
> *Udir almen ti poss'ancor.*
> *Quest'alma ai detti tuoi*
> *schiuder si vede il ciel!*

> Lost love, my only treasure,
> ah, you glory of my life!
> At least I can still hear your voice.
> At your words my soul
> sees heaven open wide!

Verdi locates these sentiments unmistakably in the world of dreams. The phrases progress in slow motion, as if the singer were under water, each musical sentence coming to a virtual halt on a final suspension. The scoring is dominated by high woodwinds (three flutes and a clarinet), which create a shimmering, diaphanous effect. Carlo has entirely forgotten the brassy political oaths he shouted with Rodrigo in the previous scene.

From this realm of nostalgic reverie he enters a visionary trance: fourteen measures in what Budden aptly calls "the 'illusory' D flat major," at the end of which he actually loses consciousness. Words are more than usually inadequate to describe the unearthly effect of Verdi's exquisite shift here from B flat major to D flat major, but that it signifies Carlo's further alienation from reality is apparent to every listener. The momentum slows, the scoring becomes yet more ethereal (harp arpeggios and very high strings), and Carlo is reduced to barely sequential ejaculations, each confined to a single note or interval, the voice seeming to sink lower with every utterance, until he finally collapses:

> *O prodigio! . . . Il mio cor . . .*
> *s'affida, . . . si consola; . . .*
> *il sovvenir . . . del dolor . . . s'invola, . . .*
> *il ciel . . . il ciel . . . pietà sentì di tanto duol.*
> *Isabella . . . al tuo pie' . . . morir . . . io vo' . . . d'amor.*

> A miracle! . . . My heart . . .
> gains hope, . . . is consoled; . . .
> the memory . . . of grief . . . vanishes . . .
> Heaven . . . heaven . . . has pitied so much pain.
> Isabella . . . at your feet . . . I want . . . to die . . . of love.

As Carlo regains consciousness, it marks not a return to reality but the final stage of his alienation. He has now passed into a delirium, which has been compared to Tristan's delirium in the third act of Wagner's opera. Like Tristan, he imagines himself actually present at the events that he had earlier visited only in memory: he is transported back to the forest of Fontainebleau and the vernal moment of his meeting with Elisabeth:

> *Ah! il ciel s'illuminò,*
> *la selva rifiorì!*
> *O mio tesor! sei tu—*
> *mio dolce amor! Sei tu!—*
> *bell'adorata,*
> *bell'adorata, sei tu, sei tu!*

> Oh, the sky is all aglow,
> the forest has bloomed again!
> Oh, my darling! It is you—
> my sweet love! It is you!—
> beautiful adored one,
> beautiful adored one, it is you, it is you!

Appropriate to a delirium, Verdi's music here modulates with almost every phrase; we have entered a completely psychic world, and all sense of fixed harmonic location is lost. Likewise, the orchestral writing reaches an eerie extreme, with tremolos, pizzicati, and harmonics in the strings. The passage also marks the only moment in which Verdi abandons the duet's stately 4/4 meter: nine bars in 3/4 time add yet further to the sense of instability and unreality.

Having passed from reverie to trance and finally to delirium, Carlo comes to his senses in the last portion of the duet (the cabaletta), but only to make the sort of wild declarations that confirm our sense of his precarious psychological estate. All emotional control lapses as he blurts out his feelings. "For me the world has vanished from existence," he says all too accurately, and he tells Elisabeth repeatedly that he loves her. The music here reverts to more familiar Verdian habits (it is sonorous, headlong, and regular), but the turbulent pace and violent orchestration accurately reflect Carlo's orgy of self-indulgence. It serves equally well for Elisabeth (a restraining influence throughout the duet), who now seizes the initiative and fulfills the promise of her Oedipal greeting with a hair-raising injunction:

> *Compi l'opra, a svenar corri il padre,*
> *ed allor del suo sangue macchiato,*
> *all'altar puoi menare la madre,*
> *ed allor all'altar puoi menare la madre!*
> *Va, va, va e svena tuo padre!*
>
> Finish your work, hurry to kill your father,
> and then, spattered with his blood,
> you can lead your mother to the altar,
> then you can lead your mother to the altar!
> Go, go, go and kill your father!

The effect of this long duet is to expose Carlo as a creature of sensibility, living in an inward world of dreams and romantic hyperbole, a figure no more suited to politics than Goethe's Werther. In fact, the duet has taken us about as far from political reality as one can imagine. Psychologically, Carlo has more in common with Pelléas than with Rodrigo, and given a few adjustments, one can almost imagine his music—at least that of his trance and delirium—integrated into the Debussy opera, where Rodrigo's would be unthinkable. Implicitly, moreover, the duet offers an ironic comment on Rodrigo's own political intelligence. Verdi heightens our sense of Rodrigo's impracticality by showing Carlo to be such an utterly inadequate vessel for the cause of Flemish liberty. The *Realpolitiker* casts a withering musical glance on this partnership between visionary idealist and romantic solipcist.

Philip

Philip is the richest character in *Don Carlo* and the one who most completely embodies Verdi's mature view of politics. He is, above all, a realist, a man who understands power. At the same time, however, he also suffers greatly from the exercise of power. One might say that his psychic life has something of the affective depths into which his son has fallen so completely. Thus he differs from Rodrigo not merely by virtue of his realism but also because, unlike Rodrigo, he is aware of the psychological costs of a political existence. Were he to indulge himself, one senses, he could become as much a creature of sensibility as his son.

Verdi's treatment of Philip thus differs considerably from Schiller's. As a document of the Enlightenment, Schiller's drama naturally focuses on the conflict between liberty and tyranny, and Philip, while not unsympathetic, plays the role of intolerant autocrat. By way of contrast, Verdi's opera, composed in the era of *Realpolitik,* takes a ruler's-eye view of the proceedings, and Philip thus emerges less a tyrant than a victim. He is a hero of sublimation, a man whom Verdi admires not merely for his intelligence but also for his conscious sacrifice of private happiness to the preservation of the state. In this respect he has something in common with Wagner's Hans Sachs.

He is, moreover, a figure who is richly prefigured in the Verdi canon. One can chart an ever-growing sympathy in the Verdi operas for the leader who gives up personal (usually romantic) satisfaction for the burdens of statesmanship. Philip's immediate precursor is Simon Boccanegra, whose political ambition effectively robs him of his family, and to whom Verdi extends enormous musical sympathy. But perhaps even more intriguing is the figure of Charles V in *Ernani,* an opera that is separated from *Don Carlo* by more than two decades. Charles V was Holy Roman Emperor from 1519 to 1556, when he abdicated to enter the Monastery of San Yuste. He was also, of course, the father of Philip II, and he actually appears in *Don Carlo* (or so the participants believe, despite the fact that its events transpire several years after his death) in the guise of a monk who, at the end of the opera, drags Don Carlo into the cloister. He thus bears both a genealogical and a dramatic relation to the figures in *Don Carlo,* and it seems fitting that he should provide Verdi with one of his earliest operatic occasions for the theme of sacrificial leadership.

The circumstances in *Ernani* are hardly designed to gain Charles our sympathy. *Ernani* is very much a Risorgimento opera, in which the subjection of sixteenth-century Spain under the Hapsburgs serves as a metaphor for Italy's subjugation under Austria in the nineteenth century. The Spanish outlaw Ernani becomes a spokesman for national liberation, while Charles is the representative of imperial despotism. Excoriated in a patriotic chorus ("Si ridesti il Leon di Castiglia") by a group of Castilian rebels, he is also Ernani's romantic antagonist.

The scene of Charles's election as Holy Roman Emperor, however, reverses our established emotional attachments. Here we witness a self-absorbed private citizen transformed into a political leader. Charles enters the tomb of his ancestor Charlemagne and sings an aria that anticipates the change he is about to undergo:

> *Oh, de' verd'anni miei*
> *sogni e bugiarde larve,*
> *se troppo vi credei,*
> *l'incanto ora disparve.*
>
> *S'ora chiamato sono,*
> *al più sublime trono,*
> *della virtù com'aquila*
> *sui vanni m'alzerò, ah,*
>
> *e vincitor de' secoli*
> *il nome mio farò.*

> Oh, dreams and lying forms
> of my youthful years,
> if I believed in you too much,
> the spell now has vanished.
>
> If now I am called
> to the most sublime throne,
> like an eagle I will rise
> on the pinions of virtue, ah,
>
> and I will make my name
> conqueror of the centuries.

The text is less than distinguished, but Verdi sets it to a noble high-baritone melody, with a hint of resignation, opening up in the last two lines into a series of magnificently sweeping phrases that pay musical tribute to the sublimation of private emotion (the "dreams and lying forms of my youthful years") into a grand public task. In the ensemble that follows (after three cannon shots have announced his elevation to Emperor), Charles leaves his private self, with its loves and hates, behind him in order to assume the responsibilities of a political existence. First he turns away from everybody present to apostrophize his great ancestor:

> *O sommo Carlo, più del tuo nome*
> *le tue virtudi aver vogl'io,*
> *sarò, lo giuro a te ed a Dio,*
> *delle tue gesta imitator.*

> O great Charles, more than your name
> I want to have your virtues;
> I shall be—I swear to you and to God—
> imitator of your achievements.

He then realizes his political identity in three gestures. To the conspirators he says: "I forgive all," magnificent in its brevity and lack of qualification. Then to himself: "I have mastered my desires," virtually a programmatic statement of the costs of political life. And, finally, to Ernani and the woman they both love: "You shall marry; love each other always," again a clipped and rending formulation of the romantic ideal that in that very moment he abandons for the good of the state. Having shown Charles's political transformation, Verdi proceeds to show the response to that transformation. Charles once again addresses the tomb of his ancestor:

> *A Carlo Magno sia gloria e onor!*

> To Charlemagne glory and honor!

to which every person on stage—all humanity, one senses—responds:

> *A Carlo Quinto sia gloria e onor!*

> To Charles the Fifth glory and honor!

The orchestra rushes downward in a series of earth-shaking scales, launching the final ensemble in celebration of the Emperor's greatness. For me it is the most thrilling moment in all of early Verdi, because it so exactly captures a profound psychological truth. I don't think one need know anything about the self-sacrificing career of the real

Charles V to share emotionally in Verdi's insight here into the costs of leadership.

In *Don Carlo,* not surprisingly, the theme of sacrificial leadership receives a considerably more probing, nuanced, and ultimately tragic representation. Charles V stands at the outset of his public career, and while his sacrifice is somberly recorded by Verdi, it is also celebrated in the splendid ensemble that concludes the scene on a note of exaltation. For Philip II there are no such musical rewards. Leadership for him is not a burden to be nobly assumed but a weary reality, which has already exacted its psychological price. Because there is no public to pay tribute to his sacrifice, the emphasis in the later opera is more unambiguously on the ruler's sorrows. Besides the instinctual renunciation stoically anticipated by the newly elected Emperor ("I have mastered my desires"), Philip has learned that rulership also brings unremitting loneliness.

Verdi signals this darker perspective by assigning Philip to a bass rather than a baritone. I argued earlier that the high baritone was his characteristic vehicle for political expression, and indeed Rodrigo, in *Don Carlo,* can legitimately be regarded as heir to the tradition of baritone politicians. But Verdi makes an exception for Philip. Only the bass voice, he seems to have known, could convey the King's gravity and black despair. Significantly, Philip is the only bass in all the Verdi operas who is made the center of psychological interest.

Although the King's loneliness is felt throughout the opera, it is explored most intensely in his fourth-act monologue, which, along with the death of Boris Godunov—another troubled ruler—is widely regarded as the greatest scene for bass voice in opera. Musically, it is composed of four parts: an orchestral introduction, a recitative, an aria (in the classic A-B-A form), and a brief coda in which we hear condensed versions of the B section of the aria and the recitative. The King is on stage alone for over ten minutes as this elaborate, patient, and entirely audible musical structure unfolds. In his study, as dawn breaks after a sleepless night, he muses on his unhappiness, giving explicit articulation to the theme of political sacrifice.

Most Verdi scholars have emphasized the motifs of sadness, loneliness, and obsessiveness in this famous scene. In doing so, I would argue, they have overlooked the equally important theme of royal power. The neglect is, in a sense, understandable because the representation of the King's power is an entirely musical achievement—the text hardly alludes to it. The music, however, is altogether unambiguous on the subject. Moreover, the musical reminders of his power are essential to Verdi's argument. Philip's unhappiness is not of the garden variety to which any of us might fall victim. Rather, he is sad, lonely, and obsessive because he has donned the royal mantle.

In the scene's thirty-two-bar orchestral introduction Verdi manages to conjure up the King's state of mind even before a word has been spoken. The ideas of sadness, loneliness, and obsessiveness are readily identified with its three musical ideas. Sadness is conveyed by what in technical language are called acciaccature. The acciaccatura is a device conventionally used to suggest weeping, an association based on the sonic resemblance between its two components—a tone preceded by a grace note on the semitone just below it—and the characteristic broken sound of a sob. The introduction begins with six of these musical sobs—six acciaccature octaves—played by horns, bassoons, and strings. Loneliness is suggested primarily by the solo cello that enters immediately after the last of these six acciaccature octaves. It does so by playing, quite literally, alone: in bars 5 to 8, 10 to 13, and 21 to 24 it is entirely unaccompanied, leading commentators to refer to this cello solo as a "soliloquy." Finally, obsessiveness is represented by a circling figure in the violins (beginning in bar 14), a figure that, like the acciaccatura, recurs throughout the scene. This reiterated violin pattern is the musical counterpart of the mind's going over a single thought again and again.

At the same time, the music of the introduction also creates a sense of the King's might. Indeed, the theme of power is already announced in the six acciaccature octaves with which the introduction begins. These are not pathetic little sobs, but loud and weighty orchestral utterances. Their extremely low pitch (extending downward over two octaves from the A below middle C), heavy scoring (four horns, four bassoons, the full component of strings), and substantial volume speak with incontrovertible authority. The person we are about to meet may be melancholy, but he is unmistakably potent.

Two other characteristics of the introduction further suggest a sense of power, although perhaps not so obviously. One of these is the music's stately pace. The introduction, and in fact the whole scene, has great rhythmic dignity. More subtly, Verdi creates an impression of spaciousness. At one level this is the dark, sepulchral spaciousness of the King's study in Madrid. But the largeness of the place is also a reflection of the largeness of the man, and it ultimately contributes to our sense of Philip's stature.

Verdi conveys this feeling of spaciousness most simply by leaving space in the music—i.e., through rests. We hear the opening octave three times, followed by a half measure of silence, in which the orchestral sound echoes as in a vast room. The pattern is immediately repeated: three octaves, played *forte,* and then silence. A similar gap follows each of the solo cello's phrases. Spaciousness is further conveyed by a musical procedure that will figure prominently throughout the scene: the exploitation of an extremely wide range of pitches. Instead of congregating in the same area, the different orchestral voices are set at great distances from one another—leaving, as it were, large sonic gaps between them. Thus after the low opening octaves, the solo cello enters nearly an octave above on a note that lies rather high in its range, from which it descends over two and a half octaves to a low C sharp. Thereafter the obsessive violin figures start more than two octaves above the solo cello's last note and proceed even higher. The music thus boasts a great vertical range, suggesting the architectural height of the room and translating, metaphorically, into a subliminal awareness of the King's stature. In the vocal writing that follows, Verdi will use the same technique to convey Philip's authority: the singer will repeatedly be asked to move over the widest possible range of pitches, often in a relatively short melodic compass.

The monologue proper has two great themes: loneliness and sleeplessness. One might say it covers the full spectrum of deprivations that the monarch must endure when he abdicates his private existence. He sacrifices both significant human relationships—love and friendship—and the more mundane physical gratifications—such as undisturbed sleep—that the ordinary citizen takes for granted. As the recitative begins, the King is "lost in thought," expressing himself only in broken phrases:

> *Ella giammai m'amò!*
> *No, quel cor chiuso è a me,*
> *amor per me non ha!*

> She never loved me!
> No, her heart is closed to me,
> she feels no love for me!

Save for the final line (which is repeated three times), Philip's music is confined to a few pitches. The musical interest of the passage remains in the accompaniment, which is composed of the three elements already familiar to us from the orchestral introduction: sobbing acciaccature, the cello melody, and the obsessive circling figures in the violins. Philip seems broken like his phrases, rising to significant musical statement only in the masochistic repetition of "amor per me non ha!"

The King then "recovers himself"—he comes out of his reverie to take note of the dawn—and he turns to his second theme: sleeplessness. At first his vocal manner is unchanged: he continues to sing in broken phrases, each keeping to a narrow compass of pitches. Suddenly, however, there is a burst of energy: in a five-bar passage marked "more animated," he takes charge of the music, subordinating the orchestra, like his subjects, and rising assertively into the upper register, from which he descends in the first of those majestic arpeggiated chords with which I have associated his authority. In this instance the voice sweeps downward from a sustained high D through a G major chord to low G an octave and a half beneath. The text to which this grand phrase is composed would seem to call for something altogether more recessive:

> *Passar veggo i miei giorni lenti!*
> *Il sonno, o Dio,*
> *sparì da' miei occhi languenti.*

> I see my days passing slowly!
> Sleep, Oh God,
> has vanished from my weary eyelids.

Verdi, however, insists on a kind of ostentatious flexing of the vocal muscles. Kings, it seems, express themselves majestically even on the subject of sleeplessness.

As with Hamlet, thoughts of sleep lead to thoughts of death and the peace of mind that it alone can assure. This is the subject of the A portion of Philip's aria, whose two phrases, sung quietly, move downward in a weary melodic declension from dominant A to tonic D:

> *Dormirò sol nel manto mio regal,*
> *quando la mia giornata è giunta a sera,*
> *dormirò sol sotto la vôlta nera,*
> *dormirò sotto la vôlta nera*
> *là nell'avello dell'Escurial.*

> I shall sleep in my royal mantle
> only when I attain the evening of my days,
> I shall sleep only beneath the black vault,

I shall sleep beneath the black vault
there, in my tomb in the Escurial.

Text, tonality (D minor), melody, and accompaniment combine to make this the central statement of Philip's sacrifice. The sobbing acciaccature now appear in the high woodwinds, and the obsessively circling violin figure has been refashioned into French horn harmonies beneath the King's lament.

The morose utterances of the aria's first section are followed by a passage whose musical effect is exactly the opposite. As in the final phrases of the recitative, the text hardly seems to call for a change:

Se il serto regal a me desse il poter,
di leggere nei cor, che Dio può sol
può sol veder.

If the royal crown could but give me the power
to read human hearts, which God
alone can see!

But Verdi again disregards the libretto. If the text alludes to a power the King doesn't have, the music speaks boldly of the power he in fact possesses. His confident B flat major melody, marked *forte,* is doubled emphatically in the lower strings and bassoon, as the violins and violas pound out staccato sextuplet rhythms, whose energy and assertiveness stand in direct contrast to the obsessively circling legato figures they play elsewhere. Most important, Philip's vocal line is composed entirely of the sweeping, athletic arpeggios that were heard originally at the end of the introductory recitative. The first two phrases carry the voice down and up a spacious B flat major chord; the last moves from a long-held high D flat down through a D flat major arpeggio to a gravelly low A flat, as the *fortissimo* orchestra suddenly breaks off and lets us hear the solo bass sweep majestically through its full compass. Each of these musical gestures has an almost ritualistic grandeur about it. The B section of the aria thus insists as clearly on the King's power as the A section insists on his unhappiness, and the musical juxtaposition makes us aware of their psychological interdependence.

Following the full repetition of "Dormirò sol," Verdi completes the scene with a pregnantly abbreviated representation of his great antithesis. The sonorous arpeggiated melody associated with the King's power returns, now transposed into D major. But after four measures, with the bass singing *fortissimo* on high D, the music is suddenly broken off, as the thunderous sound echoes out into empty space. There is a "long silence," like the silence following the opening chords—a silence that, in Julian Budden's words, "says clearly, 'What is the use?'" Philip then lapses into the broken phrases of the recitative—"Ella giammai m'amò"—as misery follows swiftly on the heels of authority. The argument is thus brought full circle, like the obsessive violin figures in the accompaniment. Power and agony are ineluctably linked.

The Grand Inquisitor

Philip's monologue is followed by a scene that, to my knowledge, has no parallel in operatic literature: the interview between the King and the Grand Inquisitor. Verdi's prelate, unlike Dostoevsky's, is not so much a person as a force. The Grand Inquisitor is of course Rodrigo's ideological antithesis—the spokesman for obscurantism and authoritarian reaction—and, appropriately, in the interview he demands that Rodrigo be handed over to the Inquisition. But Verdi does not treat the two men symmetrically. Rodrigo, for all his devotion to principle, is shown to be capable of friendship; we are made conscious of him as a psychological being, even if most of his emotional life has been sublimated into politics. By way of contrast, the Grand Inquisitor is so completely identified with his public role that the thought of him as a man with needs and desires—in other words, with any kind of psychological life—seems ludicrous.

Moreover, his principles, unlike Rodrigo's, are not to be taken at face value, since they serve only to mask his deeper concern for power. Verdi makes no effort, as he does with Rodrigo, to fashion a musical vocabulary that will bring the Inquisitor's supposed ideals—those of Roman Catholic orthodoxy—to life. He may speak the language of religion, but his true interest is in rulership. Hence, although the scene is often characterized as a musical distillation of the conflict between Church and State, Verdi, as a *Realpolitiker*, views the clash in entirely profane terms. His music does not associate one figure with the spiritual and the other with the temporal (as does Mozart's, for example, in the analogous vocal confrontation between Don Giovanni and the ghost of the Commendatore at the end of *Don Giovanni*). Instead of representatives of the City of God and the City of Man, we are shown two willful individuals struggling to control human destinies here on earth. Genuine spirituality in the opera is represented not by the Grand Inquisitor but by the ghostly Monk, whose beautiful, resigned music in Act II proclaims the vanity of earthly greatness.

Schiller's Grand Inquisitor, interestingly, is much more of an ideologue than Verdi's. In the play the interview between king and prelate takes place *after* Rodrigo's death, and the Inquisitor's main complaint is that the King has wantonly murdered Rodrigo instead of allowing the Holy Office to put him to good ideological use:

INQUISITOR:
God granted him unto this epoch's need
To make of swaggering Reason an example
By formal degradation of his mind.
That was my well considered plan. And now
It lies wiped out, my work of many years!
We have been cheated, robbed, and you have nothing
But bloody hands.

These hateful sentiments are a characteristic product of the Enlightenment's anticlericalism, and they find no place in the opera.

Verdi's utterly secular attitude toward the conflict determines the interview's musical organization. Everything about the scene is arranged to make us conscious of the essential similarity of the protagonists. Most important, Verdi assigns both parts to voices of identical range and format: both are basses of the darkest and heaviest variety. In terms of volume, breath control, and every other technical consideration, the parts call for vocalists with identical skills—which explains why singers who take on the Grand Inquisitor commonly graduate to the role of the King. In theory, such a protracted dialogue between two basses should be an operatic impossibility. Any confrontation between voices of similar range and caliber runs the risk of monotony, indeed of confusion, and basses are apt to sound even more alike than do singers belonging to other vocal categories, probably because our ears are less sensitive to nuance at these lower frequencies. But Verdi risks this unlikely pairing in order to make an intellectual, as well as an emotional, point.

His musical choice is especially remarkable when one considers that the Grand Inquisitor is in no sense the King's physical equal: he is ninety years old, blind, and must be supported by two Dominican monks as he shuffles into the room. From his appearance we might expect him to sound like Puccini's ancient Emperor Altoum in *Turandot:* the mere shell of a voice, his tenor pinched and tremulous, more squeaking than singing. But Verdi is not the least interested in verisimilitude. He has his mind set on a symbolic representation of the clash between two great forces. Since both singers wield the uniquely plangent and authoritative vocal equipment of a basso profondo, we experience their interview as a struggle between titans.

Even more so than in Philip's monologue, Verdi enlarges the characters by exploiting an unusually wide tonal spectrum. Each singer is asked to move his voice through the full compass of the bass's range, with individual phrases embracing an octave, an octave and a half, or even (in the case of the King's final line) two full octaves. Philip's part stretches from f' to F, and the Grand Inquisitor's from f' to low E (a half tone more than two octaves). Moreover, the notes at both extremes of the register must be fully and honestly sung: they are sustained tones that can't be negotiated with approximate vocal gestures. Hence the irony that Verdi's ninety-year-old ecclesiastic needs to be cast with a bass in his vocal prime. The rest of his body may be decrepit, but the vocal chords are those of a vigorous young man. The Grand Inquisitor spends less than ten minutes on stage, but the role can be done justice only by a basso of the first rank.

Like the voices, the orchestral writing is spread over a wide tonal spectrum. We are given an immediate taste of this in the opening bars: the Grand Inquisitor enters to a sepulchral theme that begins (on double basses and contrabassoon) three octaves below middle C— a note so deep that it reverberates like an organ pedal point. At the other extreme stands the moment when, as Philip reflects on the hopelessness of friendship, Verdi has the piccolo move up the scale to c'''', three octaves *above* middle C, and hence a full six octaves higher than the first tones on double bass and contrabassoon. He thus creates an enormous vertical space in which to locate his superhuman adversaries.

More than anything else, however, our sense that we are witnessing a confrontation between two men of power depends on the sheer athleticism of their singing. In order to make themselves heard above Verdi's dark and weighty orchestra—dominated by low strings, bassoons, trombones, and timpani—both basses must produce huge volumes of sound, singing at full tilt over a brutally extended range. Throughout the scene we are aware of the great physical effort both must exert—of the tremendous vocal power that each singer must command—and that awareness translates readily into the metaphor of politics.

The interview witnesses the gradual ascendancy of the Grand

Inquisitor over the King. Musically, the piece is a symmetrical structure comprising five parts. In the two outer units and the short central passage the tempo is slow and the singing about equally divided between the two antagonists. While hardly conversational, there is a feeling of verbal give-and-take. In the longer second and fourth movements, however, fast tempos prevail, and the music is devoted to the mounting arguments—and accusations—of the Inquisitor.

At first the King addresses the Inquisitor in the latter's capacity as theologian, asking whether he can in good conscience have his own son put to death for treason. The Inquisitor responds with casuistical justifications. Although the musical interest here lies primarily in the lumbering theme of the cellos, basses, bassoons, and contrabassoon, the vocal writing establishes the absolute parity of the two antagonists. They speak in alternating phrases confined to one or two tones and ending in an athletic downward interval of a fifth or an octave (as if they were flexing their vocal muscles for the battle to ensue). We are conscious that each singer begins virtually every phrase on the same note with which the previous singer ended and then proceeds to raise the pitch by half a tone. The result is a kind of musical thrust and parry. The exchanges begin in the vocally relaxed area between F and A, but as the interlocutors become more heated they move into the demanding B flat to D flat region, where a sense of strain becomes audible in both voices. In short, the King and the Grand Inquisitor speak to one another as musical equals. Both are potentates.

Philip thinks the interview is over, but instead of leaving, the old man says that he has a topic of his own he wishes to discuss. This announcement is converted into a musical insult, as the Inquisitor addresses the King ("Sire") on a characteristic octave drop, from E in the middle of the bass clef to a sub-basement E an octave beneath. It is the lowest note in the scene, indeed so low that it sounds more like a belch than a tone. Verdi cuts off the orchestra to let this sneer echo out into the house.

The Inquisitor then seizes the melodic initiative. In a series of brief, jab-like phrases, he delivers a sarcastic homily in which he upbraids the King for befriending the heretic Rodrigo. The redoubled tempo and forthright melody convey an immediate impression of his energy. There follows a disingenuous self-accusation, which is in reality a grand musical celebration of his own importance, beginning with a shamelessly reiterated personal pronoun:

> *Ed io, l'Inquisitor,*
> *io che levai sovente*
> *sopra orde vil' di rei*
> *la mano mia possente,*
> *pei grandi di quaggiù,*
> *scordando la mia fè*
> *tranquilli lascio andar*
> *un gran ribelle . . . e il Re!*

> And I, the Inquisitor,
> I who have often raised
> against the vile hordes of miscreants
> my powerful hand,
> for the great men here below,
> forgetful of my faith
> allow to go uncurbed
> a dangerous rebel . . . and the King!

Verdi provides the Inquisitor's veiled threats with music of the utmost forcibleness. The passage is composed in seven roughly parallel phrases, most of them ending in the (by now) familiar athletic downward interval and each seeming to rise higher than its predecessor until the voice is carried over a strangulating top F. The murderous tessitura and the deafening orchestral rattle (culminating in vicious brass octaves) designate the Inquisitor as very much a sovereign of this world.

Rather like his son, Philip retreats from this display of vocal power into the realm of fantasy. He thinks almost wistfully about the friendship he must now abjure. The sonorous cadences of the Inquisitor's speech give way to a thin descending line in the high violins, against which Verdi sets a rising scale in the flute and piccolo. The music has an eerie unreality, as if the idea of the King's having a true friend were the height of folly, a momentary lapse into an imaginary universe where even kings enjoy the familiar pleasures of a private existence.

The Grand Inquisitor, the least spiritual of creatures, has neither intellectual nor musical interest in such fantastical thoughts. His mind, like his music, belongs to the all-too-solid world of politics. Why should Philip need a friend? Why does he call himself King if lesser men are his equal? He interrupts the King's reverie with two characteristically athletic musical gestures, the first a downward octave leap, the second a vigorous arpeggio from a sustained high E flat down through the notes of an E flat major chord, supported by a series of earthly blasts from the trombones, tuba, and bassoons. The passage, one might say, marks a musical reversal of roles: the King sings of spiritual values to a mystical accompaniment of high strings and woodwinds, while the Inquisitor's sarcastic questions are bellowed out above emphatic, no-nonsense chords in the lower winds and brass.

The Inquisitor's second long speech is set to even faster music, thus confirming our sense of his extraordinary energy. He begins with three parallel phrases that push the voice toward its upper reaches, denouncing the King for wishing to break the power of the Church with his "feeble hand" (which stands in obvious contrast to his own "powerful hand"). Then, in a sudden shift of tactics, he turns to wheedling. The music remains brisk, but the Inquisitor adopts a mock-lyrical style. Accompanied by saccharine thirds and sixths in the high woodwinds, his voice drops to *pianissimo* and confines itself to a narrow compass of pitches in its sweet upper-middle register:

> *Ritorna al tuo dover;*
> *la Chiesa all'uom che spera,*
> *a chi si pente,*
> *puote offrir la venia intera.*

> Return to your duty;
> to the man who has hope in her,
> to him who repents,
> the Church offers complete forgiveness.

His smarmy vocal manner calls to mind another great ecclesiastical politician, the Jesuit Rangoni in Musorgsky's *Boris Godunov*. The voice dies out almost to a whisper, as he demands (on repeated G flats, marked *ppp*) that Rodrigo be handed over to the Inquisition.

The next thirty-seven bars witness an unrelenting intensification of verbal and musical violence. Forgetting Rodrigo, the Inquisitor now threatens to bring the King himself before the Inquisition. The pace is quickened to nearly three times the original *largo*, and, once again, we hear a series of short, jab-like phrases, rising to a mercilessly sustained top F and ending in a flamboyant octave-and-a-half descent through a B flat minor arpeggio. Finally, every theological pretense is abandoned, and the Inquisitor speaks openly and unapologetically in the brutal language of politics:

> *Dato ho finor due regi*
> *al regno tuo possente!*
> *L'opra di tanti dì*
> *tu vuoi strugger, demente!*

> I have already given two kings
> to your mighty realm!
> Madman, do you want to
> destroy the work of years?

Verdi pulls out all the musical stops for this last pronouncement. The Inquisitor's phrases are whiplashed by descending chromatic scales in the low strings, and he rises a final time into the bass's uppermost register, sustaining a high E for a full measure on the second syllable of "demente" ("madman"). (In the original French libretto this sustained E falls even more effectively on the word "destroy"—"détruire.") Text and music place him unambiguously in the realm of the profane, a man infinitely more concerned with the fate of the Spanish Empire than with the Kingdom of Heaven.

The interview ends on a note of operatic détente. As the double bass and contrabassoon figure reemerges in the orchestra, the music retreats from its splendid bombast to the broken phrases with which it began. The King asks for reconciliation, and the Inquisitor answers with an enigmatic "Perhaps." Philip's utter collapse seems registered in his final line, which he sings as the Inquisitor moves offstage, supported by his two Dominicans:

> *Dunque il trono piegar dovrà*
> *sempre all'altare!*

> So the throne must
> always bow to the altar!

But as he had done in the middle section of the King's monologue, Verdi again disregards his libretto to transform this textual defeat into a musical victory. He sets the line to a diapason F major arpeggio sung across two complete octaves from sustained high F at the very top of the voice to an even longer low F at the very bottom. It is the most spectacular vocal display in the opera and the logical fulfillment of the reiterated association of the arpeggio with political power. In a single musical stroke, Philip's authority is restored and the balance of power redressed.

CONCLUSION

"No single opera of Verdi's has undergone such a drastic reappraisal over the last twenty-five years as *Don Carlos*. From being regarded as gloomy, diffuse and musically unequal, despite many fine moments, it is now considered by many as Verdi's masterpiece." The words are Julian Budden's. *Don Carlo* enjoys its current esteem for a wide variety of reasons. In view of its musical splendor and psychological subtlety, its earlier unpopularity seems even more curious than the neglect still suffered by Berlioz's *The Trojans*. Nonetheless, I can't escape the suspicion that we respond more gratefully to it than did previous generations because at some level we find its vision of the world more like our own. Its unrelenting sobriety—its refusal to indulge in wishful thinking—speaks directly to the hardened sensibilities of a world that has seen two global conflicts as well as heretofore inconceivable atrocities, and that considers politics at best the maintenance of the balance of terror. Such a world appreciates the essential wisdom of Verdi's political judgments in the opera, and it finds solace in the extraordinary beauty with which those judgments are rendered.

Beneath this affinity, doubtless, lies an affinity between the age that gave rise to Verdi's masterpiece and our own. There is, in fact, an analogous pattern in the political trajectories of the nineteenth and the twentieth centuries. In both cases ideological politics during the first half of the century give way to pragmatic politics during the second half. In the nineteenth century the great political battles between liberalism and conservatism, culminating in the revolution of 1848, were succeeded by a half century of pragmatic compromise on the issues of representative government, nationhood, and industrialization. In our own time, the rabid ideological conflicts of the first half of the century, most notably the clash between communism and fascism, have dissolved into nearly four decades of post-ideological politics, for which the phrase "the end of ideology" has become the accepted label.

More so than our immediate forebears, then, we respond to the fundamental truth of Verdi's gallery of political portraits. Like him, we are inclined to take a slightly jaundiced view of idealists like Rodrigo, even while retaining a certain nostalgia for their undaunted belief in the power of convictions. We, too, congratulate ourselves on seeing through the theological pronouncements of the Grand Inquisitors of this world to the mean-spirited, profane motives that lie beneath. Self-indulgent romantics we regard as political incompetents and candidates for the psychiatrist's couch, and here again Verdi's portrait of the Infante seems only too accurate. But above all the sacrificial leader, however flawed, appeals to us, as he did to Verdi, as the only authentic hero in a world that has outlived idealism. To accept the responsibilities of power, as well as its extravagant emotional costs, is the sort of unglamorous heroism that we can still believe in. More than anything else, therefore, the great portrait of Philip II at the work's psychological and musical heart has made *Don Carlo* an opera for our time.

Art, Psyche, and Society

Richard Wagner's
> *Die Meistersinger*
and Richard Strauss's
> *Der Rosenkavalier*

I began this book by comparing two comic operas that span the gap between the eighteenth and the nineteenth centuries: Mozart's *Marriage of Figaro* and Rossini's *Barber of Seville,* the former a representative document of the Enlightenment, the latter a hardly less representative document of the revolt against the Enlightenment. I would like to end with an analogous comparison between two comic operas spanning, in this instance, the gap between the late nineteenth and the early twentieth centuries. Wagner's *Die Meistersinger von Nürnberg* and Strauss's *Der Rosenkavalier* are separated by just over four decades (the Mozart and Rossini are precisely three decades apart), but they occupy conceptual and moral universes as distinct from each other as Mozart's is from Rossini's.

A comparison of *Die Meistersinger* and *Der Rosenkavalier* will, on the surface, seem to have less to recommend it than a comparison of *The Marriage of Figaro* and *The Barber of Seville.* Mozart's and Rossini's operas, after all, are based on dramas by the same author and share a good deal of overlapping personnel. In fact, the characters and situations in the two works frequently get confused in the operagoer's mind. No such ambiguity afflicts *Die Meistersinger* and *Der Rosenkavalier,* the former about a singing contest in Reformation Nuremberg, the latter about romantic attachments and intrigues in the Vienna of Maria Theresa. The one portrays a robust bourgeois world of cobblers, goldsmiths, and town clerks, united in the cultivation of prosperity and art, the other a decadent world of self-indulgent aristocrats and *arrivistes,* largely concerned with erotic titillation and social maneuvering.

On the other hand, the operas have a number of things in common. They are probably the two most popular German operas in the repertory, and in my experience the same people who like the one are very apt to like the other. With rare exceptions the two operas also enjoy as much respect within the critical establishment as among the public at large. Both, moreover, are philosophical comedies. To be sure, Strauss is somewhat more given to slapstick than Wagner (though we must not forget the brutal treatment, both physical and musical, to which Wagner subjects Beckmesser at the end of the second act). Still, even *The Marriage of Figaro* (not to mention *The Barber of Seville*) is a fairly ribald entertainment alongside either one of them. More self-consciously than Mozart, they seek to address serious human problems within a comic format, and as a result they are the least funny and, for some, the most affecting comedies in the repertory.

There is an important structural consideration that makes a comparison of these two operas even more promising. At the emotional heart of each, I believe, lies an almost identical situation. Both are operas of romantic sacrifice, and that sacrifice, which is the source of their power to move us, takes the same form in each. Wagner and Strauss construct a romantic triangle of identical components: an older person and two younger persons. The romantic action of both operas is also the same: the older person (Hans Sachs, the Marschallin) is romantically attached to one of the younger persons (Eva, Octavian) but relinquishes his or her claim in favor of the other younger person (Walther, Sophie). The difference in the sexual composition of the two triangles is less important than their structural identity. As much as anything else, that difference reflects Wagner's partiality for the male voice and Strauss's even greater partiality for the female voice— which he compounds by assigning the one male character in his triangle to a mezzo-soprano.

The similarity extends to the triangle's emotional valence as well. Each composer's sympathies are lodged unambiguously with the older member of the triangle, whose heroism provides the drama with its finest moments. Hans Sachs and the Marschallin are in fact among the most admirable characters in opera. They are dignified, generous, insightful, self-mocking, and vulnerable, and we are deeply gratified when, in the course of the opera, their goodness comes to be acknowledged. For both, the events of the drama mark a moment of personal reckoning, although those events effect no fundamental alteration in them. Their circumstances are merely clarified.

At the opposite end of the spectrum stands the new romantic object, who is in both cases the least sympathetic, the least interesting, of the three characters. Walther von Stolzing impresses us as a callow young man, gifted but insensitive, and his melodies, for all their surface glamour, begin to cloy when heard alongside the nuanced and deeply beautiful music Wagner writes for Hans Sachs; by the end of the opera we have listened to his prize song at least once too often, in spite of the subtle variations that Wagner works into its repetitions. For her part, Sophie von Faninal is an empty-headed girl who has little to recommend her beyond youth, prettiness, and, I suppose, innocence. She pales beside the mature beauty and psychological depth of the Marschallin, and her music, like Walther's, is distinguished by a kind of agreeable tunefulness that is no match for the Marschallin's delicately contoured melodies and complex harmonies.

Appropriately, the young person who stands between these two and with whom both are in love also stands between them in the affections of the composer. Eva and Octavian are enriched by ambiguities untasted by their eventual mates, precisely because they have loved and in turn been loved by the older protagonists, whose full merit they come to appreciate. By virtue of that love, one senses, both of them have experienced a depth of existence that Walther and Sophie will never know. When one tries to picture their marital life, one can't avoid feeling that there will always be a gap in understanding and perhaps even a certain resentment. Both Wagner and Strauss foster this impression by writing music for Eva and Octavian that is tinged with melancholy and by giving them moments of singular dramatic or lyric eloquence in which they apotheosize their former lover.

Some readers will object to the notion of Eva as Hans Sachs's "former lover." And of course one of the most important differences between the two operas—a difference that obviously bears on their historical location—lies in the realm of sexual etiquette. *Die Meistersinger* adheres to a strict Victorian code in such matters, while *Der Rosenkavalier* flaunts its modern frankness about sexuality. Strauss's opera opens with the Marschallin and Octavian in bed together, after a prelude manifestly intended to represent their early-morning orgasm (or, if we follow William Mann, Octavian's premature ejaculation).

The relationship between Eva and Sachs, on the other hand, is utterly chaste. Indeed, it has a distinctly familial cast, not merely because of the difference in age between the two but because Wagner's text makes explicit that it began when Eva was still a child. Yet his text makes equally explicit that the relationship has in the meantime blossomed into an adult romance and that, until Walther's appearance, both Sachs and Eva anticipated it would end in marriage. To be sure, Sachs tries to make light of the proposition, as in the following exchange from Act II:

> EVA: *Da dacht' ich aus,*
> *ihr nähm't mich für Weib und Kind ins Haus.*
> SACHS: *Da hätt' ich ein Kind, und auch ein Weib:*
> *'s wär' gar ein lieber Zeitvertreib!*

> EVA: Then I thought:
> you might take me for wife and child into your
> house.
> SACHS: Then I should have a child, and a wife too:
> that would indeed be a pleasant pastime!

Like the Marschallin, Sachs knows all along that the relationship has no future, but also like the Marschallin, he would be less than human did he not occasionally indulge the prospect of its fulfillment. Thus if we set aside the question of sexual intimacy, the bond between Sachs and Eva is in fact remarkably similar to that between the Marschallin and Octavian.

The striking parallel between the two operas extends even to the fourth principals in the two dramas: Beckmesser and Ochs. Each is, of course, the main comic figure in his respective opera. More important, each bears the same relation to the opera's primary triangle: both are false pretenders to the affections of one of its members (although Beckmesser pursues the middle figure in the triad—Eva—while Ochs pursues the ingénue). Furthermore, both Beckmesser and Ochs are motivated in their courtship by extrinsic—that is to say, nonpsychological—considerations. To be precise, both are motivated by greed: Eva is the daughter of Nuremberg's richest citizen, the goldsmith Veit Pogner, while Sophie is the daughter of the wealthy parvenu Herr von Faninal.

Just as they are romantic interlopers, Beckmesser and Ochs also serve as parallel antagonists to Wagner's and Strauss's philosophical spokesmen. One might say that they occupy the same place in the argument of their respective operas. Beckmesser is Hans Sachs's intellectual adversary, the man who pointedly fails to grasp the organic relation between tradition and innovation, and who works to frustrate Sachs's painstaking efforts to assure Nuremberg's cultural renewal. Ochs stands in an analogously antagonistic relation to the Marschallin: he is as obtuse about the psychological imperatives of growing old as she is sensitive to them, for he finds nothing at all unsuitable in his prospective marriage to the innocent young Sophie. Indeed, precisely his boorishness prompts the Marschallin to her grave reflections about time and age in the final moments of the opera's first act. We appreciate the wisdom and generosity of Sachs and the Marschallin all the more because they are set in opposition to the stupidity and self-servingness of Beckmesser and Ochs. There is, moreover, even a musical similarity between these two "villains." Although Ochs is a more grateful role and lies considerably lower than Beckmesser, both parts call for "singing actors," and their music is accordingly more declamatory than that of the other principals. Not surprisingly, both roles are often taken on by singers whose vocal resources are relatively limited but who boast the histrionic skill to make an effective impression in the theater. Neither, in other words, inhabits the unambiguously lyrical world to which the members of the primary triangle belong.

I have called *Die Meistersinger* and *Der Rosenkavalier* operas of romantic sacrifice. Appropriately, the moment in which their sacrificial actions are concentrated elicits a similar musical response from the two composers. That moment comes at the end of the first scene of Act III in *Die Meistersinger* and at the end of the entire opera in *Der Rosenkavalier*. The different placement of this emotional crux reflects, as we shall see, the single most important difference in the operas' intellectual assumptions. I would like to start, however, by calling attention to the similar dramatic and musical procedures adopted by Wagner and Strauss in their representation of this moment. Both composers begin with the sacrificial gesture itself, which they render all the more effective by treating it in a glancing, almost offhand fashion. It is followed by an apotheosis of the sacrificial protagonist sung by the onetime lover. And, finally, the scene culminates in a musical event of striking beauty and elaborateness—a quintet in Wagner, a trio in Strauss—whose effect is to reward the protagonist's generous act with a musical celebration.

In Act III, Scene 1, of *Die Meistersinger*, Eva has come to the cobbler Sachs in the hope of finding out what happened to Walther during the Midsummer Eve riot. She is unaware that the young knight is actually present in the house, but she apparently senses that Sachs knows something. Their exchange is conducted entirely in terms of what might be called the opera's economic metaphor: they discuss Eva's shoes, whose contradictorily unsatisfactory condition (at once too loose and too tight) is an obvious, and perhaps excessively coy, reference to her love for Walther and the foiled elopement of the previous evening.

While Sachs is bending over one of the troublesome shoes, Walther appears in the doorway behind his back. Eva lets out a stifled cry as Wagner's orchestra breaks into the rapturous motive called the Magic of Midsummer Eve. Sachs knows exactly what has happened, but he feigns ignorance. As the transfixed young lovers gaze at each other, he enters upon a grumbling monologue about his profession. He even pretends to revive the idea of marrying Eva himself. One might say that he takes advantage of her oblivion to confess his true feelings, but does so in a self-deprecatory manner that marks the confession as in reality a renunciation. The effect is strangely wrenching:

> *Kind, hör' zu! Ich hab mir's überdacht,*
> *was meinem Schustern ein Ende macht:*
> *am besten, ich werbe doch noch um dich;*
> *da gewänn' ich doch 'was als Poet für mich!—*
> *Du hörst nicht d'rauf?—So sprich doch jetzt!*
> *Hast mir's ja selbst in den Kopf gesetzt?*

> Child, listen! I have thought over
> what will put an end to my cobbling:
> it will be best if I woo you after all;
> then I might still win something for myself as a poet!—
> You aren't listening?—Now say something, then!
> Wasn't it you who put the idea into my head?

The sight of Eva has inspired Walther to compose the third section of his Dream Song, which he proceeds to sing. At its conclusion, Sachs asks Eva—with the by now familiar metaphorical insinuation—whether her shoe isn't at last satisfactory. She immediately grasps the sacrifice he has made and falls against him in a violent fit of tears, which Wagner's orchestra marks with fourteen bars of *fortissimo* throbbing. Sachs copes with his dangerously exposed emotions by retreating once again into the occupational grousing that is his characteristic defense mechanism. It is the sort of embarrassed exercise in self-deprecating garrulousness that veritably begs to be interrupted.

And interrupt him Eva does, launching an exalted lyric tribute to Sachs that Ernest Newman calls "one of the blinding emotional highlights of the opera." Its opening line—"O Sachs! Mein Freund! Du teurer Mann!" ("O Sachs! My friend! You dear man!")—begins on high G and rises in the second measure (on "friend") to an ecstatic B natural. Many of its phrases embrace unusually wide intervals, carrying the voice through spans of an octave or more and thus lending Eva's thanksgiving an uncharacteristic expansiveness. They also mount in intensity (as well as in pitch) as she reveals the depth of her love:

> *O Sachs! Mein Freund! Du teurer Mann!*
> *Wie ich dir Edlem lohnen kann!*
> > *Was ohne deine Liebe,*
> > *was wär' ich ohne dich,*
> > *ob je auch Kind ich bliebe,*
> > *erwecktest du mich nicht?*
> > *Durch dich gewann ich,*
> > *was man preist,*
> > *durch dich ersann ich,*
> > *was ein Geist!*
> > *Durch dich erwacht,*
> > *durch dich nur dacht'*
> *ich edel, frei and kühn:*
> *du liessest mich erblüh'n!—*
> *Ja, lieber Meister! schilt mich nur!*
> *Ich war doch auf der rechten Spur:*
> > *denn, hatte ich die Wahl,*
> > *nur dich erwählt' ich mir:*
> > *du warest mein Gemahl,*
> > *den Preis reicht' ich nur dir!*

O Sachs! My friend! You dear man!
How can I reward you, noble man!
> What would I be without your love,
> without you?
> Wouldn't I have remained always a child
> if you had not awoken me?
> Through you I have won
> what people prize,
> through you I learnt

the workings of the mind;
by you awoken,
only through you did I think
nobly, freely and boldly:
you made me bloom!
Yes, dear Master, scold me if you will;
but I was on the right path,
for, if I had the choice,
I would choose none but you;
you were my husband,
I would give the prize to none but you!

It is an extraordinary speech to make in front of one's future mate, and, indeed, without having addressed so much as a word to him. Eva's language is surprisingly erotic, with its references to "awakening" and "blooming," and, as Newman observes, the orchestral theme that accompanies her outburst is reminiscent of *Tristan und Isolde*. Significantly, her melody is constructed from Sachs's own Resignation motive.

Eva's other great lyric moment in the opera follows soon after this tribute: her voice launches the splendid quintet "Selig, wie die Sonne" ("Blissful as the sun"), whose first twelve measures are in fact a solo for the soprano. Although the pace is more measured than that of "O Sachs! Mein Freund!" Wagner again composes her opening statement in a series of ecstatically rising phrases, carrying the voice over high A flat. Ostensibly the quintet is intended as a celebration of Walther's new song, which Sachs has just baptized the "selige Morgentraum-Deutweise" ("blessed morning-dream-interpretation-melody"), but once the other four voices have joined Eva's, not a word is intelligible. Instead we hear a long musical structure of exceptional complexity and beauty, in which the voices weave in and out of the orchestral fabric until they reach a brilliantly unanimous G flat major resolution. The opera's generally realistic temporal continuum is interrupted here as nowhere else, and we experience this sudden intrusion of polyphony as if it were a wordless, symphonic commentary on the events to which we have just been witness. Its true object of celebration, we sense, is not Walther's song but Hans Sachs's sacrifice.

Let me now turn to the comparable scene in *Der Rosenkavalier*. The Marschallin's sacrificial gesture is concentrated in the moments following the departure of Baron Ochs, above all in her brief colloquy with Sophie. As in *Die Meistersinger*, embarrassment plays a crucial role in the scene, although the embarrassment is not the Marschallin's but Octavian's, for he finds himself caught between the two women ("Der Bub, wie er verlegen da in der Mitten steht"—"How embarrassed the boy is, standing there in the middle"). In a literal sense, the Marschallin's gesture consists in rescuing him from his embarrassment. She does so by addressing Sophie, for the first time in the scene—indeed, in the entire opera. Thus Strauss, like Wagner, renders the moment all the more effective by having his protagonist act indirectly: in speaking to Sophie the Marschallin in fact speaks to Octavian, giving her blessing to his new alliance and thereby sealing her own renunciation. The music, however, is less reticent: as she turns to Sophie, the orchestra plays the theme associated with her love for Octavian.

In keeping with her exalted social estate, the Marschallin expresses herself in a more elegant fashion than the humble Hans Sachs. Where Sachs was all bourgeois awkwardness, the Marschallin is arch, even slightly condescending. The libretto indicates that she is to look at Sophie "critically but kindly" ("prüfend aber gütig"). Her remarks are set to the music from Act I with which she had said that parting must be taken lightly, "with light heart and light hands":

> *Red' Sie nur nicht zu viel, Sie ist ja hübsch genug!*
> *Und gegen den Herrn Papa sein Übel weiss ich etwa eine*
>   *Medizin.*
> *Ich geh' jetzt da hinein zu ihm und lad' ihn ein,*
> *Mit mir und Ihr und dem Herrn Grafen da*
> *In meinem Wagen heimzufahren—meint Sie nicht,*
> *Dass ihn das rekreieren wird. und allbereits*
> *Ein wenig munter machen?*

> Don't talk too much. You are pretty enough as it is.
> And as for your father's illness, I think I know the cure.
> I will go in to him now and invite him
> to drive home in my carriage with me
> and you and the Count there—don't you think
> that will restore him, and quickly
> raise his spirits?

The actual substance of her speech is as insignificant, as circumstantial, as Sachs's monologue about Eva's shoes and the tribulations of a cobbler's existence, but the effect is no less powerful. William Mann calls it "the sweetest, most gracious and most moving speech perhaps in all opera."

Moreover, like Sachs's speech, it elicits an immediate tribute. To be precise, two tributes. First from Sophie:

> *Euer Gnaden sind die Güte selbst.*

> Your Grace is goodness itself.

And then, more significantly, from Octavian, who, although he can muster nothing so transcendent as Eva's "O Sachs! Mein Freund!" nevertheless salutes the Marschallin in three apostrophes. By setting them to an expectant dominant seventh chord, Strauss gives the impression that they are the beginnings of a longer outpouring for which Octavian can't find the words and which, in any case, would probably sound somewhat fulsome in the context of the opera's generally understated and indirect discourse. However abbreviated, they have a memorable effect:

> *Marie Theres', wie gut Sie ist.*
> *Marie Theres', ich weiss gar nicht—*

> Marie Theres', how good you are.
> Marie Theres', I do not know—

And then, simply:

> *Marie Theres'!*

This final salute announces the start of the famous trio, which resembles its counterpart in *Die Meistersinger* in a number of particulars. As with Wagner's quintet, time is halted while the characters vent their independent reflections, although the effect here is perhaps less startling, if only because Strauss, unlike Wagner, has already used this technique during the scene of the presentation of the rose in Act II. Like the quintet, the trio begins with a single soprano voice (the Marschallin's), which floats alone above the orchestra for the first twelve bars. Also like its predecessor, it is constructed as a large polyphonic tapestry—each number lasts approximately four minutes—in which the voices overlap and interweave with one another, reaching their final D flat major consonance by way of an extended chromatic resolution. The trio and the quintet are further united by their stately tempo, their major tonality (G flat major in Wagner, D flat major in Strauss), and their triple meter.

Again, the musical proceedings seem more symphonic than operatic, and, accordingly, we experience the trio as a kind of abstract celebration of the preceding events. As in "Selig, wie die Sonne," the words are virtually incomprehensible, both because of the music's contrapuntal texture and because the high female voice (much of the writing lies in the upper octave) produces the least intelligible of all operatic sounds. Nonetheless, Strauss's text, unlike Wagner's, speaks directly to the Marschallin's sacrifice, particularly in her own opening lines:

> *Hab' mir's gelobt, ihn lieb zu haben in der richtigen Weis',*
> *dass ich selbst sein Lieb' zu einer andern noch lieb hab'!*

> I vowed to love him in the right way,
> so that I would even love his love for another!

If we are especially attentive we might also catch the words of Sophie's nineteen-bar melodic paragraph, whose arching phrases twice carry the voice up over high B flat and whose text sums up the relationships of the opera:

> *Ich möcht' mich niederknie'n dort*
> *vor der Frau und möcht' ihr was antun,*
> *Denn ich spür', sie gibt mir ihn*
> *und nimmt mir was von ihm zugleich.*

> I want to kneel there before the lady
> and want to do something to her,
> because I sense that she gives him to me
> and at the same time takes something of him away from
> me.

The trio doesn't actually conclude Strauss's opera (it is followed by the duet for Octavian and Sophie), but it never fails to register as the work's musical and dramatic climax. Indeed, it holds that position more unambiguously than does the quintet in *Die Meistersinger*. The reason for this has nothing to do with the relative emotional intensity of the situations or the musical worth of the two pieces. In both respects, the trio and quintet are arguably on the same elevated plane. Yet there is an important difference in their dramatic location: Wagner's quintet is followed by the Midsummer Day festival, a scene that has no counterpart in Strauss, and in which the celebration of Hans Sachs's goodness is transferred from the private to the public realm. The difference between the two works in this respect exactly mirrors the single most important shift in aesthetic sensibility between the nineteenth and the twentieth centuries: the withering of artistic interest in the social dimension of reality and the ever more exclusive focus on the psychological—the sort of shift that one notes, for example, as one moves from the novels of Balzac and Dickens to those of Proust and Joyce.

The Marschallin's sacrifice is thus an entirely personal affair, and once it has been memorialized in Strauss's great trio there is nothing more to say. But because Sachs's sacrifice is communal as well as personal, the private memorialization of the quintet is succeeded by the grand public ceremony of the festival. As a consequence, the quintet must, so to speak, compete for a place in our affections with the equally moving tributes Sachs receives from the citizens of Nuremberg as they assemble in the meadow outside their town.

This difference between a social and a psychological perspective is already anticipated in the sacrificial scene itself. The alert operagoer will have noticed that I passed over, in my account, a crucial moment in the action between Eva's solo and the quintet: Sachs's promotion of his apprentice David to journeyman. There is a curious emotional resonance between this action and the romantic sacrifice that is the principal object of our attention during the scene. David, one might say, is the social or communal equivalent of Eva: although he stands in an essentially economic relation to Sachs (as apprentice to master), the act of elevating him to journeyman entails an identical severing of deeply felt and long-established personal ties. Henceforth, like Eva, he will be independent of Sachs, free to pursue his career and to marry. The moment never fails to tug at the heart, precisely because David's promotion shows us another instance of Sachs's renouncing a relationship that had been a major source of comfort to him.

In the Marschallin's universe, however, there is no one even remotely comparable to David, for the simple reason that it is a universe shorn of significant social relationships. To be sure, the characters in the opera all have identifiable social positions, but about none of them are we made to feel anything more than indifferent. Instead, the meaningful bonds in *Der Rosenkavalier* are entirely psychological in nature. As a result both the Marschallin's character and Strauss's opera suffer a relative emotional impoverishment, and the climactic trio must bear a correspondingly heavier artistic burden.

The matter of David's promotion and the Midsummer festival suggests one important respect in which the theme of romantic sacrifice, otherwise so remarkably alike in the two operas, takes on different connotations as one moves from Wagner to Strauss. In the remainder of this chapter I wish to pursue the logic of this and other differences between the two works. Because the emotional triangles at the heart of *Die Meistersinger* and *Der Rosenkavalier* are so much alike, one is all the more curious to know why the works as a whole should leave such strikingly dissimilar impressions. The most interesting source of that dissimilarity, I'm convinced, is a shift in the general climate of opinion between the late nineteenth and the early twentieth centuries. It is, in other words, a product of changes in the intellectual realm.

Art and Society

I have begun by exploring the romantic theme that *Die Meistersinger* shares with *Der Rosenkavalier*. But in terms of its larger concerns, *Die Meistersinger* might more profitably be compared to Verdi's *Don Carlo*. Like *Don Carlo* (which premiered a year before it), *Die Meistersinger* addresses fundamental issues of public order and justice. At its center, as in *Don Carlo,* stands an essentially political protagonist, the revered city elder of Nuremberg, Hans Sachs, who, like Philip II, is shown to abdicate a measure of personal happiness to fulfill his public calling. Furthermore, *Die Meistersinger* and *Don Carlo* are set in the same period: both take place in the sixteenth century, the era of European state-building.

Because Wagner's story transpires on a much smaller historical stage than Verdi's, one is apt to overlook the affinity between the two works. But the difference in scale is more apparent than real, since Nuremberg's experience is meant to be a representative one. That is, Wagner intends his little town to stand as a microcosm of German society—indeed, of the social order in its entirety. In his famous "Wahn" monologue, for instance, Sachs draws our attention to Nuremberg's representativeness by placing the town securely in Germany's heartland:

> *Wie friedsam treuer Sitten,*
> *getrost in Tat und Werk,*
> *liegt nicht in Deutschlands Mitten*
> *mein liebes Nürenberg!*

> How peacefully with its faithful customs,
> contented in deed and work,
> lies, in the middle of Germany,
> my dear Nuremberg!

Wagner underlines the importance of Sachs's reflection by composing these lines to a sequence of memorable rising phrases, above a dominant pedal that is sustained for twelve bars before it resolves, gratifyingly, into the tonic on the last word—"Nuremberg." In the elaborate symbolism of Sachs's "Schusterlied," which he sings to prevent Eva and Walther from eloping, the town is even identified with paradise: it stands, in other words, for the whole of the civilized world, beyond which lies only desert. Sachs interferes with the lovers' elopement not out of jealousy but in order to protect them from an act they would ultimately regret, since to leave Nuremberg, in effect, means to leave civilization. Nuremberg, then, is the archetypal town in the archetypal society, and Hans Sachs is its archetypal leader.

There is, however, an important difference between Verdi's and Wagner's characterization of the political order—beyond the fact that Wagner sets his drama in the intimate, microcosmic world of a small city, while Verdi's occupies the grand arena of the nation-state. In Verdi's opera we confront political power in the raw: we are shown men whose entire public lives are devoted either to the art of statecraft or to political rebellion. In *Die Meistersinger,* by way of contrast, politics are mediated by other realities. The twelve Mastersingers celebrated in the work's title are, of course, politicians: they are the town's governors, and although they may rule in a more democratic and humane spirit than Philip II, they enjoy the same sort of authority over the lives of the town's citizens as Philip II does over the subjects of the Spanish Empire. But unlike Philip, they are only part-time politicians. Indeed, their very claim to political authority is ultimately based on their accomplishments outside the political realm.

For one thing, the Mastersingers are also businessmen. Besides running the town's government, they are the backbone of its economy. Their number includes a shoemaker, a goldsmith, a furrier, a tinsmith, a baker, a pewterer, a grocer, a tailor, a soapmaker, a stocking-weaver, and a coppersmith. Significantly, only Sixtus Beckmesser is without an independent economic identity: he is the town clerk and thus the sole full-time politician in the opera—a circumstance that has obviously proved detrimental to his character.

Even more important, these urban politicians are also artists. They are all poets, composers, and, of course, singers. Each of them has earned the title of Mastersinger through arduous training and testing of his artistic skills. Moreover, they are not merely artists in their spare time—in the way that a modern businessman might take up tennis or golf or bridge. Just as their right to rule depends on their achievements in the commercial realm, so they must prove themselves Mastersingers if their political authority is to enjoy true legitimacy. Wagner's Nuremberg, then, is a town governed not merely by its leading entrepreneurs but by its leading artists as well. At the heart of his conceit rests the unlikely proposition that political leadership, economic success, and artistic creativity should be united in the very same individuals. Karl Marx, no doubt, would be amused to find the great bourgeois ideal of the division of labor so flagrantly violated in Wagner's middle-class paradise. But one can just as well argue that no work of art gives clearer illustration of the essential identity of bourgeois political, economic, and cultural aspirations—which was, of course, one of Marx's great themes.

Although I have characterized Wagner's proposition in *Die Meistersinger* as "unlikely," in fact his vision of a union of political, economic, and artistic values was anything but an isolated phenomenon in the culture of the later nineteenth century. The very same ideal provided the inspiration for the widespread artistic and intellectual movement that generally goes by the name of aestheticism. The movement is most closely associated with a group of English thinkers, of whom John Ruskin is doubtless the best known. Alongside Ruskin, the aestheticist tradition included such other adepts as the socialist William Morris (the founder of the Arts and Crafts movement) and the poets and painters allied with Dante Gabriel Rossetti in the Pre-Raphaelite Brotherhood. Its ideas also found resonance in the writings of Friedrich Nietzsche, especially Nietzsche's philosophical analysis of Greek art and civilization in *The Birth of Tragedy* (1872). It extended, in a looser fashion, to embrace a whole roster of *fin de siècle* literary and artistic figures.

The common assumption shared by all the representatives of the aestheticist tradition was a conviction that art and society are intimately linked. They insisted that the vitality of one could not be considered in isolation from that of the other: social well-being and artistic excellence were mutually dependent. Ruskin, for example, held that the artistic worth of any object was a function of the pleasure its maker obtained in creating it. "I believe the right question to ask, respecting all ornament," he wrote, "is simply this: Was it done with enjoyment—was the carver happy while he was about it?" A work of art that resulted from toil or alienated labor was for him without aesthetic merit—a judgment he extended with courageous consistency to the Egyptian pyramids. It followed that a social order based on exploitation—whether it be that of ancient Egypt or of modern industrial England—could create nothing of artistic value. Beauty, one might say, was a function of justice.

Moreover, the inverse proposition was also true: exactly as art depended for its worth on the social order that gave rise to it, so social well-being in turn depended on the cultivation of beauty. A society that did not honor and cultivate art was doomed: it inevitably grew oppressive and finally collapsed under its own weight. Thus Ruskin rejected the notion of art as a decorative luxury, an "extra" (comparable, say, to a fine cuisine) that lent society a certain glamour and refinement, but that could ultimately be dispensed with. On the contrary, art was a matter of the gravest urgency. It held the key to a society's survival.

Ruskin was thinking primarily of the Christian Middle Ages in this analysis, which received its most forcible expression in his three-volume work *The Stones of Venice* (1851–1853), especially the chapter entitled "The Nature of Gothic." He found in the civilization that built the Gothic cathedrals a perfect model of what the relation between art and society ought to be. The medieval artisans created ornaments of genuine beauty because they worked with pleasure, and the society based on such artisan labor was informed throughout by a sense of justice and proportion. It was, of course, a hierarchical society, in which masters, journeymen, and apprentices all had their proper place. But in contrast to the regimented democracy of modern capitalism—which produced nothing but ugliness and depended on brutal exploitation—the civilization of the Middle Ages represented a peak of artistic achievement and social harmony. Moreover, if society was ever to be made whole again, according to Ruskin, art would have to be restored to its wonted dignity.

Wagner's *Die Meistersinger* might almost be thought of as an operatic demonstration of the theory of art and society articulated by Ruskin in *The Stones of Venice*. I am not aware that Wagner ever read Ruskin, or that he was at all familiar with the broader intellectual movement of which Ruskin was the leading spirit. But his opera couldn't be better designed to illustrate the aestheticists' ideas about the relation of artistic creativity to social well-being. In common with aestheticist doctrine, *Die Meistersinger* identifies art with craft: its artists are also businessmen, who produce not only songs but shoes, and who consider the latter just as worthy of their creative energies as the former. Even more important, the opera proposes, just as Ruskin did, that bad art leads to social disintegration, while good art provides the cement that alone can result in social harmony. This thesis is argued not merely in Wagner's text but in his music as well.

It is represented most schematically in the opera's grand, symbolic opposition between Midsummer Eve, the subject of its second act, and the festival of Midsummer Day, with which the opera concludes.

Midsummer Eve and Social Disintegration

Act II of *Die Meistersinger* culminates in a scene of social disintegration: the Midsummer Eve riot. At precisely the moment when all the citizens of Nuremberg should be sound asleep, they in fact erupt into a street brawl. Moreover, although the immediate causes of the riot are clearly identified, they are in no sense adequate to explain why these men and women should rise in the middle of the night to curse and pummel one another with such abandon. This is not a riot, in other words, like the one that occurs during the Council Chamber scene of Verdi's *Simon Boccanegra,* where the representatives of different factions (the "patricians" and the "people") give vent to objective social and political grievances. Rather, as Sachs muses the following morning, the Midsummer Eve riot appears a product of sheer madness. Its inexplicability, furthermore, is very much to the point: it reminds us of the barely repressed hostilities that lie beneath society's civilized veneer and that threaten to explode it. There can be little doubt that Wagner in fact wishes to show us a society coming apart at the seams. Social cohesion, he suggests, is a precarious achievement, which can at any minute dissolve into a cauldron of murderous antagonisms. The scene brings to mind Freud's argument in *Civilization and Its Discontents* about the implacable hatreds hidden behind civilization's irenic facade.

If we examine the circumstances that precede the riot and that are its immediate, though hardly adequate, cause, we see that they are all manifestations of egoism, of the assertion of private desire over the claims of society. In the background (both literally and figuratively) are the two young lovers, Eva and Walther: throughout the scene they huddle upstage in the bushes behind a linden tree, their elopement confounded first by Sachs, then by Beckmesser, and ultimately by the outbreak of the riot. But primary responsibility for the unleashing of social chaos belongs to Beckmesser himself, who has come with his lute to serenade Eva, and who imprudently agrees to allow Sachs (whose shop lies across the alley from the Pogner residence) to "mark" the errors in his song with a stroke of the shoemaker's hammer. Beckmesser, of course, commits so many errors that there is a veritable orgy of hammering, and in his increasing agitation he sings louder and louder. It is not long before the neighbors begin to stir, especially after David, mistakenly thinking that Beckmesser's serenade is intended for his beloved Magdalena, throws himself on the hapless town clerk with a cudgel. Magdalena screams for help, and now all hell breaks loose. The town's bedrooms are emptied, its citizens spill onto the stage, and the full-scale riot is launched.

Appropriately, not a word can be understood in the bedlam that ensues, although Wagner has in fact written an elaborate rhymed text for his rioters, taking up over one hundred lines in the libretto. He divides them into five groups: the Neighbors, the Apprentices, the Journeymen, the Masters, and the Women (who don't actually partic-ipate in the scuffling but shriek at one another from the windows and ultimately pour water on the men below). Everyone takes advantage of the occasion to repay some private grudge, acting out hostilities that in the daylight hours would have been repressed. "I've owed you this for a long time," they yell at one another. And we read—although we can't hear—remarks like the following:

> *Seht dort den Christian, er walkt den Peter ab!*
> *Mein! Dort den Michel seht, der haut dem Steffen eins!*

> Look at Christian, he's thrashing Peter!
> My, look at Michel, he's clubbing Steffen!

The various occupational groups take turns blaming each other: "Don't we know those locksmiths? They're sure to have started it! . . . It's the weavers! It's the tanners!" Even the Masters, who begin by calling for order, eventually give in to the madness: "Now there's nothing for it, Masters! Hit out yourselves!"

Anyone who has seen a performance of *Die Meistersinger* will easily remember the visual image of social disorder created by this scene, with its vast numbers of people rushing about the stage, shouting in all directions, and drubbing one another indiscriminately. Wagner's music for the riot is brilliantly crafted to enhance this impression of disorder. Indeed, he has found the perfect musical vehicle to represent social breakdown: he composes the riot as a massive fugue. In reality, of course, his music is not chaotic at all, since a fugue is one of the most organized and disciplined of musical structures. But it serves splendidly to convey a sonic *impression* of chaos. It does so by pitting the various voices against one another in what sounds very much like a musical battle. (Verdi uses a fugue to similar effect in the battle scene at the end of *Macbeth*.) The musical phrases, like the citizens of Nuremberg, move at cross-purposes, intersecting one another, overlapping, and becoming ever more entangled. The score reveals the extraordinary complexity of Wagner's contrapuntal tour de force, which sometimes contains as many as sixteen distinct vocal lines.

The fugue also conveys an alarmingly explicit message: it explains to us, in musical language, that the social breakdown to which we are witness is attributable to none other than Sixtus Beckmesser. Indeed, it announces by its musical organization that the cause of the disorder is precisely Beckmesser's false conception of art. Here, perhaps more unambiguously than anywhere else in the opera, we find evidence of Wagner's adherence to the ideas about art and society associated with John Ruskin and the aestheticist movement. In the riot scene he contrives a musical demonstration of the connection between bad art and social disintegration.

He does so, quite simply, by using the melody of Beckmesser's serenade as the thematic base for the fugue to which the riot is set. It is almost as if he had drawn a musical finger that pointed accusingly from the riot back to its perpetrator. Beckmesser, of course, has been identified from early on with the most hidebound and mechanical conception of art. Indeed, Wagner uses him quite shamelessly as an exponent of musical pedantry. (As is well known, he is modeled on the critic Eduard Hanslick, one of Wagner's outspoken opponents.) Music for Beckmesser is a matter of following rules. In his capacity as "Marker," he had scornfully recorded the many deviations from those rules in Walther's first-act trial song, "Fanget an!" and his own serenade to Eva on Midsummer Eve is audibly a product of the same unimaginative musical values that made him deaf to the beauty of Walther's creation.

One senses his severe aesthetic limitations already in the serenade's poetry, which is distinguished by jangling rhymes, banal metaphors, and pointless inversions:

> *Den Tag seh' ich erscheinen,*
> *der mir wohl gefall'n tut;*
> *da fasst mein Herz sich einen*
> *guten und frischen Mut.*

> The day I see appear,
> which pleases me well;
> then my heart takes to itself a
> good and fresh courage.

The serenade goes on in this vein at some length, and Wagner provides it with a wonderfully appropriate musical setting. The challenge he faced was extremely delicate, and his solution one of the most ingenious things in the opera: he needed to compose something that would be sufficiently lame to convey Beckmesser's artistic ineptitude, yet still sufficiently attractive (or at least interesting) to provide the thematic basis for an extended musical episode. It is one thing to write a piece of music that will sound funny; it is quite another to write funny music that an audience will enjoy listening to for up to a quarter of an hour (which is how long the serenade and riot last).

The melody of Beckmesser's serenade is like nothing else in the Wagner corpus. It might be described as botched coloratura: the voice makes its way, by fits and starts, through an excessively ornate musical line, which contains far too many notes for the text. Its lurching phrases typically culminate in an awkward downward interval of a fourth, after which they suddenly reach up for a sustained note that makes neither musical nor textual sense. These sustained notes seem musically incongruous because they are never the logical terminus of a recognizable melodic or harmonic progression. Instead one gets the impression that they have been selected quite arbitrarily. They also lie rather high in the singer's register (most of them are C's, D's, and E's), which makes them sound rather like an effortful braying. Textually, the sustained tones usually find Beckmesser giving undue emphasis to a weak syllable or lingering over a particularly insignificant word. In the opening quatrain, for example, the musical line comes to rest, absurdly, on the word "a" ("einen").

As the serenade progresses (and as Sachs's hammered criticisms become more insistent), the "rules" call for ever more ludicrous coloratura feats. Individual syllables are sustained through long, ugly melismas containing as many as two dozen notes. The most horrendous of these displays comes at the end of a spectacular non sequitur, which Beckmesser has obviously included in his serenade purely for the sake of the rhyme:

> *Wer sich getrau',*
> *der komm' und schau'*
> *da steh'n die hold lieblich Jungfrau,*
> *auf die ich all' mein' Hoffnung bau':*
> *darum is der Tag so schön blau.*

> Let him who dares
> come and see
> standing there the good, dear maiden,
> on whom I set all my hope:
> therefore is the day so beautifully blue.

All of the rhyming "au" words find the singer stuck, like a broken record, on a whining high E, from which he descends through a sequence of clumsy fourths, creating an effect that reminds the modern listener of nothing so much as a car's dead battery. On the last of them, "blau," Beckmesser practically asphyxiates himself as he sustains the irrelevant word through a full two measures and over a sequence of twenty-five sixteenth notes. He sounds like a bass-baritone Lucia di Lammermoor.

It is, in short, the sort of music to drive one mad—which, of course, is precisely the effect it has on Beckmesser's fellow citizens. The ensuing riot can be accurately described, from a musical point of view, as Beckmesser's serenade writ large. Virtually every line of it is derived from some portion of his ungainly romance. It is dominated by the running sixteenth-note figures, especially the descending fourths, that proliferate ever more luxuriantly as the serenade progresses. The same jagged intervals are preserved, as are its unexpected, and ultimately irrational, sustained tones—although when set to the fugue's brisker pace they achieve a vigor, even a jauntiness, entirely absent from Beckmesser's mincing original. Moreover, the musical filiation of the riot from the serenade is not merely a matter of score-watching. It is vividly heard and felt by everyone in the audience, both because the riot emerges organically out of the music of the serenade and, more important, because the serenade's full melodic line is made to sound out repeatedly in the cellos, basses, bassoons, horns, and tuba, as well as in the lower male voices of the chorus. These forces combine throughout the riot to provide the contrapuntal edifice with a firm "Beckmesserian" foundation. It is one of the most remarkably pointed instances of musical argumentation in opera, almost syllogistic in its explicitness. Bad art, it announces, leads to social breakdown.

Midsummer Day and Social Cohesion

In contrast to the chaos of Midsummer Eve stands the order of Midsummer Day. The familiar artistic association of night with evil and day with goodness provides the metaphorical background for this antithesis. In *Tristan und Isolde,* of course, Wagner had inverted this formula, associating the day with pain, the night with bliss. But in *Die Meistersinger* he was working within a more conventional symbolic framework. He also had an immediate operatic source for the conceit in Mozart's *The Magic Flute,* where the malignant forces of the Queen of the Night are sent down to defeat by the Sarastro's priests of Enlightenment:

THE QUEEN, HER LADIES, AND MONOSTATOS:

> *Zerschmettert, zernichtet ist unsere Macht,*
> *Wir alle gestürzet in ewige Nacht.*

> Shattered, destroyed is our might,
> We are all plunged into eternal night.

SARASTRO:

> *Die Strahlen der Sonne vertreiben die Nacht,*
> *Zernichten der Heuchler erschlichene Macht.*

> The sun's rays drive away the night,
> Destroy the evil power of the dissembler.

In *The Magic Flute* this transformation is the work of two couplets: Sarastro's luminous E flat major harmonies follow directly on the heels of the routed Queen's sinking diminished sevenths. Wagner, naturally, develops the idea in a more leisurely fashion, but the metaphorical opposition between night and day has exactly the same intellectual function in both operas.

The Midsummer Day festival consists of a series of primarily ceremonial activities, all of which can fairly be described as emblems of social cohesion. The very same populace that the previous evening had seemed on the verge of self-destruction is shown now to have been transformed into a harmonious unity, bound by ties of affection and respect. The agency of this transformation is, of course, art. Just as the false art of Beckmesser had brought Nuremberg to the brink of disintegration, the true art of Hans Sachs heals the wounds of egotism and restores society to wholeness.

The events of the scene are skillfully arranged to create a growing sense of that wholeness. First we see the individual guilds, their members dressed in holiday attire, as they march into the meadow outside the town. For three of them—the cobblers, the tailors, and the bakers—Wagner composes songs honoring their distinctive contributions to the town's prosperity. The cobblers eulogize St. Crispin, their patron, who made shoes even for those who couldn't afford them, stealing the leather when necessary; the tailors sing of an unnamed forebear who stitched himself inside a goatskin and then walked along the city walls to scare away the enemy; the bakers—somewhat less imaginatively—remind everyone that they daily save the town from starvation. The skull-bashing of the previous evening has given way to harmless boosterism and civic rivalry, which are nicely suggested by the competitive wordplay as well as the parallel (and finally overlapping) musical construction of the three songs. We still see Nuremberg as a society of parts, but the parts now relate to one another in an orderly fashion.

Wagner continues his argument at what might be called the gestural level. Following the guildsmen's songs come first a dance and then a procession, both of which represent physical antitheses of the riot. Where Midsummer Eve found everyone indulging his anarchic passions, the dance and the procession display just the opposite: each citizen now subordinates his movements to a collective pattern. They are balletic symbols, one might say, of social cohesion. The dance— the only ballet music in any of the Wagner operas after *Tannhäuser*— is a charming and lighthearted waltz, inspired by the arrival of a boatful of girls from Fürth. The sense of communal harmony implicit in its choreography is only mildly disturbed by the competition between apprentices and journeymen for the girls' attentions.

The waltz is interrupted by the arrival of the Mastersingers. For their entrance Wagner composes a grand march, whose tunes are already familiar to us from the opera's Prelude. Here they are worked up into a long orchestral episode of mounting excitement and splendor. Unlike Berlioz's headlong Trojan March, the march of the Mastersingers is all pomp and dignity. With its stately tempo, firm beat, and resolute C major tonality (the second theme consists largely of rising C major chords), it seems the musical embodiment of social consonance. At its conclusion we find ourselves facing a stage picture of remarkable symmetry: the citizens of Nuremberg have arrayed themselves by ranks—Mastersingers on their benches, journeymen standing behind them, apprentices before. The chaos of Midsummer Eve has yielded to an image of balance and order worthy of a Renaissance painting.

With everyone in place, the apprentices urge all to silence ("Silentium!"), and the strains of the march die away. There is a stillness about the moment, as if the townsfolk, like the worshipers on Keats's Grecian Urn, had been frozen into this tableau for eternity. We have reached the epiphany marking the complete integration of Nuremberg's citizens into a communal whole. As Hans Sachs rises and steps forward, he is greated ecstatically by his fellow citizens, who join their voices in a grand hymn, "Wach' auf!" Just as the dance and the procession represent the gestural opposites of the riot, so the hymn represents its musical opposite: the men and women who had been set against one another in contrapuntal battle are now united in gloriously emphatic harmony. Once the rebellious canaille, they have been transformed into a choir, whose music bears close (and not accidental) resemblance to the chorales Bach wrote for his community of believers in the *Passion According to St. Matthew*.

The text of the hymn was composed by the real Hans Sachs, a Nuremberg poet of the sixteenth century, who intended it as a greeting to Martin Luther and the Reformation. Its celebration of "the fiery sunrise" is perfectly suited to Wagner's metaphorical antithesis of night and day:

> *Wach' auf! es nahet gen den Tag;*
> *Ich hör' singen im grünen Hag*
> *Ein' wonnigliche Nachtigal,*
> *Ihr' Stimm' durchdringet Berg und Tal;*
> *Die Nacht neigt sich zum Occident,*
> *Der Tag geht auf vom Orient,*
> *Die rotbrünstige Morgenröt'*
> *Her durch die trüben Wolken geht.*

> Awake! The day draws near;
> I hear singing in the green grove
> A blissful nightingale,
> Its voice rings through hill and valley;
> Night is sinking in the west,
> The day arises in the east,
> The fiery sunrise
> Pierces the gloomy clouds.

The hymn's function as a musical symbol of cohesion is felt most dramatically in its opening phrase, "Wach' auf!" On the first of those words, "Wach'," all Nuremberg joins in a unison D natural, which is sustained *fortissimo* by the full chorus. It is, one might say, the most primitive conceivable expression of musical unanimity: a single note, sung to a single syllable by every voice on stage. Wagner even silences the orchestra, so that no other sound can compromise the impression of unity. On the second word, "auf," the unison D natural gives way to an even more resonant expression of the town's newfound solidarity: the voices of the chorus fan into a brilliant G major chord, which is sustained at yet greater length. The chord reflects a higher, more complex form of cohesion. Its harmony—a division of vocal labor, so to speak—symbolizes the integration of complementary parts into the social whole.

In the succeeding chorale, although the vocal lines sometimes move independently, we are made intensely conscious of their vertical consonance. The effect is of hearing all the forces on stage united from top to bottom in articulating a common text—singing as if with one mind. As the chorale moves majestically toward its resolution, it seems to dissolve the boundaries of individuality, molding Nuremberg's citizens into an ever more perfect union. Like the fugue Wagner composes for his riot, the music of the hymn is remarkably explicit in its social commentary.

Indeed, it is explicit even to the point of identifying the source of the social cohesion it embodies. If the riot directed our musical attention to Beckmesser, the chorale directs that attention to Hans Sachs. The great poignancy of the moment derives in considerable part from our awareness that the chorale is also an act of gratitude: in lending their voices to Sachs's poem, the citizens of Nuremberg at once realize their union and honor its progenitor.

The chorale is, in fact, the public counterpart of the quintet at the end of the preceding scene. Remarkably, although the citizens of Nuremberg know nothing about the particulars of Sachs's romantic sacrifice, they nonetheless hail him—"Nuremberg's dear Sachs," they shout at the chorale's conclusion—as a civic martyr. They are of course entirely correct in their intuition. For it is Wagner's contention that Sachs's sacrifice bears on the well-being of the entire community. Walther is not merely a handsome young man who will make a more fitting husband for Eva than would Sachs himself (that is the theme of *Der Rosenkavalier*), but an artist, whose genius is essential to Nuremberg's cultural revitalization, and thus to its very existence. By renouncing Eva, Sachs claims Walther for the community. Hence both the appropriateness and the emotional power of the community's spontaneous tribute: their collective voicing of "Wach' auf!" honors the creator and the vehicle—the artist and his artwork—of their communal survival.

Hans Sachs as Artistic Mediator

All of the Mastersingers recognize the vital social function of art. But Hans Sachs is the hero of *Die Meistersinger* because he alone appreciates the legitimate claims of tradition and novelty. He serves as mediator between the inflexible defenders of the old and the mindless proponents of the new. Without an openness to novelty, he contends, art grows stultified and mechanical, as illustrated by Beckmesser and above all by his serenade in the second act. But without respect for tradition there is no continuity, no creative bond with the artistic achievements of former generations, on which all successful innovation must rest. The art that preserves and revitalizes society must maintain a delicate balance between conservation and invention.

There is a striking similarity between Sachs's aesthetic philosophy and the attitude toward innovation and tradition one finds in John Ruskin and his circle. Ruskin, Morris, & Co are most often associated with a revival of medievalism—a renewed appreciation, in other words, for Europe's oldest artistic traditions. It is less often remembered that their medievalism was coupled with an enthusiasm for some of the most advanced artistic ideas and practices. Ruskin in particular was an outspoken defender of J. M. W. Turner, whose daringly impressionistic landscapes and (more important) seascapes he championed as superior in their fidelity to visual truth than the geometrically perfect abstractions of Raphael. One might say that Raphael occupied the same place in Ruskin's mental universe that Beckmesser does in Wagner's: he stands as an example of tradition grown oppressive, stylized into ugliness. "To this day," writes Ruskin, "the clear and tasteless poison of the art of Raphael infects with sleep of infidelity the hearts of millions of Christians."

Sachs's actions throughout the opera are guided by an aesthetic evenhandedness that Ruskin might have envied. Artistic novelty in *Die Meistersinger* is represented by Walther, who comes to Nuremberg from the outside world and brings with him a new song as well as a new way of singing. He is distrusted by the townfolk because he is an aristocrat, a member of the social class against which the burghers have had to struggle to obtain their municipal freedom. But at a more basic level, Wagner associates Walther with nature and the world of instinct: he embodies a precultural impulse whose energy is essential to Nuremberg's artistic renewal. Sachs's motivation in preventing the elopement of Walther and Eva is thus twofold: the young lovers must not be allowed to leave paradise, but at the same time Nuremberg must not be allowed to lose the young poet who brings with him the promise of regeneration.

Sachs's role as artistic mediator is most clearly on display in two of his great speeches: the so-called "Fliedermonolog" of Act II and the long solo with which the opera closes, "Verachtet mir die Meister nicht." These statements perfectly balance each other, the former exhibiting his receptivity to artistic innovation, the latter his enlightened defense of tradition. For both, Wagner composes music that nicely reflects these complementary attitudes: the style of the "Fliedermonolog" is modern, that of "Verachtet mir die Meister nicht" old-fashioned. Sachs is an artistic mediator not merely in what he says but in the way he says it as well.

In the "Fliedermonolog" he is reflecting on the events of that afternoon, when Walther's song "Fanget an!" had been so rudely dismissed by Beckmesser and the other Mastersingers. He wants very much to get on with his work ("I would do better to stretch leather and give up all poetry"), but the melody of the song returns again and again to haunt him. The haunting is of course literal, as snatches from Walther's melody accompany his ruminations:

> *Und doch, 's will halt nicht geh'n.*
> *Ich fühl's, und kann's nicht versteh'n;*
> *kann's nicht behalten, doch auch nicht vergessen;*
> *und fass' ich es ganz, kann ich's nicht messen!*

> And yet, it just won't go.
> I feel it, and cannot understand it;
> I cannot hold on to it, nor yet forget it;
> and if I grasp it, I cannot measure it!

The emphasis is always on the song's ineffability—its resistance to accepted canons of interpretation—a quality that Sachs proceeds to identify with the mysterious forces of nature. Although it followed none of the rules, the song sounded both old and new, "like birdsong in sweet May." "Spring's command" or "sweet necessity," he deduces, must have been its inspiration. And to a particularly lovely melodic line, over a pulsing dominant in the horns, he refers to Walther himself as a bird:

> *Dem Vogel, der heut' sang,*
> *dem war der Schnabel hold gewachsen . . .*

> The bird that sang today
> has a well-formed beak . . .

The "well-formed beak" is an allusion to Walther's handsomeness and reminds us of the romantic sacrifice Sachs is preparing himself to make. Walther's song may have disarmed the other Mastersingers, he concludes, but Hans Sachs liked it very much indeed.

Appropriate to Sachs's aesthetic open-mindedness in this monologue, its music is written in Wagner's most advanced idiom. Indeed, it is a good deal more modern even than the song that supposedly inspired it, Walther's "Fanget an!" which, while extremely beautiful, remains very much a traditional strophic piece, its predictable (and repetitive) melody supported by a steady rhythm and familiar harmonies. In the "Fliedermonolog," by way of contrast, all such traditional procedures are abandoned. Instead the melody, harmony, and rhythm of each line are carefully sculpted to fit the text. The great flexibility of Wagner's compositional method is suggested by the monologue's frequent shifts in meter, tempo, and tonality: its ninety-seven bars require less than four minutes to sing, but within that brief span the key changes four times, the meter eight times, and the tempo at least thirteen times. Taken in conjunction with the many variations in orchestration and dynamics, these result in a piece of music that seems to emerge organically from the text, responsive to its many nuances and multiple layers of meaning. The monologue, in other words, is written in the "conversational" style urged on composers by the realistic aesthetic of the nineteenth century—the style one hears in Verdi's final works and in the operas of Richard Strauss.

At the opposite extreme, both ideologically and compositionally, stands "Verachtet mir die Meister nicht." Here Sachs's role as mediator requires that he rehearse the virtues of tradition. Walther has proved victorious at the songfest and is about to be accepted into the society of Mastersingers—which will also permit him to marry Eva. But in a fit of pique he recalls his humiliation of the previous day and declares that he has no need of such recognition. Sachs, however, urges Walther to change his mind. Indeed, he proceeds to give him a lecture on the importance of tradition. Art, he argues, does not live by genius alone. It also must have its rules and its craftsmen to sustain it, especially in periods of inspirational drought and political upheaval:

> *Verachtet mir die Meister nicht,*
> *und ehrt mir ihre Kunst!* . . .
> *Dass uns're Meister sie gepflegt,*
> *g'rad' recht nach ihrer Art,*
> *nach ihrem Sinne treu gehegt,*
> *das hat sie echt bewahrt.*

> Do not despise the Masters,
> and pay honor to their art! . . .
> Our Masters have tended it
> rightly in their own way,

cherished it truly as they thought best—
that has kept it geniune.

Save for the middle section, with its warning against "foreign influences," the form of this monologue is, one might say, perfectly suited to its subject. For Sachs's appreciation of tradition Wagner composes, in effect, traditional music. That is, he writes a foursquare tune, whose clear shape, marked parallels, and frequent repetitions allow us to anticipate exactly where its music is going. Ambiguity is held to a minimum: the tonality is a resonant C major, the meter an unvarying 4/4, the harmony unadventuresome. The compositional assumptions of the piece, in sum, have much more in common with the music of the past than with the music of the future. Everything about it is familiar and reassuring, its aural effect—just like its argument—exactly opposite from that of the "Fliedermonolog." The contrast between Sachs's two monologues—the one a paean to novelty, the other to tradition—is thus as sharply etched as is the analogous contrast between the fugue of Midsummer Eve and the chorale of Midsummer Day.

The special poignancy of Hans Sachs lies in the intersection of abstract and personal—public and private—motives. Knowing that it is in the best interests of both art and society to make room for genius, he defends Walther against the myopia of the guildsmen. But at the same time he defends the latter against Walther's anarchical contention that genius is sufficient unto itself. Wagner, moreover, supplies Sachs with the musical ammunition necessary to transform his philosophical vision into a concrete artistic reality: Sachs doesn't merely *assert* the complementary virtues of novelty and tradition, he demonstrates them in his own music, particularly that of the two monologues to which I have drawn attention. Among operatic characters his only rivals either as an aesthetician or as a social critic are Hector Berlioz's Benvenuto Cellini and Hans Pfitzner's Palestrina.

Such wisdom and foresight make him an admirable character, but not necessarily a moving one. The latter he becomes because we recognize that in honoring the precepts of his social and artistic vision he is, at every point, undermining his personal happiness. Had he sided with the other Mastersingers in condemning Walther, Nuremberg might be the poorer, but he at least would have had Eva for himself. Nor does he act in his own best interests when, in the opera's closing moments, he reconciles the impetuous young knight to the legitimate claims of the Masters and hence to the social order they represent. He is truly, in the final words of his fellow townsmen, "Nürnbergs teu'rem Sachs"—"Nuremberg's dear Sachs."

THE SELF AND TIME

Where *Die Meistersinger* is an opera about society, *Der Rosenkavalier* is an opera about the self: its subject, in the last analysis, is human psychology. This fact, perhaps more than any other, marks it as a work of the twentieth century. Nearly all students of our cultural and intellectual life agree that the emergence of an essentially psychological point of view has been the distinguishing feature of the modern era. Needless to say, earlier generations were also concerned with psychology, but in the twentieth century it has become an obsession. The sociologist Philip Rieff, for example, speaks of our dominant preoccupation with "psychological man," who has replaced the economic man of the nineteenth century and the political man of the eighteenth century. Characteristically, the art and thought of the twentieth century—the art and thought of Modernism—have drawn attention to internal states; they have specialized in introspection; and, at least by comparison with the art and thought of the nineteenth century, they have shown relatively little interest in the social and political realms. Sigmund Freud—whose distinctive achievement was to insist on the autonomy and preeminence of the psychological—is in this view the archetypal modern intellectual, just as Karl Marx might be considered the archetypal thinker of the nineteenth century.

In *Der Rosenkavalier,* as in all of Strauss's operas, society is no longer a subject of serious artistic interest. Social relations are represented in only two ways in the opera: either they are trivialized by being made to seem purely decorative—little more than an extension of the characters' costumes—or, to the degree that they are allowed any real weight, they are made to appear oppressive and inauthentic. The aristocratic world of Maria Theresa's Vienna, unlike the bourgeois world of Hans Sachs's Nuremberg, functions strictly as the opera's "setting." That is, we are not invited to understand how this society works, merely to observe how it looks and sounds: we attend to its manner of speech, its interiors, its costumes, and its stylized rituals. When the Marschallin and Octavian settle down for their postcoital breakfast, we almost expect to catch the aroma of Viennese coffee. The composer's interest, in other words, is that of a historicist, and we enter his operatic universe rather as we might a museum. The prevailing spirit is nostalgic.

This archaizing mentality is completely absent from *Die Meistersinger,* which is not at all concerned with recapturing the flavor of small-town Germany in the sixteenth century, but instead uses the particular historical case of Reformation Nuremberg to address universal questions about art and society. Moreover, Strauss's archaism is related, as we shall see, to his underlying fascination with the issue of time and its passing, and it is reflected in his music as well as Hofmannsthal's libretto.

The sense of being in a historical museum is felt most strongly in the first act of *Der Rosenkavalier.* Indeed, during the Marschallin's long levée, we are treated, one might say, to a museum within a museum: just as those of us in the audience observe the curious behavior of this eighteenth-century aristocratic woman, she in turn observes the even more curious carryings-on of an extraordinary array of morning visitors, among them three "noble" orphans begging for money, a milliner and an animal vendor hawking their respective goods, and, most strikingly, an Italian tenor, who proceeds to sing an outrageously beautiful aria. The tenor, like any opera singer, pretends to entertain sentiments he doesn't feel, and Strauss pretends, momentarily, to be an Italian composer. All of these figures are, as it were, on stage before the Marschallin, just as she is on stage before us. The opera inhabits a world of display, and display within display. We see not the substance but the form of social relationships, not their essence but their outward shape.

To the extent that certain figures in *Der Rosenkavalier* do take social relationships seriously, it is a measure of their inauthenticity— the authentic being understood in a characteristically modern fashion as the purely psychological. The Marschallin, Octavian, and, in her less sophisticated way, Sophie are the only genuine characters in the opera, since they care about nothing except what is in their hearts. Theirs is a life of love, jealousy, anxiety, and self-awareness. Those feelings are variously evaluated by the composer, but in no case are we allowed to think that they serve merely to disguise grosser motives, such as the desire for wealth or social advancement. Wealth and position hold no charm for them, since the social realm counts for nothing in their purely psychological view of the world.

In contrast to the Marschallin, Octavian, and Sophie, the other characters in the opera think *only* of wealth and position. Strauss presents them as if they were without a genuine emotional life.

Moreover, the opera's view of such characters is entirely negative. At their head stands Baron Ochs, who opera lovers like to tell us is a real gentleman and therefore mustn't be played too broadly. He is indeed a gentleman—in which capacity he has his own niche in Strauss's historical museum—but his motives never rise above the epicurean. He is interested in his own pleasure and in money. Sophie matters to him first for her dowry and second for her pretty face. But from the start he is represented as a man incapable of authentic feeling.

On a somewhat lower level of boorishness is Sophie's parvenu father, Herr von Faninal. In the end he discovers the remnants of a sense of decency and paternal obligation. But his primary function in the opera is to represent blind social ambition. Throughout the second act he insists that his daughter accept Ochs's proposal in spite of the overwhelming evidence of the latter's unsuitability. Like Ochs himself, Faninal is psychologically impoverished; his life is one of externalities.

While there is at least a veneer of civility to Ochs and Faninal, everyone else we see in the opera is selling commodities or services. At the head of this crowd stand the intriguers Valzacchi and Annina, whose preoccupations are entirely mercenary and who will stoop to any depth. In the same company belongs the gang that shows up at the Marschallin's levée, as well as the waiters, musicians, and assorted hangers-on who contribute to Baron Ochs's discomfiture in Act III. All of them are infected with rapaciousness and sour humor. In other words, anyone "doing a job" (as opposed to "entertaining a sentiment") is made to seem corrupt and vaguely subhuman. Authenticity belongs only to those without visible economic functions or concerns—to the Marschallin, Octavian, and Sophie, who enjoy the luxury of a purely affective existence. We have, I hardly need say, traveled light-years from the world of Hans Sachs and the Nuremberg Mastersingers, for whom doing a job and the love of beauty—not to mention the love of one's fellowman—were not merely compatible with one another but inseparable. In effect, we have traveled from the nineteenth century to the twentieth, from the world of Ruskin to that of Freud.

Aging

Der Rosenkavalier has two great themes, both of them psychological and both related to the issue of time. The first is aging—or, to speak more precisely, age-consciousness. The second is young love, which, in Strauss's representation, is shown to be the exact antithesis of aging. Octavian and Sophie are utterly indifferent to the passing of time, and their indifference is a necessary precondition of their romance. The Marschallin, by way of contrast, is as sensitive to time as the young lovers are ignorant of it. Indeed, time-consciousness stands at the very heart of her experience. The conflict between these two sensibilities provides the opera with its essential psychological tension as well as its most haunting music.

One does only slight injustice to *Der Rosenkavalier* in saying that it is an opera about growing old gracefully. Its preoccupation with aging, moreover, gives it an unmistakably modern flavor. Since aging is a universal human experience, it of course finds its place in the concerns of every important artist. Mozart's Countess asks where the beautiful moments of sweetness and pleasure have fled and—more pointedly—why their memory refuses to fade; Verdi's King Philip laments the slow passing of his days as he recollects his young queen's sad face gazing on his white hair; and Wagner's Hans Sachs alludes several times to the awkwardness of an old man's courting a young woman. But aging for these figures is not life's central problem, only incidental to it. Least of all do Mozart, Verdi, or Wagner suggest that the great challenge facing their respective protagonists is to come to terms with the inevitability of growing old, to adjust to its inexorable realities with dignity and good humor. Yet that is exactly the principal drama in the life of Strauss's Marschallin, who, though in actuality still quite a young woman (Strauss suggests about thirty-two), is terrified by her awareness of time's passing.

A heightened sensitivity to age is one of the most striking aspects of modern consciousness. It was, of course, already beginning to emerge as an important fixation among the Romantics (one thinks, for example, of the poignant sense of evanescing youth recorded in a poem like Wordsworth's "Tintern Abbey"). But in the twentieth century it has virtually overwhelmed all other measures of identity. This can be calculated in many ways, but one of the most telling, I feel, is the order in which we regularly inform ourselves about the vital statistics of another human being. Once we have ascertained the person's sex, usually the next thing we want to know is how old he or she is. The same prejudice is revealed in our newspapers and magazines, which, when introducing a character, rarely fail to indicate his or her age, often making it the first order of business. Everyone, in other words, must be located on a chronological continuum, which, whether we are aware of it or not, has become the primary index of modern identity. Age, in this respect, has overtaken such traditional categories of identification as occupation, character, and religious persuasion, which, while they retain various degrees of importance, have had to forgo pride of place.

Modern age-consciousness, moreover, is profoundly tendentious. In all of its conventions, it assumes that youth is preferable to maturity, and that what comes after youth can be assessed only in terms of loss. Every protest against these assumptions (a protest that, in recent years, has solidified into the critique of "ageism") merely serves to confirm their existence. Yet we know that the assumptions are historically conditioned, that earlier generations didn't always look back with regret toward their lost youth (or at least not so compulsively as we do). Rather, they were more inclined to regard life's early decades as a precarious and troubled time from which, if lucky, one escaped into the security, composure, and wisdom of full adulthood.

The historian can only speculate as to why age has become so important to us and why youth in particular has achieved its privileged status. In general he is apt to relate age-consciousness to the greatly increased pace of social, political, and technological change in modern times. The world that an older person now looks back on is truly more alien than was the world his counterpart looked back on in the years before the democratic and industrial revolutions. Today one's youth is often associated with things that have indeed altered radically or even disappeared, things that would more likely have remained the same as one moved from childhood to old age in a previous era. Hence, more so than ever before, the loss of one's youth is the loss of a whole order of being, and this historical fact has perhaps served to increase our sensitivity to age as well as our seeming overvaluation of youth.

Of course, youth *is* superior to maturity in a number of fairly obvious ways, most notably in strength and vitality. In fact, I am inclined to attribute our modern age-consciousness above all else to the heightened value we place on the body. In the twentieth century the body has come to enjoy a kind of parity with the spirit, and its claims are taken a good deal more seriously than they were in earlier times. In particular, the claims of sexuality are given greater attention than they used to be, and our heightened appreciation of sex has contributed to the prevailing cult of youth. Masters and Johnson may tell us that sex in old age need be no less ecstatic than in adolescence, but few of us can embrace that proposition in more than a theoretical fashion. The *recherche du temps perdu* with which we moderns are obsessed is, I believe, to a considerable extent a search for the real or imagined orgasmic potency that we inescapably associate with youth.

These reflections may seem to have taken us some distance from Richard Strauss's opera. But in fact, the predicament from which the Marschallin so gracefully extricates herself in *Der Rosenkavalier* makes no sense outside the context of our modern preconceptions about age and its significance. That she should attain a kind of heroism simply by accepting the realities of aging presupposes that age and age-consciousness have achieved heretofore unknown psychological weight. In this respect, the sexual explicitness of the opera is probably intrinsic to its effect. By making the Marschallin and Octavian lovers—indeed, by showing them in bed—Strauss draws attention to precisely that realm where differences in age have come to seem most crucial. By way of contrast, the sublimation of eroticism in *Die Meistersinger* serves to diminish the significance of this theme in Wagner's opera, where it is made subservient to the composer's larger argument about art and society.

Growing old gracefully, then, is the Marschallin's great accomplishment, and nowhere in the opera are we made more aware of that accomplishment than in the closing scene of the first act, when, her levée complete and the Baron dismissed, she bids farewell to her lover—ostensibly for the day, but in reality for life. The scene is, in effect, a long meditation on the subject of time's passing, and it represents the opera's intellectual and emotional center. No nineteenth-century composer would even have conceived of such a scene, at least not on so grand a scale (it takes up the last twenty-five minutes of what is already a very long act), just as no nineteenth-century writer would have conceived of a work like Thomas Mann's *The Magic Mountain,* in which page after page of what purports to be a conventional novel is devoted to philosophical ruminations about the nature of time.

The Marschallin's reflections might be said to comprise three psychological moments: first, a sense of identity confusion as her thoughts about time and aging are made explicit; then a deepening anxiety about the transitoriness of all things; and finally (and most importantly) a stoic refusal to succumb to the despair and self-pity that tempt her so seductively. These themes come to the fore one after the other as we move from her opening monologue, through her central disquisition, to her preview of the day's events at the close. But the full progression from confusion through anxiety to disciplined good humor is also anticipated in each of the first two episodes (the monologue and the disquisition), which thus become miniature refractions of the scene's larger psychological and musical trajectory.

Throughout, Octavian serves as an emotional foil to the Marschallin, and Strauss composes music for him that nicely suggests the young man's ardor, incomprehension, and egoism, all of which stand in opposition to her composure, reflectiveness, and generosity.

The Marschallin begins by pondering the mysteries of age and identity in a lengthy, and entirely explicit, monologue. For some critics, indeed, it is so explicit as to cross the fine line dividing self-awareness from sentimentality. But if the Marschallin is to be represented as a hero of time (and that, I believe, is Strauss's ultimate intent), she must at least be *tempted* by sentimentality. Alone in her bedroom, she takes her mirror in hand and asks:

> *Wo ist die jetzt? Ja,*
> *such' dir den Schnee vom vergangenen Jahr!*
> *Das sag' ich so:*
> *Aber wie kann das wirklich sein,*
> *dass ich die kleine Resi war*
> *und dass ich auch einmal die alte Frau sein werd'* . . .
> *Die alte Frau, die alte Marschallin!*
> *"Siegst es, da geht die alte Fürstin Resi!"*
> *Wie kann denn das geschehen?*
> *Wie macht denn das der liebe Gott?*
> *Wo ich doch immer die gleiche bin.*

> Where is she now? Yes,
> seek the snows of yesteryear!
> It is easily said:
> but how can it really be,
> that I was once the little Resi
> and that I will one day become the old woman . . .
> The old woman, the old Marschallin!
> "Look you, there she goes, the old Princess Resi!"
> How can it happen?
> How does our dear Lord make it so?
> While I always remain the same.

The most striking thing about Strauss's setting for these musings is its careful understatement. The whole passage is composed in an astringent conversational manner, with only rare gestures of melodic expansion that might tempt a singer to "operatic" self-indulgence. The tempo is moderate, the scoring recessive, and the phrases generally short-winded. The vocal line, moreover, lies remarkably low, its uppermost sustained note being an F, thus denying the soprano access to her most potent register. In effect, the music acts as an antidote to the maudlin proclivities of the text. Put another way, the music carries the burden of Strauss's larger proposition about the Marschallin's heroic equanimity in the face of time's threatening ravages. Needless to say, with so few vocal opportunities (it is, technically speaking, one of the easiest important soprano roles in the standard repertory), the part calls for a singing actress of exceptional presence.

The monologue ends, like the scene as a whole, on a characteristically disciplined and sanguine note, but not before we are plunged, however briefly, into the deeper waters of anxiety. What truly frightens her, the Marschallin confesses, is not aging itself but being forced to observe herself in the process. Self-consciousness, in other words, is the ultimate terror:

> *Und wenn er's schon so machen muss,*
> *warum lasst er mich zuschau'n dabei*
> *mit gar so klarem Sinn? Warum versteckt er's nicht vor mir?*
> *Das alles ist geheim, so viel geheim.*

> And if He has to do it like this,
> why does He let me watch it happen
> with such clear senses? Why doesn't He hide it from me?
> It is all a mystery, so deep a mystery.

The tonality here turns distinctly minor, the orchestration thins, and the soprano's broken phrases (several of which are sung unaccompanied) descend into her lowest register, culminating in a sequence of repeated low C's. This is as close as the Marschallin will come to despair. But since her heroism consists in refusing to wallow in such dark thoughts, they are banished as the melody associated with her love for Octavian enters in the oboe and the French horns modulate upward into a confident C sharp major triad. The mystery, she says, is there to be endured:

> *Und in dem "Wie"*
> *da liegt der ganze Unterschied—*

> And in the "how"
> there lies the whole difference—

Strauss's phrase, tripping lightly down one arpeggio and up another, perfectly captures her determined cheerfulness. She will not let herself be paralyzed by the fears about aging to which all of us are regularly subject.

In the middle of the scene, after Octavian has rejoined her, the Marschallin's somber thoughts well up again and receive fuller exposition. Indeed, they are made the subject of what amounts to an old-fashioned aria—or the closest approximation thereto that Strauss allows his heroine. What had been touched on only in passing during the monologue is now contemplated unblinkingly and at length. The effect is of looking into the abyss, of refusing to avert one's eyes from the awful truth. Thus the Marschallin treats her unwilling auditor— and, more important, herself—to a sustained discourse on the painful mystery of time.

Time, she observes, becomes a source of agony for us only when we grow conscious of it. The effort to "get hold" of it results paradoxically in a heightened sense of its elusiveness. It is at once everywhere and nowhere, dramatically present and no less dramatically absent. Above all it is forever slipping away. Again and again the Marschallin returns to the idea that, although overwhelmingly real, time always escapes us:

> *Die Zeit, die ist ein sonderbar' Ding.*
> *Wenn man so hinlebt, ist sie rein gar nichts.*
> *Aber dann auf einmal, da spürt man nichts als sie.*
> *Sie ist um uns herum, sie ist auch in uns drinnen.*
> *In den Gesichtern rieselt sie,*
> *im Spiegel da rieselt sie,*
> *in meinen Schläfen fliesst sie.*
> *Und zwischen mir und dir*
> *da fliesst sie wieder, lautlos, wie eine Sanduhr.*
> *Oh, Quinquin! Manchmal hör' ich sie fliessen—*
> *unaufhaltsam.*

> Time is a strange thing.
> When one lives heedlessly, time means nothing.
> But then suddenly, one is aware of nothing else.
> It is all around us, it is also inside us.
> It trickles in our faces,
> it trickles in the looking glass,
> it flows through my temples.
> And between me and you
> it flows again, silently, like an hourglass.
> Oh, Quinquin! Sometimes I hear it flowing—
> staunchlessly.

To convey an impression of the staunchless flowing and of the anxiety to which it gives rise, Strauss sets these lines to slithering scale-like figures, now rising now falling, that make their way, in ever-changing manifestations, through the orchestral fabric and ultimately entrap even the singer herself. The harmonic structure, too, is appropriately unstable, and the constant shifting of melodic responsibility from one instrumental choir to another contributes further to the overpowering sense of transience.

The Marschallin then confesses to having tried to stem her panic through a manifestly irrational gesture:

> *Manchmal steh' ich auf mitten in der Nacht*
> *und lass' die Uhren alle, alle steh'n.*

> Sometimes I rise in the middle of the night
> and stop all, all the clocks.

Suddenly the restless chromatic harmonies and meandering vocal line give way to perfectly regular G naturals (thirteen of them, to be exact), in the harp and celesta, and the soprano restricts herself almost entirely to repeated G's and D's at the bottom of her register. The music's hushed regularity seems to interrupt time's nervous flow, but the chime-like G naturals allude unambiguously to clocks not yet stopped. One might say that the passage makes aurally concrete the Marschallin's fantasy of halting time, while simultaneously exposing its irrationality. The effect is chilling, and it establishes clearly both the neurotic intensity of her fears and her vulnerability to self-delusion.

As in the opening monologue, however, the most desperate revelation is followed immediately by a willful reassertion of discipline. In this instance the Marschallin has recourse to an ordinary piety:

> *Allein man muss sich auch vor ihr nicht fürchten.*
> *Auch sie ist ein Geschöpf des Vaters, der uns alle erschaffen*
> *hat.*

> And yet one must not be afraid of it.
> Time, too, is a creation of the Father who has created us
> all.

Like any good modern, Strauss takes no interest in the Marschallin's theology, which, it seems fair to presume, she wears rather lightly. Her remark is important only because of its conventionality: having come to the brink of self-pity, she rescues herself with a cliché. Appropriately, Strauss supplies it with a reassuringly conventional harmonic underpinning, including an especially radiant E flat major triad for the phrase "Auch sie."

He adopts a similar musical procedure for the Marschallin's last extended speech, which is devoted entirely to reinforcing our sense of her sublime equanimity. The confusions and doubts to which she has given expression in the earlier episodes are now put behind her, as both text and music work to create a picture of resolute composure. The libretto achieves this through its utter matter-of-factness. All weighty pronouncements—all probings into the desperate heart of things—are banished in favor of an offhand account of the forthcoming day's inconsequential events—a visit to church, lunch with a relative, a drive in the afternoon:

> *Ich werd' jetzt in die Kirchen geh'n,*
> *und später fahr' ich zum Onkel Greifenklau,*
> *der alt und gelähmt ist,*
> *und ess' mit ihm: das freut den alten Mann.*
> *Und Nachmittag werd' ich Ihm einen Lauffer schicken,*
> *Quinquin, und sagen lassen,*
> *ob ich in den Prater fahr'.*
> *Und wenn ich fahr'*
> *und Er hat Lust,*
> *so wird Er auch in den Prater kommen*
> *und neben meinem Wagen reiten.*
> *Jetzt sei Er gut und folg' Er mir.*

> Now I am going to church,
> and later driving to Uncle Greifenklau,
> who is old and paralyzed,
> to eat with him: that pleases the old man.
> And in the afternoon I will send you a messenger,
> Quinquin, and leave word
> whether I shall drive to the Prater.
> And if I drive,
> and you feel so inclined,
> you will come to the Prater too
> and ride beside my carriage.
> Now be good and do as I say.

But, of course, the resolve to carry on as usual is the ultimate manifestation of the Marschallin's heroism: while the enemy can't be defeated by stopping clocks in the middle of the night, it can at least be held at bay by turning one's attention to life's quotidian responsibilities and pleasures. The very ordinariness of her remarks at once disguises and embodies her achievement.

Here, as throughout the scene, Strauss and his librettist play skillfully on the idea of "the day," which becomes the significant terrain on which time's battles are won and lost. "Today or tomorrow," the Marschallin tells Octavian, he will leave her for someone younger and prettier than herself. And when Octavian curses the "terrible day," she renders the judgment even more painful by seeming to relent: "Today or tomorrow or the day after tomorrow" ("Heut' oder morgen oder den übernächsten Tag"). As it turns out, the Marschallin's last calculation is the correct one, the events of the day after tomorrow (when Octavian presents himself to Sophie as the Rosenkavalier) marking one of those turning points in which time wins a major victory. But the day is also a terrain of victory for the self, since each of its apparently innocuous occurrences is in fact an opportunity to defeat our inclination to self-absorption. Hence the symbolic appropriateness of the Marschallin's closing survey of the day's unremarkable itinerary. These commonplace anticipations stand not in pathetic or ironic contrast to the eventful changes that actually lie in store for her, but as the only possible antidote to them.

Strauss's music for this speech, moreover, leaves little doubt as to its great psychological importance. The vocal restraint that has characterized the Marschallin throughout here becomes even more marked. Virtually the whole of it is set in the middle of the singer's register, where there is a minimal sense of strain; the pace is measured, the orchestration is exceptionally transparent, and the soprano never raises her voice above a *mezzo forte*. Moreover, the Marschallin's phrases, which have always avoided operatic expansiveness, here achieve a new level of austerity. Each line is broken into fragments, sometimes containing only a couple of words, and the fragments are given correspondingly laconic musical representation: most of them are limited to two, three, or four notes, followed by a rest. There is, in effect, a kind of musical containment that exactly corresponds to the character's emotional containment. Finally, Strauss completes the picture by setting the vocal line above quietly sustained major harmonies in the horns, and beneath delicate elaborations on the theme associated with the Marschallin's love for Octavian, scored in ingratiating thirds and sixths for clarinets, flutes, and high strings. The effect is both hushed and sweet. One might say that the music puts on a smiling face, although the smile has been artfully composed: it mirrors the Marschallin's willful triumph over her inner demons.

Strauss's success in representing his protagonist's psychological heroism depends very much on his setting her in musical and dramatic opposition to her young lover. Where she is reflective, he is obtuse; where she musters discipline, he gives way to passion; where she speaks of things slipping away, he insists on holding, clasping, keeping, and owning. Octavian's very first observation is representative of his behavior throughout: he succeeds in misconstruing the situation entirely, and does so in a fashion that draws attention to himself. Entering the room after the Marschallin's monologue, he announces confidently that he knows the reason for her pensiveness: the arrival of Baron Ochs, he says, had made her anxious for her lover's safety:

> *du hast Angst gehabt,*
> *du Süsse, du Liebe,*
> *um mich, um mich!*

> you were afraid,
> my sweet, my darling,
> for me, for me!

Strauss here establishes a musical pattern that he will use again and again in the scene: when Octavian responds to the Marschallin, his outbursts are invariably loud and rapturous. Moreover, they generally culminate in sustained notes near the top of the singer's register, and these strenuous, emphatically sung high notes tend to be lavished on solipsistic (and repeated) personal pronouns. In the present instance, "um mich, um mich!" rises first to a sustained high F sharp and then to an even longer high G sharp. Moments later Octavian sings:

> *du gehörst mir, du gehörst mir!*

> you belong to me, you belong to me!

and the second "mir" again brings him up to a *forte* G sharp. The Marschallin manages only two lines before he once more assails the upper register to reiterate his claim:

> *Sag', dass du mir gehörst! Mir!*

> Say that you belong to me! To me!

Here the repeated "to me's" are on G and E flat. Finally comes "Sie gehört zu mir! . . . Sie ist mein!" ("She belongs to me! . . . She is mine!"), the "me" held for four beats on upper E, "mine" for the same duration on the by now familiar high G sharp.

Not all of Octavian's exclamations are so shamelessly self-regarding, but they typically follow an assertive upward trajectory that, when contrasted with the Marschallin's vocal moderation, conveys an unmistakable impression of egoism. In a colloquy where the Marschallin sustains nothing higher than two F sharps (and both of those *piano*), Octavian essays six F sharps, four G's, three G sharps, and three high A's, all of them loud, and all held between one and a half and four beats. The sense of vocal abandon is exacerbated by the fact that Octavian is assigned by Strauss to a mezzo-soprano, whose natural range lies a note or more below that of the soprano voice for which the Marschallin's role is written. Octavian's F sharps, G's, G sharps, and A's thus require decidedly greater vocal effort than is exerted by the soprano, and this reversal in vocal postures contributes further to our sense of the Marschallin's composure and Octavian's impetuousness.

With Octavian's departure to assume his responsibilities as Rosenkavalier for Baron Ochs, the essential psychodrama of Strauss's Marschallin is complete. To be sure, she regresses momentarily in the act's closing moments, voicing sentiments more appropriate to Octavian ("Ich hab' ihn fortgeh'n lassen und ihn nicht einmal geküsst!"—"I have let him go, and not even kissed him!"), and singing with uncharacteristic vigor. But in effect, her story has now been told. She will make no appearance at all in Act II, and when she returns at the end of the opera, it will be to play out the role she has anticipated in all its emotional particulars in the scene we have just examined. Having explored her psychological circumstances to the fullest, Strauss now turns to his counterproposition, the timelessness of young love.

Young Love

The second act of *Der Rosenkavalier* is generally thought to belong to Baron Ochs. And, indeed, the greater part of it is devoted to Ochs's ill-mannered carryings-on in the home of his prospective bride, and its music is saturated with the famous waltzes that have become his signature tunes. Nonetheless, the most memorable moment in the act has nothing to do with the Baron. I have in mind the scene of the presentation of the rose. Amidst the act's generally scabrous proceedings and often lowbrow music, it stands out as a moment of ethereal beauty and transcendence. Above all it concentrates into a single musical episode a realm of experience diametrically opposed to the time-drenched consciousness of the Marschallin.

The presentation of the rose is a ceremonial prerequisite of the

Baron's suit, and the Marschallin has prevailed upon Octavian (just as she was prevailed upon by Ochs) to assume this task. Strauss and Hofmannsthal exploit the occasion to an ironically contradictory end: they use it to show Octavian and Sophie falling suddenly and abjectly in love. "Falling in love" rather distorts what actually transpires, since the phrase carries a suggestion of process or development, even if a precipitate one. The love that simultaneously infects these two young people, however, is of its very essence timeless. It is based on no anterior persuasion, since Octavian knows absolutely nothing about Sophie, and what little Sophie knows about Octavian she has gleaned from the "Austrian Almanac of Honors." It also requires no room for growth, but seems to exist full-blown at the very instant they come into one another's presence. Furthermore, it obliterates all previous experience: Octavian's affair with the Marschallin counts for nothing in this moment, and Strauss makes no effort to distinguish him, either musically or dramatically, from Sophie. If their romance can be said to have a history at all, it is in some unspecified, mythical past, perhaps even in a previous existence ("Wo war ich schon einmal und war so selig?"—"Where was I once before and was so happy?")—that is to say, outside of time. It is, moreover, without ambiguity, qualification, or limits—exactly opposite, in every essential, from the contingent, attenuated, time-bound experience of the Marschallin.

In the Marschallin's farewell to Octavian at the end of Act I, the burden of argument is shared more or less equally by Strauss's music and Hofmannsthal's libretto. Although the music lends remarkably precise expression to the Marschallin's fears as well as her dispassionate self-control, by itself it lacks the requisite specificity to translate her thoughts in all their complexity. Because the scene's effectiveness depends very much on our entering into those thoughts, Hofmannsthal's often poetic text is crucial to its success. Indeed, one of the reasons—technical rather than emotional—for the part's low tessitura is to ensure that the text remain as intelligible as possible.

No such parity between words and music exists in the scene of the presentation of the rose. Here nearly all the work must be done by Strauss's score. This is no reflection on Hofmannsthal: the situation simply lacks the dramatic momentum or intellectual substance that might permit the librettist to contribute importantly to its effect. Most of what gets said is either inconsequential or unintelligible. When, after the formal presentation of the rose (with both parties reading their set speeches) and an exchange of pleasantries, Sophie and

Octavian finally give expression to their feelings, their voices join in the sort of high female harmony that leaves nearly every word incomprehensible.

None of this matters, however, because Strauss succeeds so extraordinarily in bringing the moment to life musically. In effect, his music does for the young lovers what the Marschallin was unable to do for herself when she awoke in the middle of the night to stop all the clocks: it brings time to a halt. Although the room is full of onlookers, they are frozen out of existence as the stage—indeed, the whole world—belongs suddenly and entirely to the two young lovers. The moment hangs in trance-like suspension, as if it had been bracketed off from the ordinary flow of events. It is the sort of musical episode that sends one searching for transcendental analogies: a revelation, an epiphany.

In the fourth act of *The Trojans,* Berlioz managed to conjure up the eternal world of romance by gradually slowing the act's pulse; when we finally reach the love duet, "Nuit d'ivresse," the musical clock seems to have been brought to a standstill. Strauss achieves a similar effect in the scene of the presentation of the rose, but he does so by opposite means. Instead of a gradual progression toward entropy, he exploits a radical contrast between highly eventful music on the one hand and, on the other, music in which both rhythmic and harmonic activity has been drastically curtailed. The presentation of the rose is thus set in stark opposition to the immediately preceding scene, where, in anticipation of Octavian's coming, the Faninal household bustles about to music that grows ever louder and more agitated. The sense of time is very much upon us here, as scurrying sixteenth notes in the orchestra suggest the household's frantic last-minute preparations, until an enormous crescendo and a set of brilliant F sharp major fanfares mark the actual moment of the young man's arrival. Then, as if by magic, the orchestral racket suddenly dies away to nothing, the music's pulse evaporates, and we find ourselves in an utterly transfigured musical landscape—ethereal, shimmering, motionless. We are in the timeless realm of young love, where there is neither tomorrow nor yesterday, but only an everlasting now.

Many aspects of Strauss's compositional procedure contribute to the sense of being suspended beyond time. Among the most subtle is his treatment of rhythm. As one would expect, the tempo for the entire scene is quite slow. By itself, however, a slow tempo would not guarantee the remarkable feeling of suspension that Strauss here achieves. More critical, I believe, is his habit of "covering over" the beat, so that the music's pulse is left relatively uninflected. That is, movement in the musical line often takes place between beats, with the effect that our sense of regular forward movement is blurred. Thus in the principal melody associated with the opening part of the scene—an arpeggiated figure heard originally in the oboe and then repeated more than a dozen times on various instruments—the sustained tone about which the phrase turns is twice carried over the beat. Similarly, in the memorable phrase that introduces the duet proper ("Wo war ich schon einmal und war so selig?"), the melody's two longest notes have an equally ambiguous rhythmic location: the first starts on an upbeat, the second on the final third of a triplet. The pulse is further undermined by Strauss's tendency to launch these significant phrases in the middle or (more often) toward the end of the bar, and, indeed, to alter the launching spot from one incarnation to the next. When we consider, finally, the prominence of sustained tones in the orchestral background—the violins play a tremolo C sharp for twenty-seven measures at the start of the scene—we begin to understand how the temporal flow has been interdicted.

The unusual orchestration also contributes to the timeless associations of the scene. The most striking thing about Strauss's scoring here is its top-heaviness: the lower instruments are largely silenced, and the others are assigned responsibilities that fall toward the upper end of their registers. A related feature of the orchestration is the prominence of high-pitched percussion instruments, notably harp, celesta, triangle, and glockenspiel. All of these instruments produce somewhat brittle, tinkling sounds. The latter quality suggests, almost literally, the specific effect Strauss is after: he wants a shimmering, metallic sonority, brilliant but with a certain chilliness. His allusion, moreover, is fairly clear: the music is intended to represent the silver rose that Octavian carries and that becomes ineluctably associated in our minds with the love of the two young people.

The rose is a particularly apt emblem of that love and of the place of young love in the psychological scheme of Strauss's opera. Roses are conventional symbols of passion, but the crucial thing about Octavian's rose is that it's made of silver. Unlike an ordinary flower, it is not subject to the process of maturation and decay that weighs so heavily on the mind of the Marschallin. From an ordinary human perspective, it might be said to partake of the eternal. Moreover, what is true of the rose is also true of Strauss's musical evocation of it. The cool, metallic shimmer of his orchestra, whether we are aware of it or not, underlines the identification of the rose with eternity. Not merely the relative stillness of the musical proceedings, but their pervasive timbre—shining yet somehow austere—brings to mind the timeless innocence of young love.

The top-heaviness of the orchestration—and of the singing as well—has, I believe, a further relevant association, one explicitly suggested by Hofmannsthal's text: namely, with the world beyond. Smelling the rose, Sophie observes:

> *Hat einen starken Geruch, wie Rosen, wie lebendige.*

> It has a strong scent of roses—real ones.

But the fragrance, she learns, is from a drop of Persian rose attar, and this intelligence causes her to alter her simile. Now she thinks not of living roses but of heavenly ones:

> *Wie himmlische, nicht irdische, wie Rosen*
> *vom hochheiligen Paradies.*

> Like heavenly, not earthly roses, like roses
> from the heavenly kingdom of Paradise.

Her voice soars toward the empyrean on the word "himmlische," carrying the soprano over a rapturous high B, and making musically explicit the rose's otherworldly connotations. The distinctively elevated orchestration that we hear throughout the scene bears the same significance: it is a sonic image of "hochheiligen Paradies," lifting our imaginations from the earth to the firmament, from the transitory to the eternal. Appropriately, "Ewigkeit" ("eternity") is one of Sophie's favorite words. When she sings, "This is Time and Eternity in one blessed moment" ("Ist Zeit und Ewigkeit in einem sel'gen Augenblick"), Strauss composes her most exalted musical paragraph, sustaining the word "Ewigkeit" through a long melodic arc reaching over high C sharp. It is a word, one feels instinctively, that would stick in the Marschallin's throat.

I have left until last the single most important, as well as disturbing, component of Strauss's musical portrait of young love. What virtually every listener finds unforgettable about this scene is its euphoniousness. Even in the generally ingratiating context of the opera as a whole, its sheer musical consonance sets it categorically apart. Understanding how Strauss achieves this effect is not especially difficult, but specifying how it contributes to the opera's larger argument (as I think it unmistakably does) will take us on a more speculative course, and one with far-reaching implications for our understanding of Strauss's art and its place in modern cultural history.

The key to the scene's euphoniousness is the harmonic scheme Strauss adopts. One remembers the presentation of the rose above all as a sequence of ravishing progressions, of glorious modulations, now familiar now surprising, but always supremely gratifying. By way of contrast, the scene's melodies are far less remarkable. They hang like beautiful filigree upon the harmonic edifice; stripped from it, they lose the better part of their charm.

The scene falls naturally into two distinct harmonic moments. The first section, during which the rose is presented and commented on by the young lovers, is distinguished by its exceptional harmonic simplicity. In nearly thirty-six of its forty-six bars we hear little more than a repeated rocking back and forth between tonic and dominant. Over and over again Strauss exploits this most primitive, most archaic, and (in a sense) most satisfying of harmonic progressions. Even the two brief passages that deviate from the tonic-dominant-tonic pattern stick to closely related tonalities: to the relative minor (D sharp) and the subdominant (B major). Moreover, Strauss intensifies the sense of harmonic simplification by assigning special importance to the fifth (C sharp), the one note that is a component of both tonic and dominant triads. Thus the shifting back and forth between tonic and dominant takes place, for the most part, over sustained fifths, and the melodic line, likewise, tends to hover about the same note. The shared C sharps minimize the sense of harmonic movement and lend the passage its distinctively suspended effect, as would not be the case had Strauss chosen to emphasize the home tone of F sharp.*

The effect of these procedures is to create a smooth cushion of triadic sound whose unvarying consonance and harmonic stability imply a reality at once lovely and immutable. The music seems as impervious to change as the silver rose, an eternally recurring pattern of archetypal familiarity. Harmonically as well as psychologically, Octavian and Sophie inhabit a world without ambiguity.

The second portion of the scene—the duet proper—makes up in

---

* There is one notable deviation from the tonic-dominant-tonic rule: the curious sequence of dissonant eighth-note chords, played on flute, celesta, harps, and high muted violins, following each statement of the principal theme. These are rather like a modernistic appendage to what is otherwise a very old-fashioned harmonic event—Strauss's effort, one might say, to reclaim the musical proceedings for the twentieth century. They have no structural role in the harmonic organization of the scene, their function being purely decorative. With their high metallic timbre, they are intended to suggest the glistening reflections of the silver rose, and they remind us, in a rather self-conscious fashion, that Strauss knows how to write "modern" music.

the extravagance of its harmonic progressions for the austerity of the first portion. As the lovers give private voice to their ecstasy, every third bar seems to bring a modulation to some yet more exotic tonality. Each of these modulations sounds more rapturous, more exalted than its predecessor, until at last the music returns to its original F sharp major, allowing Strauss to end the scene in a long orchestral postlude of tonic-dominant-tonic sequences such as we heard at the outset.

Strauss intends the second part of the scene to remind us that young love is ecstatic as well as innocent. The riot of modulations combines with a warmer orchestral timbre (the strings, for example, come down from their silvery heights) to give the young lovers a distinctly more human cast. They may not yet be Tristan and Isolde, but they sing here as creatures of passion. In one all-important respect, however, Strauss's harmonic procedures for even this more animated portion of the scene are of a piece with what has gone before: he continues to overwhelm us with consonance, with an almost oppressive euphony. The progressions we hear are often deliciously unexpected, but they invariably move from one pleasing triadic formation to another. Dissonance has no place in the harmonic scheme.

In part, the avoidance of dissonance throughout this scene is obviously meant to suggest the unqualified rapture of the young lovers. Since young love is uncorrupted by experience, it knows nothing of the reservations, anxieties, or scars that dissonance might imply. At another level, however, the scene's prevailing consonance is part of Strauss's systematic effort to associate young love with timelessness. The important consideration here is the musical context within which we experience this oasis of triadic sweetness. The immediate context, of course, is the harmonic ambiance of the opera as a whole. *Der Rosenkavalier* is hardly a dissonant opera, but its ordinary harmonic manner is nonetheless considerably more complex, more astringent, more "modern" than what we hear during the presentation of the rose. The final adjective, "modern," provides the key to the larger and ultimately more important musical context against which we experience the scene: we can't hear it, I'm convinced, without becoming conscious of its anomalous location in the history of Western music. If our ears are at all attuned to music's historical development, we will know that this kind of unqualified euphony belongs to the musical vocabulary not of the twentieth century but of the eighteenth, and even if our knowledge of musical history is limited, the harmonic manner that prevails elsewhere in the opera functions to place the scene in historical italics. By means of its relentless consonance, the scene has the effect of taking us out of our own musical time (the time to which much of the rest of the opera belongs) and transporting us to the remote past, to an era when such triadic harmony was not the exception but the rule. In the spirit of Hofmannsthal's libretto, Strauss's music reaches back to the harmonic gratifications of an earlier age.

That Strauss should indulge this historicizing proclivity most blatantly in the scene of the presentation of the rose is altogether appropriate to the portrait of young love he wishes to draw. Young love, he suggests, shows as little respect for musical time as it does for psychological time. Without any sense of implausibility, it can flout the historical imperatives to which music is normally subject, singing its song to the harmonies of one age just as easily as another. More particularly, it sings its song to harmonies out of the distant past, harmonies that remind us of a time when (or so we like to think) music was as innocent, as beautiful, as untainted as young love itself. Strauss's harmonic scheme for the presentation of the rose is thus integral to the opera's larger obsession. It is a harmonic variation on his great theme of time-consciousness, drawing our attention once again, as do the scene's rhythmic patterns and scoring, to the blessed indifference that categorically separates the young lovers from the Marschallin.

Harmonic anachronism, then, is a technique that Strauss uses in a calculated and dispassionate manner to suggest a particular state of mind. He deploys it as a kind of musical code for youth's temporal insouciance. But it is a good deal more than that. It also points to certain crucial autobiographical realities, exposing the central predicament in Strauss's artistic career. Strauss was himself deeply entangled in the very issue that his opera explores. His artistic situation was strikingly similar to the Marschallin's romantic situation: as a composer of a certain age and with a substantial musical past, he had arrived at a point where he had to make some important decisions about the direction his art would take. In fact, *Der Rosenkavalier* might be said to mark a kind of mid-life crisis. At stake in the crisis, appropriately, was the question of his relation to music's past and its future—the question, in other words, of his place in musical time.

Before the appearance of *Der Rosenkavalier* Strauss was generally regarded as Europe's foremost avant-garde composer. *Salome* (1905) and *Elektra* (1909), in particular, had earned him a reputation as an adventuresome pioneer in the art of dissonance, a man seemingly destined (or condemned) to lead music into the new century. Yet that is precisely what he failed to do. With *Der Rosenkavalier* he relinquished his leadership to a group of younger composers, turning his back on the movement he seemed appointed to guide, and becoming instead the most notorious musical reactionary of his day. In the two years immediately following the opera's premiere in January 1911, Arnold Schoenberg's *Pierrot Lunaire* and Igor Stravinsky's *Rite of Spring* would launch the modernist movement on its dissonant course. Strauss's career after *Der Rosenkavalier*, on the other hand, led from one euphonious triumph to another. Many of the later operas repeat the successful formula that he and Hofmannsthal had hit upon in *Der Rosenkavalier*, and all of them exhibit the ingratiating harmonic manner that so clearly distinguishes *Rosenkavalier* from its two predecessors. From the perspective of the main developments in twentieth-century music, his evolution after 1911 appears an uninterrupted retreat into the past, culminating in the *Four Last Songs* (1948)—a work of almost unbearable loveliness, but one whose harmonic idiom belongs to another age. Not surprisingly, this artistic about-face thoroughly tarnished his reputation among musical progressives, and to this day a cloud hangs over him in the musicological establishment.

In effect, Strauss pointedly failed to follow the example of his own Marschallin. If the Marschallin is a hero of time, Strauss himself must be judged considerably less than heroic in this respect: growing old gracefully (in musical terms) is exactly what he refused to do. Instead, he sought to make the musical clock stand still, even to turn it back. His fascination with the Marschallin, I suspect, was as much a matter of envy as identification.

But more important than the particular choice Strauss made is the fact that he felt obliged to choose at all. It bespeaks a much more self-conscious relation to the musical past than was known to composers before the twentieth century. Indeed, we can't even conceive of Mozart, Beethoven, or Wagner pursuing the sort of historicizing career that Strauss ultimately opted for. It is not that they necessarily possessed a quality of artistic integrity that he somehow lacked, but rather that they belonged to an age entirely comfortable with the notion of music as a developmental phenomenon, propelled by some mysterious aesthetic logic from the past into the future. They knew instinctively that the art of one era cannot duplicate that of another, and their knowledge seems to have given them little pause.

By way of contrast, the modern composer is cursed with a heightened sensitivity to the process of musical aging. The past has become problematic for him in a way it never was for his forebears, and as a result he is always in danger of being seduced into an orgy of musical nostalgia. Strauss is only the most extreme example of this sort of artistic regression; forays into history have become a regular feature of the modern composer's musical biography. This fateful preoccupation with the past is, it seems to me, the artistic analogue of our century's pervasive age-consciousness. The modern composer experiences the same sort of anxieties about the process of artistic growth—of movement out of the artistic past into the artistic future—as all of us now experience about biological growth. The musical past haunts him just as the personal past haunts each one of us, and he is forever tempted to escape into that past just as we escape into morbid reflections about our vanished youth. From this perspective, *Der Rosenkavalier* is a uniquely rich and symptomatic document of the modern temperament, exploring the theme of age-consciousness in its story even as it succumbs to the artistic correlate of age-consciousness—the retreat into history—in its music. Like Proust's *Remembrance of Things Past*, it pays tribute to the anxious preoccupation with one's place on the temporal continuum—be it the continuum of a single life or of an artistic tradition—that has become the hallmark of our century.

Postscript

In these studies I have tried to suggest a number of ways in which ideas impinge upon opera and become an integral part of its aesthetic fabric. Ideas, of course, are not equally important to all operas. Composers differ in their responsiveness to intellectual life, and even works by the same composer vary considerably in their intellectual texture and intensity. In the cases I have examined, the intellectual factor impresses me as extremely important, but there are others, obviously, where it counts for a good deal less.

Moreover, whatever the inclinations of individual composers, not all aspects of intellectual life lend themselves to operatic representation. Indeed, one can easily compile a list of ideas or traditions of thought that have figured prominently in our intellectual history but that are resolutely unoperatic. Opera, for example, is not prepared to enter into negotiations with the labor theory of value, the idea of natural selection, or the doctrine of utility.

There is, then, no neat and continuous fit between intellectual and operatic history, and one might legitimately wonder what principle, if any, governs their relations. Is opera drawn to certain *kinds* of ideas, for which it is an especially appropriate vehicle? Are certain intellectual traditions, or perhaps whole ages in the history of thought, inherently more operatic than others? On the basis of the limited number of cases I have examined in this book, I would be rash to

offer anything more than tentative answers to such questions. Nonetheless, my cases do suggest certain patterns, and in this Postscript I
would like to speculate briefly about the nature and logic of those
patterns.

To begin with, opera appears to respond most vigorously to
ideas that might broadly be called psychological. I have in mind not
only conceptions of the self and its vicissitudes, but also ideas about
love, friendship, parenthood, and the like. In my first chapter, for
example, I argued that Mozart's *Marriage of Figaro* and Rossini's
Barber of Seville reflect a major shift in psychological values between
the Enlightenment and the conservative Reaction. Mozart gives operatic
articulation to a psychology of reconciliation, Rossini to one of
antagonism and emotional withdrawal. The operas aren't able to
address the explicit *political* doctrines that separate the Enlightenment
and the Reaction—not musically, at least—but they convey a vigorous
impression of the antithetical conceptions of personality and human
relations that underlie those political differences.

One might expect, then, that periods notably concerned with
psychological issues would be likely to invite operatic engagement.
That is, to the degree that a historical culture has an important
subjective component, the relations between musical and intellectual
life ought to flourish. Such, it seems to me, is indeed the case in the
first half of both the nineteenth and the twentieth centuries, when
one observes a broad shift away from the political and scientific
interests of the immediately preceding eras and a concentration of
intellectual energies on the self—in the one instance on the Romantic
self seeking transcendence in nature, in the other on the modern self
looking to recapture its past. Schubert's song cycles and Strauss's
Rosenkavalier give appropriate musical expression to these contrasting
moments, and each, I would argue, enjoys intimate ties with the
intellectual concerns of its time precisely because, in both instances,
those concerns were intensely psychological.

Something like the opposite situation might be said to prevail in
the closing decades of the nineteenth century. Especially after the
publication of Darwin's *Origin of Species* in 1859, European intellectual
life came to be dominated by a set of assumptions that were
profoundly antipsychological. At their most extravagant, the thinkers
of the era sought to explain human behavior in terms of the materialistic
categories of natural science. This positivist ideal was embodied, for
example, in the Helmholtzian medical tradition, where Sigmund Freud
received his training, and it also found expression in the imaginative

literature of the period. Thus Émile Zola could write of the protagonists in his novel *Thérèse Raquin* (1868): "I simply applied to two living bodies the analytic method that surgeons apply to corpses." In such a climate of opinion, it is not surprising that the ties between operatic and intellectual life began to loosen. Indeed, the notion of a positivist opera seems almost a contradiction in terms. By and large, composers in the late nineteenth century (I am thinking especially of Massenet and Puccini) were forced to pursue their way independently of so uncongenial a *Zeitgeist,* and one might even argue that the absence of a strong intellectual impulse in their operas accounts in part for their lesser artistic stature.

The affinity of opera for psychological ideas rests on the unique power of music to express emotions. Even though language—especially the language of poetry—can circumscribe and gesture toward the emotions, music has privileged access to them. Perhaps this is because the emotions belong to an essentially subverbal realm, and music works its appeal at the same level of experience. Through music's emotional eloquence, opera is able to address the great subjects of psychological life—desire and fulfillment, anxiety and relief, despair and ecstasy—with unparalleled immediacy. It thereby touches the core of sentiment informing different ideals of selfhood and personal relations. The observation is hardly earth-shattering, but it provides one important answer to the question of what principle governs the relations between opera and ideas.

That opera and intellectual life intersect in the domain of psychology is not, however, the full story. At least three of the cases I have examined—Berlioz's *The Trojans,* Verdi's *Don Carlo,* and Wagner's *Die Meistersinger*—embody ideas that transcend the purely psychological. Admittedly, these operas don't neglect psychology, but their principal bond with the intellectual life of their time does not lie in a representation of ideas about the self or human relations. *The Trojans,* I've argued, reflects the peculiar historical consciousness of the nineteenth century—the notion of history as a powerful developmental force shaping all human experience. *Don Carlo,* for its part, engages one of the great political themes of the age, the doctrine of *Realpolitik.* And *Die Meistersinger* explores ideas about art and community that also find expression in an important nineteenth-century tradition of social criticism. In each of these instances, the confluence of operatic and intellectual life occurs beyond or above the realm of psychology. Opera here enters into communion with ideas about the past, about politics, and about society.

In my discussion of Berlioz, Verdi, and Wagner, I emphasized that such ideas find expression not merely in the texts of the operas but above all in their music. Clearly, however, music cannot articulate notions about the past, politics, and society with anything like the precision or detail achieved by philosophers, political theorists, and social critics. Indeed, in most respects it seems a hopelessly blunt intellectual instrument. But where the discursive particulars of intellectual life are beyond its reach, it is uniquely empowered to evoke the structural core of certain ideas—to convey their deepest and most abstract logic. This is so, I believe, because music creates patterns of sound that echo the conceptual patterns embedded in those ideas. The essential elements of musical expression—rhythm, melody, harmony, volume, timbre—combine to fashion sonic structures that, in certain instances at least, mirror the conceptual structures implicit in ideas.

In *The Trojans,* for example, the structural pattern linking the musical and conceptual realms is the opposition between movement and stasis. At the conceptual core of the nineteenth-century idea of history is a sense of inevitable forward momentum, which stands in tension-ridden antithesis to the forces of inertia. Berlioz's music, especially through its manipulation of rhythm, is able to capture precisely this opposition between movement and stasis. The opera's fundamental musical conceit, one might say, echoes the conceptual structure inherent in the Hegelian theory of history. In Verdi's case, a different antithesis provides the meeting ground for idea and music, namely, that between power and impotence. Much of the interest in *Don Carlo,* of course, lies in the psychological implications of this antithesis, but the opera's music also succeeds in evoking an abstract, depersonalized representation of force and its depletion, especially through dramatic contrasts in orchestral volume and vocal intensity. It thereby takes us to the structural heart of *Realpolitik.* Analogously, it is music's ability to represent images of order and chaos that explains the affinity between Wagner's *Die Meistersinger* and Ruskinian social criticism. A fear of disintegration and a longing for unity lie at the conceptual center of that criticism, and music is richly endowed with means—rhythmic, harmonic, and timbral—to express this fundamental antithesis. Once again, music and ideas intersect in a common structural pattern.

If I am correct, therefore, opera and ideas are most likely to generate ties at the two extreme poles of mental life: in the concrete realm of emotion or in the disembodied realm of advanced abstraction.

Moreover, this duality exactly corresponds to an essential division in the expressive powers of music. Of all forms of human expression, music is distinguished by being at once the most concrete and the most abstract. It is concrete in its immediate sensuousness: in listening to music we are beguiled by the sheer physical pleasure of certain kinds of sounds, sounds to which we attach no representational significance. From this perspective, music is characterized by its radical specificity and its aversion to representation. At the same time, however, music is also highly abstract in that it forces us to attend to structural patterns whose logic is purely formal. Some of these structural patterns are local and relatively simple: the way, for example, that two adjacent phrases are heard to parallel one another. Others are large and complex, as when we note in listening to a symphonic movement that material from the beginning of the piece returns again toward the end, thereby lending the whole a grand symmetrical design. Because music constantly draws our attention to such processes of formal patterning, philosophers since Plato have often compared it to mathematics. In exactly this spirit, Kierkergaard contends that *Don Juan* is the ideal operatic subject, because both its theme ("sensuous genius") and its medium (music) are completely abstract: "The most abstract idea conceivable is sensuous genius. But in what medium is this idea expressible? Solely in music." Similarly, Thomas Mann calls music "the kingdom of a purer, profounder, more absolute logic than that which shapes our verbal conceptions and thoughts."

Music, then, has an affinity for ideas that might be described as subverbal on the one hand and supraverbal on the other. It can touch feelings too deep for thought and conceptions too elevated for words. What it seems poorly equipped to express—and what opera therefore leaves relatively unexplored—is the realm of ideas that fall between the emotionally concrete and the structurally abstract. Such middle-level ideas might be characterized as discursive or representational: they are sufficiently disembodied to have lost touch with the concrete world of the emotions, yet they don't achieve the exalted degree of abstraction where ideas again invite musical evocation. They are ideas condemned to a purely verbal existence, without hope of taking wing in song—ideas like the labor theory of value, natural selection, and the principle of utility. Needless to say, many of the ideas with which intellectual historians concern themselves—especially in political theory, science, and technical philosophy—belong to this discursive middle ground, and herein, I believe, lies the most important reason why operatic and intellectual life echo one another only imperfectly.

The distinction I have drawn between a concrete-abstract intellectual syndrome susceptible to operatic expression and a discursive one inimical to it must remain exasperatingly imprecise, but it is nonetheless suggestive. It helps us understand why opera can recount only part of our intellectual history, but also why it recounts that part with singular directness and power. Much is left out, but what remains is brought to life before our eyes and ears—and in our minds—as in no other medium.

Notes

These notes identify direct quotations from sources other than those (such as libretti) that are widely accessible.

1: Enlightenment and Reaction

p. 18 Joseph Kerman, *Opera as Drama* (New York, 1956), p. 107.

p. 45 Ernest Newman, *Great Operas*, vol. 1 (New York, 1958), p. 67.

p. 57 Stendhal, *Life of Rossini*, trans. by Richard N. Coe (Seattle, 1970), p. 3.

2. The Self and Nature

p. 59 Donald Jay Grout, *A Short History of Opera*, 2nd ed. (New York, 1965), pp. 323–24.

p. 64 Letter to John Hamilton Reynolds, August 24, 1819, in *The Selected Letters of John Keats*, ed. by Lionel Trilling (New York, 1951), p. 237.

p. 67 M. H. Abrams, *Natural Supernaturalism* (New York, 1971), p. 197.

p. 69 Samuel Taylor Coleridge, *The Literary Remains*, vol. 2 [1836] (New York, 1969), p. 66.

3: The Idea of History

p. 108 Hegel, *Lectures on the Philosophy of History*, trans. by J. Sibree (London, 1902), pp. 30, 34.

p. 127 Thomas Carlyle, *On Heroes, Hero-Worship, and the Heroic in History* (Lincoln, Neb., 1966), p. 13.

p. 136 Letter to Adèle Berlioz, February 25, 1857, cited in the Philips recording of *The Trojans*, p. 8.

p. 137 Ernest Newman, *Seventeen Famous Operas* (New York, 1955), p. 288.

p. 140 Ibid., p. 293.

p. 143 Hegel, *Philosophy of History*, p. 28.

4: Realpolitik

p. 156 Letter to Francesco Maria Piave, April 21, 1848, quoted in Frank Walker, *The Man Verdi* (New York, 1962), pp. 187–88.

p. 161 Jacob Burckhardt, *The Civilization of the Renaissance in Italy*, trans. by S. G. L. Middlemore (New York, 1935), p. 22.

p. 161 Heinrich von Treitschke, *Politics*, trans. by Blanche Dugdale and Torben de Bille, vol. 1 (London, 1916), p. 24.

p. 161 Burckhardt, *Civilization*, p. 107.

p. 162 Treitschke, *Politics*, vol. 1, p. 65.

p. 163 Isaiah Berlin, "The *Naïveté* of Verdi" [1968], in *Against the Current* (New York, 1980), p. 287.

p. 179 Letter to Franco Faccio, January 1879, quoted by Julian Budden, *The Operas of Verdi*, vol. 3 (New York, 1981), p. 29.

p. 185 Francis Toye, *Verdi: His Life and Work* (New York, 1972 [1930]), p. 342.

p. 185 Spike Hughes, *Famous Verdi Operas* (Philadelphia, 1968), p. 333.

p. 185 Budden, *Operas of Verdi*, vol. 3, p. 139.

p. 187 Ibid.

p. 190 Ibid., p. 75.

p. 201 Ibid., p. 121.

p. 208 Ibid., p. 155.

5: *Art, Psyche, and Society*

p. 216 Ernest Newman, *The Wagner Operas* (New York, 1949), p. 381.

p. 218 William Mann, *Richard Strauss: A Critical Study of the Operas* (London, 1964), p. 140.

p. 224 John Ruskin, *The Seven Lamps of Architecture* [1849] (Philadelphia, 1891), p. 165.

p. 235 Ruskin, *Modern Painters*, vol. 3 [1856] (Philadelphia, 1891), p. 84.

p. 239 Philip Rieff, *Freud: The Mind of the Moralist* (New York, 1959), p. 391.

Postscript

p. 264 Émile Zola, "Preface to the Second Edition," *Thérèse Raquin*, trans. by Leonard Tancock (Harmondsworth, Eng., 1962), p. 23.

p. 266 Søren Kierkegaard, *Either/Or* [1843], trans. by David F. Swenson and Lillian Marvin Swenson (Princeton, 1943), vol. 1, p. 55.

p. 266 Thomas Mann, *Buddenbrooks* [1901], trans. by H. T. Lowe-Porter (New York, 1924), p. 406.

Index

Library of Congress Cataloging-in-Publication Data

Robinson, Paul A., 1940–
    Opera & ideas.

    Originally published: New York : Harper & Row, c1985.
    Includes index.
    1. Opera. 2. Song cycles—History and criticism. 3. Europe—Intellectual
life. I. Title. II. Title: Opera and ideas.
ML1720.R6   1986   782.1'09   86-47637
ISBN 0-8014-9828-1